HIGHER EDUCATION
AND ITS USEFUL PAST

HIGHER EDUCATION AND
ITS USEFUL PAST

APPLIED HISTORY IN RESEARCH AND PLANNING

by
John R. Thelin

SCHENKMAN PUBLISHING COMPANY INC.
Cambridge, Massachusetts

Copyright © 1982

Schenkman Publishing Company Inc.
3 Mount Auburn Place
Cambridge, Massachusetts 02138

Library of Congress Cataloging in Publication Data
Thelin, John R., 1947-
  Higher education and its useful past.
  1. Education, Higher—History—Research.
I. Title,
LA174.T42   378'.009   81-9422
ISBN 0-87073-079-7 (pbk.)   AACR2

PRINTED IN THE UNITED STATES OF AMERICA.

Contents

For A. S. T. B.
. . . *Moja Supruga*

ABOUT THE AUTHOR

John Thelin is Associate Professor of Higher Education at the College of William and Mary. A graduate of Brown University, he received the M.A. and Ph.D. from the University of California, Berkeley. He has taught at the University of Kentucky and Claremont Graduate School, and was Assistant Dean of Admissions at Pomona College. His experience in policy analysis includes having served as Assistant Director and Research Director for the Association of Independent California Colleges and Universities. Mr. Thelin's first book, *The Cultivation of Ivy*, was published by Schenkman Publishing Company in 1976. He is married to A. Sharon Blackburn.

ACKNOWLEDGEMENTS

Writing *Higher Education and Its Useful Past* has meant bringing together materials in social and educational studies which I have encountered over several years. I am grateful for the people whose counsel assisted me in shaping the work. Jack Schuster of Claremont Graduate School, my teaching partner, commented on the design of Higher Education doctoral programs. David Riesman of Harvard University always found time to write perceptive replies to my letters. Charles Elton of the University of Kentucky encouraged me to use unorthodox sources in teaching and research. Morgan Odell, Kenneth Beyer, and Jonathan Brown of the Association of Independent California Colleges and Universities contributed insights on policies and planning. Dean John Quinlan of Pomona College patiently introduced me to admissions research. Robert Rosenzweig, Vice President of Stanford University, reaffirmed my conviction that good conversation and an eye for social and historical detail have an important place in administration. I wish to thank Dean James Yankovich and Mary Ann Sagaria of the College of William and Mary for welcoming me to incorporate the book's substance and spirit into a lively doctoral program. The examples set by these mentors and colleagues suggest a bright future for leadership in higher education.

Extended discussions with friends have been close to the heart of the writing project. Arthur Levine, Stewart Edelstein, James McManus, Mark Thompson, Lawrence Murphy, Will Buck and Randall Dahl provided suggestions and arguments on various issues. Alfred Schenkman, who gave encouragement from start to finish, stands as publisher *par excellence*. Many of the ideas I present in the book were introduced in my articles for *The Review of Higher Education, Liberal Education, College and University, Journal of Educational Thought, The Educational Forum, History of Education Quarterly,* and *Educational Studies*. I thank the editors for having permitted me to draw passages from articles. Editor

John C. Smart of *The Review of Higher Education* was especially helpful in providing a forum for developing the essayist's craft.

In the text I bring attention to the expertise which archivists contribute to the study of higher education. Beyond general praise, I am indebted to the following archivists for their help and permission to reproduce illustrations and documents: J.R.K. Kantor of the University of California, Berkeley; Dorothy O. Johansen, Reed College; Leslie A. Morris, University of Chicago; Cynthia McClelland, Princeton University; Leila W. Jamison, University of Pittsburgh; Anne Caige, UCLA; Judith A. Schiff, Yale University; Ruth Hauser and Jean Beckner, Claremont Colleges; and Wolfgang Tatsch of Tatsch Associates. The Council for Financial Aid to Education and The Advertising Council allowed me to reproduce the public service announcement appearing in Chapter 1. A research grant from the College of William and Mary enabled me to complete the manuscript.

This roster names only some of the many people who assisted me. The lengthy responses and inspired arguments which my questions elicited provide optimism that the topic of higher education need not be moribund or predictable in the 1980s.

J.R.T.
Peckwood Place
1982

Introduction

Henry Ford's quip, "History is bunk," all too often has provided a convenient excuse to exclude historical studies from the practical affairs of management and administration. My particular concern is that there is little assurance that college and university administrators have read about the history of the institutions in which they lead and serve. The oversight is ironic because Henry Ford, in fact, thought history was an important subject and was upset that it suffered from unimaginative presentation. In response to Ford's complaint, this book explores some uses of historical research and reading for those concerned with planning and administration in higher education.

Colleges and universities are fascinating places. Their charm and complexity come, in large measure, from the fact that they are *historic* institutions. I make no apologies for the awe which campuses inspire in me. Commencement processions, charter day speeches, academic gowns, monuments, legends, and renovated buildings have provided me a happy combination of idle curiosity and professional observation. The artifacts and events of campus life have induced me to study closely the historical and societal influences on institutional practices. What moves this book beyond personal indulgence into contribution to the education of leaders? It is my conviction that one's decisions and actions as a president, planner, dean, department chairman, faculty member, trustee, or alumnus will be enhanced if prefaced by the historical study of higher education. On a dire note, I warn that neglect of the historical dimension may cause the study of higher education to compete with Economics as "the dismal science."

Higher Education and Its Useful Past advances the notion of *applied history*. I hope that readers will become comfortable with the logic of historical thinking and with the varieties of sources that can shape the ways in which they discuss higher education institutions and issues. My aim is to complicate present-minded conceptions of higher education by examining both the continuities and changes in colleges and universities. The book presents several essays, each of which discusses past and present implications of some perennial issue in higher education. Topics, for example, include certification, institutional structure, admissions and access to courses of study, and connections between national development and university-building. Chronological ordering of the studies, which have been drawn from medieval, modern European, and American history, promotes a rough sense of historical sequence. Yet the book should not be mistaken as a comprehensive survey of the history of colleges and universities. The collection of studies are intended to leave readers with two habits: the active use of the methods and strategies of historical research in approaching professional problems; second, a penchant for reading varied sources beyond the predictable chores of "keeping up in the professional journals."

I emphasize this latter habit because members of the higher education community are heirs to a rich body of fiction, lore, biography, iconography, architecture, and journalism which deals with the college and university experience. I fear that this literary and artistic legacy has been neglected. The literature about colleges and universities includes both heroes and villains, failures and successes — and so, ought not to be dismissed as a genre which promotes ancestor worship or uncritical celebration.

Messengers who bear troubling news often are blamed for having caused the problem itself. I am sorry to report that "higher education" is a confused and confusing term. My plea to grumbling editors and readers is that the situation existed long before I started writing on the topic. I alert readers to two distinctions among the multiple connotations spawned by the "higher education" term:

Higher Education refers to Institutions: Colleges and universities are the heart of higher education. They are the institutions in which undergraduate, graduate, and professional curricula are offered. They are the settings not only for research, teaching, and administration — but also, for the intricate organizational subcultures of students, faculty and staff. Colleges and universities are the object of policies and programs set up by external agencies. Campuses, of course, deal with foundations, government agencies, commissions, associations, and other organizations; hence, these latter institutions play a supporting role which at times makes them part of the higher education drama. Yet when all is said and done, colleges and universities remain central.

Since World War II the term "postsecondary education" has been used with alarming frequency in drafting legislation. Ultimately, the term may be used on campuses. It is a weak term which artificially links programs, services, and organizations having little to do with the higher education associated with colleges and universities. Perhaps the best way to deal with the term "postsecondary education" is to regard it as a government office — comparable to "Health, Education, and Welfare."

Higher Education refers to an Area of Study: The field of "Higher Education" is the systematic analysis of colleges and universities. It is an area which draws from such academic disciplines as history, sociology, economics, anthropology, and psychology. Chapter I goes into detailed discussion of the debates over "Higher Education" 's standing as an academic department and a field of study.

The chapters include many summaries of findings first advanced by scholars in journal articles and books. I acknowledge these in the notes at the end of each chapter so as to provide some guides for additional reading. I have avoided excessive notes and citations which would bog down the text. In quoting from some documents, memoranda, and publications, I have occasionally omitted the name of a particular university, location, person, or publication, especially in those instances where my intent was to illustrate a widespread practice, rather than to single out a specific incident.

A final word on perspective: thus far I have chided administrators who may have ignored or scorned historical studies as impractical. Avoidance, however, often requires tacit cooperation of two parties. Historians, too, must accept some blame for their discipline's isolation from advanced education for such fields as administration, law, medicine, public health, and city planning. *Higher Education and Its Useful Past* is an invitation for historians to acquire both courage and confidence to write for and speak to nonhistorians. My pleasant surprise has been the discovery that many prospective administrators' unfamiliarity with historical sources and issues was surpassed only by their enthusiasm for an introduction to applications of historical studies to their special fields. My role has been to act as a broker between the discipline of history and the field of higher education administration. I hope this book goes beyond such specifics to provide a model whereby many liberal arts disciplines may be incorporated into the curricula of various graduate professional schools.

1

Colleges and Universities: Peculiar Institutions

A PROSPECT FOR INSTITUTIONAL RESEARCH

In 1908 Edwin Slosson, an editor from the Midwest, set out to observe colleges and universities throughout the United States. He was intrigued by the distinctive fashions, icons, and monumental architecture which each campus spawned. While on the Pacific Coast he wrote, "I hope the Stanford museum is not neglecting to acquire some specimens, for they will be useful material for the anthropologists as well as the college historians of the future." In Philadelphia he praised the University of Pennsylvania for its unique Bureau of Publicity which collected artifacts of campus life. Slossom exclaimed, "No other university, so far as I have found, has such a complete and convenient collection of materials for the present and future study of the institution," and proposed as follows:

> In particular, let me suggest that there should be in each university a society or preferably, a person whose duty is to collect fugitive publications of all kinds, programs of clubs and festivities, snapshots of student life, and mateoric periodicals. A file of catalogues and doctor's dissertations will not satisfy the needs for future historians and biographers. They must have something more if they are to make these dry bones live.[1]

Slosson's campus profiles, originally featured as a series in *The Independent* magazine, were published in 1910 an an anthology, *Great American Universities*. They endure as a model of serious, comprehensive analysis in higher education. Not only did the profiles describe campuses during the formative years of the modern American university, but also, were Slosson's invitation for others to pursue institutional research which

5

draws from several data sources. Seventy years after Slosson's pioneering work, has his research invitation been accepted? Have higher education analysts developed methods which "make these dry bones live"?

Whereas Slosson was probing healthy institutions in 1910, the declining enrollments and financial problems of the 1980s may cast researchers into the role of pathologists whose exhumation and autopsies chart the demise of colleges and universities. Campus obituaries, however, are not the complete story today. To gauge the legacy of Slosson's research invitation, it is helpful to review higher education as an area of professional education and expertise.

HIGHER EDUCATION AS A FIELD OF STUDY

Proponents of higher education as a field of study have attempted to stake out a professional identity and a legitimate place in a university setting. The process resembles developments in graduate schools of business in the late 1920s, followed by Foundation support for setting up graduate programs, offering advanced degrees, attracting scholars, holding conferences, and establishing professional journals and associations. Since the early 1960s doctoral programs, research and development centers, consortia, state councils, and consulting firms have proliferated to contribute to "Higher Education" standing as a familiar department in American universities.

Despite such accomplishments, the study of higher education has yet to resolve identity crises. Higher education has not clearly achieved recognition as a discipline, complete with its own body of knowledge, theory, tradition, and research orientation. Much of the best writing on higher education comes from economists, sociologists, and psychologists who have no association with higher education departments. Graduate programs in the field of higher education prepare students for any number of institutional positions, yet there are no data which shows the impact of such programs on career patterns.

One problem for program review is that higher education leadership positions are subject to codes and precedents beyond the relatively new higher education graduate programs. For some university administrative appointments, selections are made from the faculty ranks. Elsewhere in the institution, the higher education profession is fragmented into such specialties as admissions, public relations, alumni programs, research, student affairs, finance, and development. One need not have completed courses or a professional degree in higher education to be a "practicing professional." A university's director of public relations, for example, may have no formal study of higher education and may feel primary affiliation with other public relations people, whether they work for banks, food franchises, or recording studios. College and university presidents, concerned about the tendency toward fragmentation, call for "professional unity" among the varied staff members who administer campus programs and services. One national organization for higher education professionals, the Council for the Advancement and Support of Education (CASE), has responded by setting up certification programs which encourage "professional growth that transcends functional specialties."[2] Such voluntary continuing education, however, lacks the esprit, rigor, and licensing authority of established professions. In contrasts, for example, with the field of law where there is tight connection between completion of law school and subsequent passage of the bar examination as requirements for professional practice.

Professionals in higher education generally perceive themselves as "managers"—an administrative designation which gives loose generic unity to disparate specialties. And, when research is used to assist decision making and administration, it is the applied research variant one associates with systems analysis and quantitative data. The sources of this role model have been borrowed from occupations outside higher education. To assess its appropriateness calls for discussion of the combined skills of management and measurement.

MANAGEMENT AND MEASUREMENT

One reason management and measurement have been attractive to higher education administrators is that these skills are associated with the mystique of business expertise. College and university presidents often are urged to emulate leadership styles practiced in industry and corporations. In 1978, for example, one university president addressed his colleagues, "Education should take a lesson from the auto industry: strive to be more efficient and more effective, instead of bigger." Such advice ignored the fact that colleges and universities operate in a setting of regulations, laws, charters, traditions, and purposes which are not the same as those for profit-production corporations. Practices which work well in one institution may not be appropriate elsewhere.

The advice also is puzzling because there is little evidence that automobile executives in the United States have themselves practiced the principles for which they were praised, i.e., they have not built enterprises which are efficient, effective, or not concerned with getting bigger. Opposite tendencies seem to hold: the major companies were reluctant to enter the small-car market, even though American consumer demand and foreign competition had shifted sales away from the large American cars. Efficiency and effectiveness do not characterize the industry, as Detroit's factories have been slow to retool production. Chrysler Corporation's dependency on government loans suggest administrative practices which would be intolerable for a college or university president. Instead of looking for heroes and models in business and other fields, colleges and universities would do well to develop their own criteria for institutional research, planning, and leadership. Preoccupation with imitating other organizations is a drain on the time, esteem, and imagination of colleges and universities.

Although most higher education administrators are not expected to be researchers, higher education doctoral programs prefer that recruits and apprentices gain familiarity with information collection strategies which provide institutional "feedback" and "feedforward" as managerial aids. In many programs, graduate students fulfill the research training component by taking statistics and research design courses, often offered under the auspices of the educational psychology department. Indicative of the applied research orientation which now is associated with professional expertise in higher education is the following job description posted in 1978:

> Director, Institute of Higher Education Management. The State University System is seeking a director of a newly established Institute of Higher Education Management to be located in the System Headquarters in the state capitol city. The director should have demonstrated leadership in management and should have knowledge of the management problems in higher education. Administrative experience in higher education is highly desirable. The Institute will develop and administer programs designed to emphasize the 'real world' problems of administering universities. Faculty for the Institute will be drawn from experts in the state and the nation under the leadership of the director.

In addition to the demand for transinstitutional and systemwide research and development at the state level, colleges and universities seek directors for in-house research, evaluation, and program planning. Here the vocabulary of expertise includes the following:

> Requires (1) Ph.D./Ed.D. in Educational Management (or related area) or equivalent experience with substantial background in statistics, (2)

some experience with data processing and computer analysis, (3) teaching experience in higher education.

Elsewhere, a director of institutional research is "responsible for the continuing development and direction of a comprehensive program of institutional research directed toward managerial decision-making at the university-wide level." Candidates for the position were warned that "knowledge or experience working with HEGIS, NACUBO, and NCHEMS is important."

Managerial studies in higher education lag behind their business and industry models. Twenty years after Peter Drucker introduced Management by Objectives (MBO) into business analysis, a journal for higher education professionals hails MBO as an appropriate innovation for colleges and universities. In the search for research strategies, the higher education profession has looked to the factory, the hospital, and the supermarket. According to the "factory model," the consequences of going to college are measured by comparison of "inputs" and "outputs" of students' characteristics. A weak research approach, it is unable to probe the structures, environment, and experiences which students encounter in the long, complicated process between entrance and departure from college.

Imitating the "hospital model" means that college students are analogous to patients: both are subject to services and treatments administered by institutional staff. Hospitals are especially suspect as models for higher education, however, because college students are not passive, short-term recipients of treatment. Students may spend more than four years immersed in an elaborate subculture with its own customs and rites, after which they may continue affiliation as alumni. Nor does the "hospital model" allow for the active role which students play in shaping the college's programs. Libraries, forensics, foreign-language study, science, laboratories, and literary studies at one time were initiated by undergraduates without the endorsement or control of campus administration.

Demand for institutional accountability has led to the "consumer model" for higher education analysis. The rationale holds that the elective system has transformed the campus into an educational supermarket, with students comparable to shoppers: their enrollment choices guide policy and planning. This simplistic analogy glosses over the historical and legal fact that colleges and universities forfeit societal trust if instruction vacillates wholly according to student demand. The ultimate "consumers" of higher education "products" are not students, but those members of the community served by university graduates.

The preceding models are inappropriate because they encourage members of colleges and universities to ignore the unique characteristics of their own institutional missions and environments. Second, the models rely heavily on questionnare data. Survey research is increasingly limited in both richness and validity, since student respondents have become uncooperative with institutional questionnaires. Survey research also is susceptible to the Heisenberg Effect—in answering a question, students may change as well as record their attitudes. Above all, survey data have difficulty incorporating the highly visual character and collective behavior of a campus. Research in higher education ought acknowledge the peculiarity of colleges and universities—special places shaped by lore, architecutre, monuments, and ceremonies. History is the discipline which can provide this perspective in institutional research.

A PLACE FOR HISTORICAL SOURCES IN INSTITUTIONAL RESEARCH

Sherlock Holmes, baffled by a case, complained to Watson that he could not continue his investigation without clues. Scrounging for evidence, he cried out, "I cannot build bricks without straw." A comparable exasperation in higher education survey research has kindled increasing respect for the historian's ability to probe institutional nooks and crannies. One project sponsored by psychologists at the Educational Testing Service sought straw for its research bricks by explicitly including a "narrative case study" and a "retrospective description." In other words, the project needed an historian who could draw from a miscellany of federal, state, and local documents the background for the survey data that the principal investigators would collect. Survey research in higher education would benefit from a supplement of the "unobtrusive measures"—artifacts, traces, and memorabilia—which allow for indirect study of what takes place in institutions. Historians should conduct such applied research because they can reconstruct and interpret organizations by using documents which many educational researchers would ignore.[3]

The implications for the adminstration of higher education are not far-fetched. Some "unobtrusive measures" of administrative attitude toward students follow: Are library stacks open or closed? Can students gain access to conference rooms, special equipment, laboratories and other facilities? Student fondness for a college might be indicated by the percentage of students who stay on campus in the evening, during weekends and vacations, or even after graduation. Universities may reveal priorities and status differentiations in parking-lot assignments. Before dismissing this last statement as frivolous, it should be recalled that Clark Kerr's *Uses of the University* cites outrage over undesirable parking assignments as one issue which united faculty at several campuses in the 1960s.

Rituals and ceremonies often reveal the respect which an institution gives (or withholds from) its members. Whereas in 17th-century Germany teachers were honored on *two* national holidays, a 19th-century Oxford don was enraged not by his low pay, but because "professors were not even prayed for in University sermons." Ceremony participation indicates the extent to which college transmits its ethos to students, faculty, and the surrounding community. Instead of distributing a questionnaire which asks instructors, "Are you satisfied with your job," one might observe who takes the trouble to march in academic processions. The clue to such a research strategy is prompted by the following passage from a 1976 memorandum sent by the Dean to the faculty at a large state university on the subject of commencement ceremonies:

> . . . faculty interest is still on the wane. To the members of the Commencement Committee and the others that have a role in the ceremony, this seems unfortunate, for Commencement is the one time we have to bid our students and the parents farewell and to show the Commonwealth what the University is! Commencement is an opportunity to present a solid front to the citizens, and its value in public relations is considerable. Accordingly, we would like to urge all the faculty to make an extra effort to attend this spring.
>
> True, you need academic dress, but you can get a cap and gown from the Bookstore up to the last minute before the ceremony begins. If you do not own a hood, you must of course place an order for one with the Bookstore (or order one for yourself) in advance, or you can rent one from the Bookstore by placing an order before the 16th of April. But you don't need a hood to attend and sit with the faculty. While the committee would like as much academic dress and color as possible, what we really want is your support and presence.

The memorandum closes with the inducement that the ceremony has been trimmed to about an hour in duration. This seemingly mundane document underscores several important issues in higher education. First, faculty lag behind students, parents, and local residents in support of ceremonies. Second, the university administration demonstrates at least mild concern about the threat of faculty absenteeism to the semblance of an academic community. No measure of gentle suasion, convenience, and appeal to faculty goodwill has been spared. An interesting sequel would be to see whether the dean later proposed that faculty attendance be mandatory.

Academic planning often includes both curricular change and campus construction. Architecture can be an index of educational planning priorities: Does a university renovate old buildings or construct new ones? Are new buildings designed in a modern or a revivalistic style? How are new structures integrated into the older campus core? Responses to these inquiries, combined with commission reports and master plans, reveal the degree of a university's concern with maintaining its historic image. Inferences about architecture and planning, however, must be guided by sound information on the limits with in which university officials must work. Renovation of old buildings for science curricula requiring laboratories and new equipment might be infeasible owing to factors of electrical wiring and structural stress limits. This was the case with the University of Pennsylvania's old dental school. When the dental school moved to new facilities, however, the vacated building was gutted and restored to make an attractive, historic home for the school of architecture and design.

One student of campus planning at the University of California, Berkeley wondered why new buildings departed from the unified, classical style of the original campus. By digging through state records and university archives, he was able to document connections between architectural planning and changes in educational funding and philosophy.[4] Whereas the university from 1902 to 1925 had supported the classical master plan of John Galen Howard, by the 1960s the State Department of Finance had criticized the expense of university construction and refused to fund structures more elaborate than other state buildings. Neither accident nor illusion had forced a decline in the attention to harmony of building styles. The university regents attempted to demonstrate fiscal responsibility to state auditors by using cheaper building materials and by excluding such academic "luxuries" as student lounges. Here is an instance in which an hypothesis relies on insight and unorthodox sources to provide evidence about the relations between policy and architecture.

If Berkeley illustrates an abandonment of original plans for an historic campus, the case of the University of Kentucky in the 1970s indicates an attempt at architectural recycling. Increased enrollments led to demolition of old buildings and construction of a seventeen-story office tower. Although the new reinforced-concrete structure departed drastically from the original buildings, university planners honored the legacy of the historic campus: the base and first two stories of the new tower were constructed with old bricks reclaimed from the razed structures.

Such isolated examples must be considered together in a conceptual framework if they are to provide accurate, systematic readings of an institution's pulse. The message, even at a rudimentary level, is that colleges and universities are historic institutions whose past influences present and future campus atmosphere.

HISTORICAL SOURCES AND QUANTITATIVE RESEARCH

An erroneous belief is that unobtrusive measures and historical sources yield "soft" data incompatible with the precision of "hard" quantitative research. To the contrary, the measures and indicators cited in the preceding discussion of rituals, policies, and architecture lend themselves to statistical analyses.[5] Historians have contributed *posopography*—collective biography and factor analysis—to the research effort. Historians of higher education now make sophisticated use of demographic, economic, and sociological data to monitor institutional change. The term *cliometrics*, which literally combines the Greek words for the muse of history and measurement, good-naturedly refers to computer history—testimony to the range of sources and strategies historians have brought into their discipline. The historian's warning is that one must understand the details of customs, culture, and context which give special connotations to sources, whether statistics or documents. Since the data never speak for themselves, research design ought to provide for social and historical background.

It is easy to forget that quantitative research can be imprecise and vague. Even if a study uses a sophisticated quantitative research technique (e.g., multiple regression anaylsis), one usually finds the project director's foreward containing the disclaimer, ". . . full account of the social, economic, and educational factors are beyond the scope of this study." In the 1960s, one famous computer company's advertisements features a lonely, pensive executive who faced the burdens of decision-making accompanied only by the slogan, "Reality, not data." Higher education research, unfortunately, seldom fulfills that promise. Social and institutional studies, regardless of methods, lean toward complexity and ambiguity and fail to provide infallible recipes for higher education policies. Incorporation of unobtrusive measures and historical sources is a mixed blessing for researchers because these factors require taking notice of dimensions of institutional life heretofore overlooked.

At one state university, a group petitioned the university regents to include a "social impact" statement in its agricultural research program. Although growers were convinced that they could ascertain the economic impact of university-developed machines, heated arguments among several groups indicated that no one knew what the social consequences of the agriculture research and development had been. According to one reporter, the university's vice president for agriculture "said he is not opposed to social impact statements in principle. However, he said—as he has in the past—that they are extremely difficult to write."[6] Rather than shy away from such difficult assignments, researchers might well combine quantitative analyses with the use of historical sources to prepare university impact studies.

To encourage such an approach it is helpful to acknowledge works which are models of research excellence. One strong contender is Carlo Cipolla's *Literacy and Development in the West,* a slim volume which took on the large task of analyzing the social and economic ramifications of reading and writing for Western civilization.[7] Whereas many education researchers conduct longitudinal studies spanning five to ten years, Cipolla opted to cover 500 years and assembled data from more than fifteen countries and empires.

Cipolla's elaborate statistics on literacy rates are especially significant because he has taken care to account for changing standards and definitions of reading and writing as they have varied over time and from one country to another. When school records were of meager validity, Cipolla imaginatively culled data from census records, parish books, courthouse registers, and prison documents. Amid the statistics he paid attention to special documents and events which signalled changing levels of and attitudes toward literacy. Whereas literacy was associated with religious orders in medieval England, by the 16th century priests and clerics had no monopoly on reading and writing skills. How did Cipolla reach this inference? He noted that legal statutes no longer granted "benefit of clergy" exemptions to convicted criminals who were literate. This is the eye for historical detail which enables research to look beyond the obvious.

There is no formula for turning out researchers who are both thorough and interesting. Cipolla is intriguing because he is an economist who acknowledges the importance of fortuna—chance—in social and institutional history. Although managerial studies strive to predict and control organizational behavior, Cipolla reminds us that such uncontrollable factors as weather have been grossly under-estimated in economic development. Cipolla's reminder may cause directors of higher education management institutes to *chafe impatiently,* but Cipolla is difficult to refute. After all, he does have the statistics to back up his argument!

THE CRITICAL EDGE: CUTTING THROUGH SLOGANS AND FADS

One strand of conventional thinking in graduate education maintains that the research effort requires ability to generate data. Equally impor-tant is the skill to repsond *critically* to the prodigious amount of institu-tional information encountered. Since much of the data are analoguous to noise, the preparation of college and university decision makers would do well to teach how to cut through nonsense.

Ours is an age of mass communication in which we are besieged with contrived images which profess to connect institutions to the sur-rounding society. Colleges and universities both generate and conern advertisements, public relations brochures, and marketing campaigns. Such information represents the "mass lore" of higher education, part of the folklore of modern organizational life. Mass lore spins a web of innuendo, illogic, and distortion. Historical research orientation is invaluable for sorting through the lore because historians pay close attention to a document's tone and origin. Historians encourage vigilance against *anachronism,* an abuse of historical logic which attributes the conditions or values of one era to another. Consider the public service announcement in Figure 1, which appeared in a national news magazine in 1976. A period-piece photograph (circa 1900) features a boy working in a factory, with the caption, "Sixty years ago, you didn't need a college education." The text elaborates as follows:

> In fact, you didn't need much of anything except a willingness to work 16 hours a day. For 8¢ an hour. Under brutal conditions. But times have changed drastically. Life for the working man is more challenging. Safer. More stimulating, and far more rewarding. Why? Many things have helped. Especially an endless flow of technological improvements and discoveries. Many of which came from college campuses, and from college-trained men and women. We must sustain this flow of ideas. Only in this way can we increase the productivity that will maintain and in-crease our standard of living. America's colleges need your help. They are in deep financial trouble. Give to the college of your choice. Now.[9]

The ad's claims about the relationships among colleges, technology, and improvements in living standards are surprising if we recall the incident cited earlier in the chapter in which a university vice-president contended that social impact statements were difficult to write. Does the public relations firm know something the university vice-president does not? One could reasonably argue that the technological innovations advanced by college-trained men and women led to establishment of the dismal factory in which this child of the industrial revolution had to work. Above all, today one still does not need a college education for factory work, or for numerous occupations. The ad's suggestions are not convincing.

Another variant in the abuse of history in higher education lore is what might be termed "negative factor analysis." One institutional brochure dramatically asked in 1977, "Suppose there were no State U?" Looking backward from the campus' 30th anniversary, it noted:

> No one can answer these questions with certainty, but there are available statistics and facts that immediately relate what the state would *miss* if the contributions and services of State U. were abruptly terminated tomorrow, and all State U. graduates now living and working in the state were to cease their labors.

The introduction is followed by a horror story of unattended patients, understaffed hospitals, uneducated children, unbuilt highways, breakdown of law and order, slowdown of business, and cancellation of cultural events. The flaw in this tract is the assumption that State U. graduates would not have been educated elsewhere if there had been no State U. Likewise, no consideration is given to the possibility that the land used for campus construction might have provided a pleasant park and metropolitan greenbelt if left in its 1947 condition. The pamphlet fails to mention that if there were no State U., American higher education might have avoided the problems of over-expansion.

American higher education has become linked to slogans about mobility and income. In the late 19th century a campaign proclaimed, "Open a school, close a prison." Reports about violence and crime in public schools of the 1970s could lead one to conclude that differences between the two institutions are negligible. There *are* connections between higher education and jobs, but they are less obvious and more interesting than the brochures would have readers and donors believe. "Going to college" has changed meaning from one era to another, creating complicated issues. Has higher education promoted social change and mobility, or are these merely products of an expanding economy? What reasons do groups have for *not* going to college?

A number of state and federal agencies now have truth-in-advertising ordinances for postsecondary education catalogues.[10] Such mild measures hardly eliminate the need for critical analysis among planners and policy-makers—otherwise one runs the risk of believing the slogans one helped to devise. The serious danger arises when large sums are invested in programs based on dubious assumptions. In 1978, for example, several foundations publicly conceded that the millions of dollars spent on compensatory education programs had accomplished few of the stated objectives. Yet funding persisted for years, buoyed by wishful thinking rather than sound evaluation. The critical edge of historical analysis can assist planning and management by testing slogans and assumptions used to justify a proposed program.

INTO THE ARCHIVES

Although historical sources have had only marginal status in higher education's applied research, Edwin Slosson's 1910 proposal for artifact preservation has not gone wholly unheeded. Archivists at colleges and universities have collected unorthodox materials which can be the "historical flesh" to carry out Slosson's plan to make dry institutional bones come to life. The unobtrusive measures found in archives include photograph albums, alumni records, year books, and memorabilia. Fascinating as these resources may be, archival materials pose problems when used to understand institutional character. The following samples illustrate the complexities of making inferences:

Photographs:

One comes across a group portrait of Yale College students, circa 1900, comparable to Figure 2. The sepia-tint picture has a stylized, formal pose which brings to mind Arrow shirt advertisements and visions of "Frank Merriwell at Yale" novels. Certainly, this photograph reassures us that all was well with golden college youth, gentlemen scoundrels who probably had spent the evening singing at Mory's.

Or does it? Close inspection shows that the famous Yale Fence appears a bit contrived. Background research reveals that the fence had been dismantled in a class rush twenty years before the photograph was taken. It was salvaged by a New Haven photographer, then later reassembled as a prop in front of a tapestry screen which depicted an idealized view of the old campus. The fence eventually ended up in the basement of a college building, set up next to a bowling alley, and was used for official photographs of Yale team captains. Research has tarnished the idyllic image of the historic campus.

What about the stately, confident students? Might we revise our initial charm for the portrait when biographical research shatters the illusion of elegant stability? Consider the following hypothetical destinies: one young man had to leave Yale a few weeks after the group portrait because his family lost their fortune in the infamous stock-market crash of 1902. The proud fellow on the far right was to die in France fighting in World War I. History also can be the art of omission. One friend of the group was unable to sit for the portrait because he had been expelled for poor grades. He missed out on the camaraderie of senior year but went on to make a fortune in South American tin mines. We do not know whether lack of a Yale College bachelor's degree hampered him in adult life, although it is possible that honorary degrees from *three* Ivy League universities in the 1950s provided him with some consolation for his early academic failure. Photographs, without supporting documents, do not tell all.[11]

Monuments and Memorials:

Campus monuments, along with photographs, give clues to higher education's visual character, and also help determine the kinds of heroes and achievements a college honors. But the reasons for erecting monuments are not obvious and are subject to national and regional peculiarities. Whereas hundreds of American towns have Civil War monuments and veterans' memorial gymnasia, we ought not assume this is a universal tendency. The city of Ljubljana in Slovenia contradicts the American town pattern: a municipal ordinance prohibits statues in honor of military figures. The result is an abundance of memorials to artists, writers, and composers, very much in character in a city which has a high literacy rate and numerous publishing houses, galleries, and concert halls. Colleges and universities follow a distinctive logic about likely subjects to honor—but generalizations are not infallible. One hypothesis posits that when a college builds a *new* structure, it encourages a sense of history by naming the building after *old* people, usually donors or prominent alumni. To go beyond such a generalization, it is useful to consider the intricacies of a particular case of monument building.

Earlier in the chapter we discussed construction and history in connection with the University of Kentucky's new office tower. During the same years, on that campus fused institutional heritage and architecture in another incident which illstrates the *historic* character of higher education. When the new Commonwealth Stadium was built in 1973 a few miles from the main campus, the university tore down the quaint old stadium known to generations of students and fans as Stoll Field. It is plausible to assume that new structures and winning teams would erase the old stadium from university life, but such was not the case. Despite popular terminology of Stoll Field to refer to the name of stadium, the *official* (and largely unknown) name was MacLean Stadium (located on Stoll Field), in honor of a player from the 1900s who had been killed in an early season game. A check of old records showed that he never had been awarded a varsity letter. So in 1975, more than a half century after MacLean's death, the president of the university and members of the athletic board found time amid pressing business to award the varsity letter to MacLean posthumously. The university had remembered!

But colleges and universities also can forget. Historical monuments can be selective and manipulative. Offended philanthropists sometimes withdraw gifts; names of buildings are changed; shrines and monuments fall into disrepair; once famous alumni sometimes fall into disrepute. Until one understands the circumstances around a monument, their names and celebrations may seem senseless.

Official histories:

Almost every college has published an official history which old grads purchase yet seldom read. These "handsomely bound, richly illustrated collector's works, suitable for coffee table display" usually are commissioned by the board of trustees, written by a professor emeritus, and published during the college's contennial celebration. The formula for the text is to narrate the college's ascent from humble beginnings through decades of struggle, growth, and triumph. The concluding chapter forecasts more growth and a bright future.

The "house history" genre assists in understanding how colleges and universities depict themselves, but such works seldom provide a comprehensive institutional profile. The scope is limited, self-congratulatory, and sanitized of scandal. Despite painfully long accounts of faculty appointments and curricula changes, the people and issues described are carefully selected. House history authors tend to lapse into historical illogic in their assumption of indefinite progress. Official chronicles reinforce the contention that colleges do devote time and energy to cultivation of historical image, even at the expense of candor and depth.

Quite apart from the house histories, historians of higher education revise and use archival materials to ask searching questions about incidents and developments within institutions. They often include reconstruction of the campus ethnography and student subcultures, analysis of institutional decision-making, admissions policies, and trends in alumni achievement. As well as critically examining the campus, historians of education often look at institutions as part of social history. Colleges and universities are studied as a factor in local, regional, or national developments.[12]

THE SAGA AND CHARTER OF COLLEGES AND UNIVERSITIES

The preceding brief samples of photographs, monuments, and chronicles hint at the care that must be taken in using unorthodox sources for organizational analysis. They hardly exhaust the research possibilities; rather, they are intended to what the appetite for the artifacts, documents, and archival materials which will be encountered in subsequent chapters. Before proceeding to the historical case studies, we seek some concept which refines the perspective such artifacts might bring to institutional studies. What follows is an attempt to incorporate Slosson's 1910 insights with the contemporary research and development effort.

A recurrent theme thus far has been that colleges and universities are special places, historic institutions whose elaborate internal life inspires strong feelings (of love and hate) among various groups. Campuses acquire distinctive images and reputations; Neither wholly rational nor efficient, their operations and affairs are determined in part by custom. Such traits bring to mind the concept of institutional *saga*—a mixture of legend and fact—of embellished and accurate history which colleges and universities cultivate over time. The saga concept, identified by sociologist Burton Clark, is crucial for understanding higher education because colleges convey a mystique, bestow (or withhold) prestige, and generate loyalty among students, alumni, faculty, and staff.[13] A concept related to saga is that of institutional charter, the distinctive reputation, expertise, privileges, traditions, and legitimacies which insiders and outsiders associate with a particular campus.[14] To illustrate the manner in which *charter* frames our expectations about organizations, consider that readily accepted is the idea that a liberal arts college behaves one way, whereas a state university behaves another; problems arise when an institution violates its charter by adding on some uncharacteristic activity. Similarly, public opinion may be outraged when an unaccredited institution claims it is a college and grants bogus degrees.

Saga and charter, which are historical dimensions of an institutional personality, are serious considerations for presidents, deans, and planners who want to work with or alter a university. Effective intervention and administration require an understanding of the peculiar legends, lore, taboos, and traditions embraced by a campus's constituents. Careful attention is devoted to vocabulary to avoid such *faux pas* as asking for directions to Harvard's "campus." In some cases, an institution which has acquired a strong sense of mission has great power to endure crises and solve problems which trouble alma mater.

Previous research dealing with saga in higher education suggested that small, distinctive colleges have an advantage over large universities—in that the former are better able to transmit to students and alumni an historic sense of being unique, a citadel continually threatened by external heathens. Decision making in small colleges was admired because it relied on consensus and informal discussion, in contrast to the alleged clumsiness of multiversity bureaucracies. That hypothesis is not wholly convincing because abundant evidence suggests that the saga of many large state universities has inspired incredible loyalty among alumni and citizens. Nonetheless, it does prompt administrators and planners to entertain the argument that the "normative bonding" of an institution's historic ceremonies, symbols, and liturgy are essential for analyzing how the organizations work.

Saga also suggests a strategy from which to approach transinstitutional studies. If a college commands strong feelings of support, perhaps equally strong emotions of rivalry and competition will develop among institutions. This holds especially when there is real or imagined pressure to attract students, donors, research grants, legislative supports, and sports fans.

Having equipped ourselves with an introduction to historical sources, methods, concepts, and research strategies, let us now get down to cases.

60 YEARS AGO, YOU DIDN'T NEED A COLLEGE EDUCATION

In fact, you didn't need much of anything except a willingness to work 16 hours a day. For 8¢ an hour. Under brutal conditions.

But times have changed drastically.

Life for the working man is more challenging. Safer. More stimulating. And far more rewarding.

Why?

Many things have helped. Especially an endless flow of technological improvements and discoveries. Many of which came from college campuses, and from college-trained men and women.

We must sustain this flow of ideas. Only in this way, can we increase the productivity that will maintain and increase our standard of living.

America's colleges need your help. They are in deep financial trouble.

GIVE TO THE COLLEGE OF YOUR CHOICE. NOW.

 Council for Financial Aid to Education, Inc.
680 Fifth Avenue, New York, N.Y. 10019

A Public Service of This Magazine & The Advertising Council

FIGURE 1

The College Contribution: Higher Education in the Public Eye

Reproduced by courtesy of the Council for Financial Aid to Education, Inc., and by The Advertising Council

FIGURE 2

"Campus Monuments and Mementos": The Famous Yale Fence, circa 1879—
used for student group portraits, later knocked down in inter-class rush, salvaged
and reconstructed as an interior set for Yale portraits (cf. Figure 7).

Courtesy and Permission of Yale University Library, Manuscripts and Archives.

2

Certification and Structure: The Medieval Universities

MIXING MODERN AND MEDIEVAL INSTITUTIONS

Modern colleges and universities are fond of invoking the legacy of medieval universities in such forms as academic gowns, commencement processions, or the Gothic towers which fill hundreds of American campuses. Nostalgia, hardly an accurate sense of history, allows medieval splendor to be carried forward several centuries and combined with modern convenience. In 1929, for example, University of Pittsburgh architects clothed a reinforced concrete skyscraper in a Gothic shell to create a monumental "cathedral of learning" (Figure 3).[1]

Instead of resurrecting medieval forms for use today, let us reserve the order and transport the present backwards. How, for example, would a 20th century accreditation team report on the 13th century universities at Paris or Bologna? What would strike them as familiar and noteworthy—the physical plant, the laboratories, students, curriculum, or the university president? Would endowments be sufficient to warrant accreditation? What would be the foremost contributions which medieval universities would make to higher education seven hundred years away? To answer such questions we must sort through complexities and inaccuracies in historical images about connections between the medieval university and its present day namesake.

The medieval university is attractive because it is inspirational. The colors, grandeur, and traditions revived in academic ceremonies are today's translations of the Middle Ages' legacy. Belief and loyalty, introduced in Chapter I as elements of organizational saga, are tempting themes for linking the medieval university to the American campus. Crises facing a college elicit strong support. It is this unbashed loyalty which we would like to think inspired Dartmouth alumnus Daniel Webster to wipe his eyes and tell the Supreme Court, "It is, Sir, as I have said, a small College. And yet, there are those who love it."[2]

A comparable sentiment stirs us in the following 14th century incident. A young count, later famous as Charles the Bold, learned that he had been disinherited by his father. Young Charles, unable to afford his retinue after money from home had been cut, bid farewell—after which the assembly of cooks, workers, and servants broke into tears and cried, "We all, we all, my lord, will live and die with thee." Charles replied, "Well, then, stay and suffer, and I will suffer for you, rather than that you should be in want."[3] Such devotion and shared adversity is at the heart of the bond which ties the American campus to its alumni.

Yet the emotions which characterized medieval life are found only rarely in modern organization. Today one does not expect blind support in the face of impending disaster. We are more apt to think of "steady state growth" and "cutting losses" in attitudes toward institutions. Sports teams, often praised as sources of civic pageantry and cohesions comparable to medieval ceremonies, usually lose fans during losing seasons. Nor do modern cities and their "home teams" in professional sports have an enduring shared fate; team owners, for example, can move a team from one city to another—from Brooklyn to Los Angeles, or from Kansas City to Oakland.

Today organizations aspire to moderation and control. A weeping executive violates the standards of sound administration. Efficiency and profit may make sense to us, but they do not fully explain the ways in which medieval people made decisions and arranged their activities. The hunt for medieval contributions to modern institutions often leads to a confusion of modern form and medieval spirit. Double entry bookkeeping, a practice cited as evidence of secular capitalism, has been traced back to the 14th century. At the same time historians were puzzled by recurrent entries of *donati deo* in counting house ledgers. The explanation was that profit-minded merchants still were very much concerned about eternal salvation—expressed by frequent gifts to the Church. The *donati deo* entries (literally, "given to God") suggest that development of a modern financial practice provided a means to record accurately—but had not eliminated—religious devotion even among bankers and merchants of the late Middle Ages.

BEYOND THE DARK AGES STEREOTYPE

The "Dark Ages" image stereotype hampers reconstruction of the character of medieval institutions. Italian writers in the 15th century who wished to inflate their own achievements first used the term; they linked themselves to the glory of Ancient Greece and Rome by belittling the Middle Ages as a period of gloom, illiteracy, and pestilence. The social order was described as a rigid hierarchy dominated by the Church and a martial nobility. Such images are misleading because they gloss over the nuances and changes of five hundred years. To speak of the Middle Ages is to refer to a period from 900 A.D. to as late as 1400—a epoch of ascent, acomplishment, excess, and decline.

For the purposes of the study of higher education, it is important to note that the university was a product of the High Middle Ages, roughly the 11th through 13th centuries; during this time the area now called Western Europe enjoyed economic recovery, growth of towns, and increased commerce within Europe and with the East. Two groups—urban merchants-craftsmen and the kings of nation-states—and the Pope gained political power at the expense of local princes and bishops. As relations among the various factions became more involved, interest in, need for, systems of law, theology, and administration increased. At the same time, exposure to (and curiosity about) ancient philosophies, grammar, and the civilizations of Arab and Mediterranean people grew.[4]

Proponents of the Dark Ages image create the impression that the people of the Middle Ages were ignorant, even stupid. This view tends to be reinforced by social science researchers of the 20th century, who have the advantage of hindsight to point out that the men and women of the 13th century had little grasp of the macro phenomena—demographic change, political consolidation, and economic forces—shaping their world. The temptation is to ridicule the medieval people for having misunderstood their own situation. A more reasonable view would hold that in any culture, medieval or modern, there is a lag between the realities of life and what people believe to be important at the moment.

In the 13th century the Christian world had much to learn from the ancient, Arabic, and Eastern civilizations, a condition which became painfully evident during the Crusades. One Greek observer described the Franks as barbarous, greedy, and laden with locusts. The following incident reported by an Arab physician suggests the limits of Western medicine and problem-solving:

> They brought before me a knight in whose leg an abscess had grown; to the knight I applied a small poultice until the abscess opened and became well. . . . Then a Frankish physician came to them and said, 'This man

knows nothing about treating them.' He then said to the knight, 'Which wouldst thou prefer, living with one leg or dying with two?' The latter replied, 'Living with one leg.' The Frankish physician said, 'Bring me a strong knight and a sharp axe.' . . . Then the physician laid the leg of the patient on a block of wood and bade the knight stride the leg with the axe and chop it off at the one blow. Accordingly, he struck it—while I was looking on—one blow, but the leg was not severed. He dealt another blow, upon which the marrow of the leg flowed out and the patient died on the spot. . . . Thereupon I asked them whether my services were needed any longer, and when they replied in the negative, I returned home, having learned of their medicine what I knew not before.[5]

For the sake of higher education's reputation, it should be noted that most medieval universities did *not* include the study of medicine. Surgeons were multitalented, as they also had the training to be barbers. Althought this incident illustrates the ignorance of science and medicine in Western Europe, most medieval scholars readily acknowledged their debt to ancient and foreign thinkers by comparing themselves to "a dwarf standing on the shoulders of a giant."

How do we best approach the charge that medieval people were uneducated? One reason there were relatively few schools was that there was little popular demand for literacy. As Carlo Cipolla has argued in his own study, acquisition of the skills to understand elaborate visual and aural symbols—icons, frescoes, stained glass, chimes, sermons, legends—was the medieval variant of public instruction and communication. Even if one did learn to read or write, the lack of books and presses would make the knowledge useless.[6] Writing, a special skill analogous to computer programming today, could be accomplished by using the services of a scribe. Parishes often did set up schools, but most parents showed little interest in having their children attend. Going to school, followed by advanced studies at a university, usually was reserved for the occasional bright boy who aspired to a career related to service of church or crown.

LOYALTY AND CEREMONY

To understand the medieval university one first must acknowledge the distinctive values and forms of medieval civilization. Elaborate rituals, costumes, and sounds marked every event of daily life. Members of guilds, professions, nobility, and even beggars and lepers proudly proclaimed their affiliations by publicly presenting themselves in uniforms and processions with well-understood connotations. According to historian Johan Huizinga, vivid pageants symptomized a culture whose events were grasped in "violent contrasts and impressive forms" which "lent a tone of excitement of passion to everyday life." Conspicuous displays of emotions at coronations and executions reaffirmed popular belief in standards of justice. Although the dramatic emotional shifts strike us as infantile and cruel, Huizinga observed that medieval people would find our deportment and justice to be timid and boring.[7]

The Middle Ages refined formalized conduct. Chivalry and courtesy, for example, referred to the codes for knights (horsemen, chevaliers) and for court members. Ceremonies for marriage, baptism, burial, knighthood, or reception of the doctorate provided explicit liturgies which elevated the social importance of the events.

Universities fit into the scheme by formalizing learning.[8] Scholars staked out a distinctive corporate identity, complete with seals, colors, symbols, guilds, and licenses. It was an age of institution building, signified most obviously by the magnificent cathedrals. The university represented the institutionalization of scholarship, a development inseparable from consolidation of authority by the Papacy and by kings. To understand the connection we turn to external features of the university.

EXTERNAL FEATURES OF THE MEDIEVAL UNIVERSITY

The founding dates for universities are not recorded with precision because many of these institutions evolved inconspicuously out of schools established by bishops, near cathedrals. The major structural gains for a university lies in its history of external relations—acquisition of privileges, exemptions, and a charter. The pattern involved three stages: first, a university gained the *ecclesiastical* status which made it immune from local secular urban jurisdiction; second, it received *royal* exemptions which meant that the king protected the university from both city authorities and the bishop; finally, a university was granted *papal* privileges, which meant that the institution was accountable to Rome, exempt even from control by a nation's king.

University privileges were often granted after a dispute between students and local authorities. Squabbles between "town and gown" gave a king a convenient excuse to intercede and to extend his own authority over a city. Philip Augustus, for example, made the following rule in favor of students at Paris in 1200:

> Neither our provost nor our judges shall lay hands on a student for any offense whatever; nor shall they place him in our prison, unless such a crime has been committed by the student that he ought to be arrested. And in

that case, our judge shall arrest him on the spot, without striking him at
all, unless he resists, and shall hand him over to the ecclesiastical judge,
who ought to guard him in order to satisfy us and the one suffering the in-
jury.[9]

Thus, students were given clerical status, accountable to ecclesiastic
authority; they were protected from civil authorities. The privilege was
set "forever by fixed law" that the university provost would affirm by
oath to the scholars to abide by the king's regulations. Similarly, in 1255
King Henry III of England protected the clerical status of scholars and
granted rights to university chancellor at Oxford. He proclaimed,
"Know that we have provided for the peace and tranquility of the
University of Scholars at Oxford." According to the document, a
layman who wounded a cleric (student) would be held in the *king's*
castle, not the town jail. Students charged with crimes against townspeople were to be held by the king's authorities, then handed over to the
university chancellor.

Local merchants and landlords who gouged students on rents and
food were subjected to royal punishments:

> The bakers and brewers of Oxford will not be punished for the first of-
> fense, but for the second they will lose their bread and for the third they
> will be sentenced to the pillory. Every baker should have his sign and mark
> his bread with it so that it can be recognized. The townsman who brews
> for sale should expose his trade sign; otherwise he loses his beer. Wine will
> be sold at Oxford in public and indiscriminately to clergy and layman
> alike after it has been tapped for retail.[10]

A university's gains in corporate privileges did not imply extensive institutional wealth. The *university* was a self-regulating association of
masters and scholars whose main power derived from a *charter* to grant
degrees (licenses) for particular curricula and professions. The university was important to society because it was directly concerned with training for professions and for the resolution of legal, administrative, and
theological issues. Its regulations for conferring degrees contributed the
idea of *certification* to formal education.

What kind of place was the university? Each one acquired from its
host city attributes which shaped institutional specialties. Southern
universities in Italy were especially important for medicine and civil
law. Northern universities, notably Paris, were famous for canon law.
The following glorified prospectus for the new University at Toulouse
intended to draw scholars away from established Paris:

. . . theologians teaching in the pulpit and preaching at the street corners, lawyers magnifying Justinian and physicians studying Galen, professors of grammar and logic, and musicians with their instruments, lectures on the books of natural philosophy, low prices, a friendly populace. . . prepared by the extirpation of heresy, and land flowing with milk and honey, Bacchus reigning in the vineyards and Ceres in the fields under the mild climate desired by the philosophers of old, with plenary indulgence for all masters and students.[11]

One student fondly recalled the activity at Paris, noting ''Happy the exile who is allowed to stay at this place.'' His praise was not universally shared, as another student observed that the university's pleasant exile was at odds with the Christian life; he exclaimed, ''Oh, Paris! How you trap and deceive the soul.'' He warned prospective students that ''life rather than lecture preaches; simplicity rather than syllogism'' was the proper education. Despite his warnings, many bright, adventurous boys and men found universities to be irresistible.

A university was a special place because it concentrated resources and attracted scholars from many regions and countries. Faculties and student groups often were organized along national or ethnic lines. Jacques de Vitry has left us this account of ''student nations'' at Paris:

They wrangled and disputed not merely about the various sects or about some discussions; but the differences between the countries also caused dissensions, hatreds, and virulent animosities among them, and they impudently uttered all kinds of affronts and insults against one another.[12]

An inventory of national and regional slurs among medieval student groups follows:

English	drunkards; have tails
French	proud; effeminate, adorned like women
Germans	obscene at feats; furious
Normans	vain and boastful
Poitevins	traitors and adventurers
Burgundians	vulgar and stupid
Bretons	fickle
Lomards	avaricious, vicious, cowardly
Romans	seditious, turbulent, slanderous
Sicilians	tyrannical and cruel
Brabants	brigands and ravishers
Flemish	fickle, pprodigal, gluttonous, slothful

One 13th century reporter said that student discussions often provoked national rivalries, and "from words they often came to blows." It seems that the national factions among students set historic precedent for the limited cooperation among the European Common Market countries of the 20th century.

INTERNAL LIFE AND REGULATIONS OF THE MEDIEVAL UNIVERSITY

The corollary to external privileges in dealings with civil authorities was that charters and codes insured that life within the university adhered to explicit regulations. Both formal codes and informal practices contributed to a distinctive institutional life. The following excerpt written by Pope Innocent III in 1209 reminded (and reprimanded) masters about proper deportment:

> . . . we learned that some recently appointed doctors of liberal arts deviated from the ways of their predecessors in three main points: the wearing of antiregulation dress; the failure to observe the accustomed order in lectures and disputations, and the neglect of the pious custom of attending the funerals of the deceased masters.[13]

The pope helped masters restore the code by having regulations written into statutes, which the masters would swear to observe. Costumes, ceremonies, certification, oaths, funerals, and piety—all general characteristics of medieval civilization—received an *academic* variant in the papal document.

According to the statutes of a papal legate, strict requirements governed the masters at Paris.[14] Those under twenty years old could not lecture in the arts; masters had to study in the arts for at least six years, promise to lecture for at least two years, and not be "smirched by infamy." A lecturer candidate had to be examined by the bishop of Paris. Teaching in the theology curriculm had the most stringent requirements: one had to be at least thirty-five years old, have completed eight years of university study, have studied theology for five years, and be "of approved character and learning." Lecturing was a public event regulated by statutes and custom.

Masters in the arts hand to wear a "cope, round and black and reaching to the heels—at least when it is new." They were required to attend student funerals and remain "until the burial is completed, unless they have some good reason." To curb corruption in examinations, the statute said, "no one is to receive a license from the chancellor or anyone else through a gift of money, or furnishing a pledge or making an agreement."

Student life was governed both by informal manuals (including John of Garland's 13th century *How The Student Should Behave*) and by university regulations. One surviving document, Robert de Sorbonne's *Statutes for a College*, dwells on dining regulations in the colleges (residential halls) and warns that "no one shall have loud shoes or clothing by which scandal might be generated in any way." Just as each guild had a trademark, each student was required to have his own mark on clothing, hood, and personal items. Membership in the college meant prohibitions; guests, women, and nonacademics could not enter college rooms. And, Sorbonne was firm in his command that "no fellow shall have a key to the kitchen."

Students also expected masters to fulfill obligations. At the start of a course, the master outlined materials to be covered, the fee schedule, provisions for review, and classroom procedures. Some masters concluded a course with a preview:

> It is an ancient custom in this city that when a book is finished, mass should be sung to the Holy Ghost, and it is a good custom and hence should be observed. But since it is the practice that doctors on finishing a book should say something of their plans, I will tell you something but not much. Next year I expect to give ordinary lectures well and lawfully, as I always have, but no extraordinary lectures, for students are not good payers, wishing to learn but not to pay, as the saying is: "All desire to know but none to pay the price." I have nothing more to say to you beyond dismissing you with God's blessing and begging you to attend the mass."[15]

A 14th century statement issued by the chancellor at Oxford attests to the importance of academic dress:

> . . . all regents in congregation assembled have ordained unanimously that a tailor when he cuts and measures the material to be distributed among the members of the University shall dispose and measure the fabric in such a way as to give the masters and bedells their robes not as short and reduced garments but as full length robes as they were wont to wear in times past. For it is decent and reasonable that those whom God has distinguished with inner qualities from laymen also be different from laymen in their appearance. If some tailor acts against this ordinance may he be punished with prison.[16]

Formality was tempered with kindness, as one chancellor allowed special summer dress: instead of heavy fabrics, "from Easter to All Saints' day, graduates and undergraduates who so wish may use silk robes, ancient custom notwithstanding."

According to documents and memoirs, a student's initiation into scholarly ranks required mastery of specified readings, attendance at lectures, and the swearing of an oath. Accurate reconstruction of *the pattern* calls for a look at a rule's intent and enforcement, as well as its formal statement. Although flagrant bribery and deceit were punished severely, evidence shows that a student could partially ease the crisis of examinations by holding a banquet for his masters. Within the university, penalties for rule breaking often *rewarded* the academic community. The statutes of the Sorbonne, for example, decreed that a fellow who attacked a servant must pay one *sester*, or four gallons of good wine—not to the injured servant, but to his own fellows.   This fine was comparable to that levied on a student caught speaking French instead of Latin in the hall or arriving late for dinner.

THE CURRICULUM

The bachelor of arts course apparently was an induction into the scholars' guild. It took about one and a half years of reading and lectures, during which the student could not teach. At the deposition, a freshman hazing where the new student had to host a banquet for fellow students and masters, he had to to swear to an oath of attendance and pay schooling fees. Afterward he received the gown called a *cappa*.

The master of arts course was longer and more important than the bachelor of arts curriculum. After having received the bachelor of arts degree, a student spent four to six years reading prescribed works and preparing for the inception—a formal, public disputation. Successful completion led to receipt of the license, in which the student marched in a solemn procession, knelt before the chancellor, and (once again) paid for the ever-popular academic banquet.

Medieval students and masters were scholars in the sense that they were learned and devoted to serious reading and disputations. Modern notions of research and expansion of information were alien, as the resolution of issues within certain logical boundaries held precedence. If there was a research mission of the advanced faculties in theology, it was to clarify issues of Christian belief via disputation. The medieval scholars were not literary figures—which has given rise to two strands of complaint.

A vocal minority of critics, notably John of Salisbury, wanted to include literature in the curricula. They were tired of disputations and complained that scholars tortured words and pondered a "small number of questions suitable for dispute on which to exercise their talents and waste their lives.'' Although the complaint was warranted, many issues which the scholars disputed were consequential—especially the reconciliation of seeming contradictions in Christian doctrine. Whereas John of Salisbury was bored with university studies, 13th century Church authorities were alarmed when Christian scholars aroused controversy by wandering from philosophy into theology. Access to translations of ancient (pagan) philosophers created a dilema for Christian belief: was Christian understanding gained through reason or revelation?

Our concern is less with an intellectual history of the university than with implications for academic structure. The university scholars embroiled in controversy with church authorities were not heretics, nor were they what we might call ''atheistic, radical free-thinkers.'' They were true believers, Christians who felt that if logic were applied to theology, doubt and disputation ultimately would confirm Christian beliefs. The organizational and professional consequences of theological disputes were in the realm of guild privileges. Masters' campaigns for recognition as a professional group with control over licensing was central to the notion of academic freedom. The scholars perceived the Church's attempts to intervene in academic disputations not only as intellectual controversies, but also as threats to their corporate professional statutes.

THE MEDIEVAL STUDENTS

The university's corporate protections shaped the academic profession and created structures within which an interesting student culture developed. Unfortunately, the medieval student world has been misrepresented and slurred. In the 1970s a number of successful (and vocal) American college football coaches defended large expenditures on intercollegiate programs on the ground that campuses would become dull, limpid refuges for ''monks'' and ''medieval scholars'' if financial support of the football programs was curtailed. Whatever the merits of football, such charges indicate a sloppy use history.

First, the tendency is to confuse and equate monasteries with medieval universities. Although both were under church auspices and had instructional provisions, each was a separate entity. Second, students at medieval universities hardly could be charged with reclusive, saintly, or ''monastic'' behavior. One 13th century chronicler recorded that university students:

> . . . go about the streets armed, attacking the citizens, breaking into houses and abusing women. They quarrel among themselves over dogs,

women, or what-not, slashing off one another's fingers with their swords, or, with only knives in their hands and nothing to protect their tonsured pates, rush into conflicts from which armed knights would hold back.[17]

Such an account suggests that American coaches would do well to borrow for their own athletes the medieval students' reckless abandon and ferocious courage in encounters which were not eased by shoulder pads, player substitution, or time-outs. Centuries before Notre Dame of South Bend, Indiana, acquired fame for football power, Notre Dame of Paris was the site of memorable student contests. Oxford's St. Scholastica's Day Riot, in which dozens of students and citizens were killed, was a big victory for Gown over Town—and makes contemporary football appear to be a tame, confined endeavor.[18]

The university's statutes did not exert complete control over students' activities. Students fended for themselves in lodgings and were under scrutiny of the masters only in certain situations. The university was not a residential campus; *colleges* or *hostels* were halls set up for indigent students, but hardly shaped the whole of student living. Within the structural ideal of proper behavior, as set forth in manuals and lists of regulations, students pursued their own interests. Diaries, poetry, chronicles, form letters to parents, and court records enable us to sketch a profile of the student culture. Along with the quarrels and rowdy fights noted earlier, students tended to be capable, serious, and learned. Readings, lectures, and examinations were rigorous. University education was not a gentleman's education. To the contrary, nobles who wished to pursue hunting, sports, martial arts, or territorial expansion had little desire to attend a university. Most crafts had their own arrangements for apprenticeship and licensing, so the medieval university was left to fulfill a few special purposes. The institution was characterized by remarkable self-selection: accessible to those who sought inclusion in the circle of scholars and teachers, it had little appeal to other groups.

University students had clerical status, yet few aspired to be ordained priests. The varieties of Church positions, ranging from teaching to the practice of canon law, brings to mind the scope of today's civil service. The terms clergy, cleric, and clerk indicate the association between church and the skills of literacy and recordkeeping, but do not imply that the university was a seminary. To the contrary, in Spain and a number of other European countries, severe problems of national economy developed when excessive numbers of young men sought to pursue professions under the auspices of church service.

Since acceptance into the university required clerical status, women were excluded by canon law from the university. Medieval students often entered the university at twelve or thirteen years of age and stayed for years, even decades. Student status overruled age differences. Although the degrees had minimum age requirements, it was not unusual to find thirty-five-year-old scholars who attended lectures and lived in hostels with fifteen-year-olds. Only in later centuries would emerge the idea of the boarding school in which young students were institutionally segregated from adults for reasons of social development, quite apart from academic considerations.[19]

Different conceptions of proper correlation between age and curricula are serious matters for higher education. Whereas the medieval universities were indifferent to studies arranged by age categories, most American colleges assumed that courses and activities would coincide with the designations of freshman, sophomore, junior, and senior. Professors expect freshman courses to be attended by seventeen and eighteen-year olds; alumni reunions emphasize class-year affiliation rather than field of study. Such internal patterns at American campuses were disrupted after World War II, when the G.I. Bill altered conventions about age-curricula correlation.[20] It was disconcerting to find a married, thirty-year-old veteran being called a freshman and being subjected to hazings conducted by a nineteen-year-old sophomore. Confusions increased in the 1970s when declining birthrates and changing career patterns induced American colleges to accommodate reentry and continuing education programs for students who had been away from school for several years.

SORTING OUT THE LEGACIES OF THE MEDIEVAL UNIVERSITY

How much, then, does the modern American university in its physical and corporate aspects really have to do with its medieval counterpart? The first difficulty in answering this question would be simply to find the medieval university within the city. No sketches, photographs, ruins, or restorations survive to guide a reconstruction of the buildings' appearance. The medieval university had no campus; chronicles and diaries indicate that hostels and colleges were undistinguished lodgings scattered throughout the town. Classrooms would be hard to locate, as each master made his own arrangements for renting lecture halls, which tended to be inexpensive, nondescript structures subject to change from term to term.

Gothic spires, glorified today as the architectural symbol of higher education in the Middle Ages, belonged to cathedrals, not to universities. According to Charles Homer Haskins, academia's fondness for Gothic Revival architecture originated at Oxford and Cambridge during the Tudor reign.[21] American higher education's fascination with medieval architecture has favored the English and Western European influence and neglected the older, advanced professional schools of universities in the southern areas of Europe. An exception is the University of California at Los Angeles, where in 1929 planners departed from the usual campus preference for Georgian brick and Gothic stone by drawing historical inspiration (but not accuracy) from the 13th century university at Bologna—an institution which, like UCLA, was located in a warm climate.[22]

Grand architecture, then, was not a product of the medieval university. Nor is there evidence of residential quadrangles, manicured lawns, research centers, playing fields, or agricultural experiment stations. Libraries were either small or nonexistent—one explanation for the popularity of lectures and note taking. Most continental universities never developed student dormitories as a formal part of the academic structure; it remained for Oxford and Cambridge in the 17th century to make residences the center of the university's instructional scheme.

The use of academic gowns and ceremonial costumes is an obvious historical continuity, yet requires careful reservation. Although medieval costumes inspire the American colleges' mortarboards and gowns, the results have been a crude approximation whose accuracy and longevity in America are exaggerated. College students and faculty in the United States did not wear caps and gowns until the 1880s. At that time, they were a fad which gave rise to debates over the propriety of academic robes. At some campuses, the robes were intended to democratize dress; elsewhere the aim was to exalt academic rank. According to one historian from Oberlin College, the colors and designs of modern hoods and gowns differ from medieval apparel. In the Middle Ages gowns were essential wear, designed to provide warmth as well as color. When American students did start to favor academic headgear, the medieval-style mortar board competed with visored hats and sailors' caps for popularity on campuses of the late 19th century.[23]

Modern evaluators probably would regard the financial and managerial arrangements of a medieval university as questionable. Conspicuously absent, by American standards, would be a board of trustees, a president, vice-presidents, development directors, or a financial planner. A chancellor or provost headed the medieval university. The office, neither permanent nor powerful, rotated among faculty members. Endowments and finances were not substantial.

The danger is our tendency to mistake peripheral support services for the essence of a university. The legacy of the medieval university is, in part, the art of omission; it may not have provided a campus or physical plant, but it did codify well-defined institutional rights. Impressive buildings would lack educational mission without the statutes and charters which were negotiated by masters and students in the 13th and 14th centuries. The university's *corporate* identity and structure of rights and authority endure beyond picturesque architecture.

The particulars of the medieval curriculum are alien to students today, even though we have adopted the "bachelor of arts" nomenclature. Liberal arts as education of the "whole person" was an educational ideal of ancient Greece or Renaissance Italy, not of the Middle Ages. There was no claim that the institution would provide "socialization" for the region's privileged youth; i.e., it was not "elite" education. The curriculum was an important influence on modern practice as evidenced by today's conventions of syllabi, lectures, examinations, and degree requirements arranged in a systematic, accountable manner.

Today one hears the lament that the Ph.D. has been debased to a union card for college teaching. In fact, that is its historic connotation. Medieval universities contributed to the formal recognition of scholarship as a profession; scholars who held degrees or licenses were a guild. Such professional licensing was taken seriously, as it gave teaching and scholarship a transcendent dignity and status. To receive the master's license meant not only that one had completed study requirements, but also that one accepted lifelong rights and obligations as an academic guild member. University licenses worked in two ways: their positive effect was to bestow honor and the privilege to teach; their negative, proscriptive dimension was to prohibit those who did not hold the degree from teaching. Thus, students were protected from educational malpractice, comparable to the protection buyers enjoyed against faulty crafts and services by tradesmen who were required to display their insignia and license.

The notion of academic certification is a medieval legacy which has expanded far beyond its original application. The academic guild was only one of many guilds in the Middle Ages, whereas in the 20th century university degrees have been extended to include nonacademic areas. Today one measure of a field's legitimacy is that its training and certification take place in a college or university. Since the late 19th century such fields as law, medicine, engineering, pharmacy, and business have shifted from apprenticeship arrangements or independent schools into university settings. A review of the range of degree programs now offered by a large state university leads one to wonder if there are any fields which now do not claim academic stature. Medieval citizens endorsed the practice that all crafts and professions should require licenses; but they would have been puzzled by Ezra Cornell's claim, "I would found an institution where anyone could study anything."

The logos, seals, and mottoes found on contemporary college diplomas are a rich inheritance from the medieval university, whose licenses asserted the standard of *pro bono publico*—"for the public good." Each American institution gives a concise statement of its educational mission via its motto. Some familiar examples, accompanied by translations from Latin to English are as follows:

> *Fiat Lux* ("Let There Be Light")—University of California
> *In Deo Speramus* ("In God We Trust")—Brown University
> *Multa Lumina, Lux Una* ("Many Lamps, One Light")—Claremont University Center
> *Veritas* ("Truth")—Harvard University
> *Lux et Veritas* ("Light and Truth")—Yale University
> *Leges Sine Moribus Vanae* ("Law Without Morals is Vain")—University of Pennsylvania
> *Incipit Vita Nova* ("A New Life Begins")—Scripps College
> *Vox Clamat Desertio* ("A Voice Cries Out in the Wilderness")—Dartmouth College

Some campuses have forsaken Latin mottoes for straightforward statements in English; Iowa State University's no-nonsense declaration on its seal is "Science with Practice." At Harvard in 1962 a controversy developed over the proposal that diplomas be worded in English rather than the traditional Latin. In any case, the medieval practice of dignifying academic certification has taken root in American life today, both inside and outside colleges and universities. An educational irony of the 1970s was that the demand for college degrees rose sharply at the same time that numerous articles featured evidence to "prove" that the college degree was an expensive investment with dubious personal and professional returns.

Those who possess a college degree often dismiss casually the stigma, whether self-inflicted or externally imposed, felt by those who do not have a diploma. One measure of the enduring prestige of academic certification in recent years has been the growth of a counterfeit diploma industry. One reporter documented a company's offer to supply a customer with a "beautiful, exacting copy" of a Stanford diploma for $45. Extras, including designation of major, department, or *cum laude*, were available at added cost. The number of complaints about the bogus degrees was so large that the State of California pressed charges against the soliciting company; individual campuses created form letters and files for dealing with "Doubtful Princetonians," "Columbia Special Cases," and other academic imposters.[24]

The booming counterfeit diploma market suggests that many people covet the college degree, if not the expense and experience of going to college. Their motives include gaining a job, impressing clients, making business deals, or being admitted to graduate programs in order to pursue another degree. The mystique and value of an academic degree might explain a peculiar syndrome: editors of Who's Who reported that many successful nominees for the biographical directory have made false claims about holding a college degree, even though their fame did not depend on formal education. Fortunately, the counterfeit degree abuses have been curbed by vigilant registrars, whose knowledgeable eyes and fidelity to the medieval preoccupation with symbols and trademarks enable them to identify inauthentic diplomas by spotting errors in signatures, dates, and departments.

Deceit, however, is not the only problem which plagues academic certification. A number of degree-granting institutions have confused the idea of what a college diploma represents and under what conditions it is awarded. Instances in which individuals and institutions worked out mutually agreeable arrangements for buying and selling diplomas indicate a warped idea of "consumerism" in higher education. One institution which was struggling to bolster its endowments ran advertisements in national literary magazines for a "genuine" honorary Ph.D., printed on the "same high-quality imitation sheepskin used by leading colleges and universities, for $150." The idea was that the institution would trust candidates to set and fulfill their own advanced study requirements; these would be duly acknowledged by the institution once the candidate had submitted his donation/processing fee. One could argue that most established colleges and universities grant honorary degrees to persons far removed from educational, academic, or intellectual pursuits.

While the preceding case represents an institution which has sought students and diplomates, the certification marketplace also has allowed the process to be reversed. The following notice suggests how one achievement-oriented individual discarded modesty to match himself with a deserving university:[25]

HONORARY DEGREE WANTED

Desire Ph.D. of honorary doctorate in business or business administration. Will gladly take necessary examinations and/or make suitable pecuniary or civic contribution to college of higher learning which is able and willing to bestow the degree on me. I am age 60, financially responsible and successful. Already have qualifications as follows: B.A. Cornell University, graduate work done at Columbia University (advertising), former president and general manager of highly successful radio-TV operation, and now president of a successful and lucrative real estate operation, 25 years resident of same city and am financial advisor to many of its local businessmen, am listed in "Who's Who in the West", 3-1/2 years member Board of Regents State Junior College, references of any nature can be supplied, good Dun and Bradstreet rating available. The worst I have ever done in breaking a law is to get one speeding ticket for going 70 miles per hour last year, no other violations whatever or ever! I should like to meet any requirement and receive sheepskin by March 25, 1978 and will not be easily available after that date. Have made many civic contributions such as founder, officer and director of local national bank, local Red Cross, city library building fund, founder and past president Rotary Club, etc. Write immediately to Box A2-105, The Chronicle of Higher Education or phone me at 801-259-5991.

Certification, which the medieval universities developed as a source of societal protection and order, has run the risk of becoming a modern liability because of the excesses of inflation, debasement, and imitation. If academic degrees lose integrity and public confidence, colleges and universities may cease to be acknowledged as *bona fide* certifying agencies. Herein lies a central feature of the medieval university—instruction and certification combined under the same auspices. It is a practice followed today at most American colleges and universities: a professor teaches a course and assigns a grade for student work, which in turn is accepted as official credit toward degree requirements. This arrangement seems familiar and obvious, yet it need not be so. At Oxford and Cambridge, for example, colleges offer residence and instruction to students, while the university administers examinations and awards degrees. German universities of the 19th century provided students with rigorous instruction, social prestige, and professional preparation, yet did not award what we would consider an undergraduate degree.

Similarly one might argue that in the United States, bar examinations, not law degrees, are the ultimate determinant of who has the right to practice as an attorney-at-law.

Declining confidence in academic degrees might promote a separation of instruction and certification. One view of contemporary American higher education might hold that certification takes place at entrance examinations, rather than after fulfillment of degree requirements. One may enter college without a high school diploma, yet may be required to take (and achieve a prescribed score) on the Scholastic Aptitude Test (SAT). High performance on the Law School Aptitude Test (LSAT) may be of paramount importance for admission to law school if grade inflation renders undergraduate transcripts invalid as a discriminating source of academic performance evaluation. It is possible that the academic guild (i.e., the faculty at colleges and universities) has abdicated a considerable part of its certification authority to such testing enterprises as the College Entrance Examination Board and American College Testing. Reliance on an external agency, rather than on the examinations and evaluations made by faculty, is a *de facto* erosion of the certification legacy handed down from the medieval university.

CONNECTING MEDIEVAL AND MODERN INSTITUTIONS

To locate the heart of the medieval university requires one to resist preoccupation with nostalgic forms. True, academic robes and gothic revival architecture provide the modern university with inspirational color and traditions. But these forms are little more than pleasant distractions if they are resurrected without connection to the legal and structural foundations of medieval life. A healthy sense of historical revivalism is to regard the pomp and ceremony as outward signs of a remarkable *corporate* legacy. The medieval university was a complex institution which formalized higher education by means of elaborate charters, codes, and statutes. Advanced instruction was fused with orderly arrangements for examination and certification. Without an appreciation of the political, legal, and social circumstances of the period 1100 to 1300, it is unlikely that we can understand the fundamental assumptions which shape the university as an institution with distinctive privileges and obligations.

FIGURE 3

The Mix of Modern and Medieval Forms in the American University: "Girder Gothic" Construction of the University of Pittsburgh's remarkable "Cathedral of Learning," circa 1929.

Reproduced courtesy of the University of Pittsburgh Libraries, Department of Special Collections.

3

The Collegiate Ideal: The Oxford-Cambridge Legacy

Oxford and Cambridge, consciously and unwittingly, have provided American higher education with symbols, forms, and vocabulary for much that is cited as the ultimate good in undergraduate education. These two British universities have come to stand for the "collegiate ideal," whose features include residential education, tutorial instruction, attention to campus landscape, and construction of quadrangles. The ideal suggests nonprofessional education for the gentleman-scholar, whose academic achievement is fused with "character."[1]

One might also add such trappings as crew races, pipe-smoking, tweed jackets, and an elaborate extracurriculum, although a list of components alone fails to congeal the elusive collegiate ideal. The Oxford-Cambridge legacy includes a spiritual dimension—the symbolic associations which led Frank Aydelotte to initiate an honors program and selective admissions at Swarthmore in the 1920s, or which imply prestige when California's Claremont Colleges are nicknamed the "Oxford of the Orange Belt." The British collegiate ideal was cited to inspire and explain the "cluster-college" phenomenon of the 1960s, a strategy for institutional alchemy by which Clark Kerr hoped to make the American university appear smaller as it grew larger. And in the 1970s, Oxford and Cambridge are the historical inspiration for St. Mary's College of Maryland, an institution which has taken on the exciting task of creating a quality residential liberal-arts college in the public sector.

Celebration of Oxford and Cambridge as models for American higher-education innovation has been accompanied by equally strong dissent, which adheres to a predictable, recurrent formula:

And what, indeed, are these prescriptions? They are adaptations of the courses of study originated in European, especially English, universities. Basically, they represent the sort of thing required to educate the son of an English gentleman, that is to say, an English man who has inherited money. . . But it is applied to the education of the sons of American farmers, store-keepers, plumbers, policemen, and street-car conductors who have not inherited money and have made enough to send their boys to college only by years of intense concentration on their jobs, to the exclusion of purely intellectual interests.[2]

The significant social fact of these debates is that both sides know their lines sufficiently well that the British collegiate ideal is discussed in symbolic shorthand. All the connotations and implications are captured in the term *Oxbridge*, which compresses centuries of institutional history into a single image. One problematic side effect has been that American students and educators tend to mistake Oxford and Cambridge for the whole story of British higher education, to the neglect of identities and innovations at more than forty other colleges and universities. The imbalance and distortion has been such that administrators of the Fulbright awards and Marshall scholarships were prompted to put out descriptive brochures after they noted that only the University of London had managed to attract a sizable number of American fellowship applicants away from Cambridge and Oxford.[3]

The term also glosses over differences between Oxford and Cambridge. As Noel Annan, a Cambridge graduate, observed, "Although the ancient universities resemble each other more than they do any other university, their alumni love to depict the subtle distinctions which evoke in Cambridge an ethos different from that in Oxford."[4] Oxford, whose reputation is that of a flamboyant, worldy mother of statesmen and public servants, contrasts markedly with Cambridge's reknown as an austere home for the science. The two universities have differential exposure; Annan summed up his contrasts with the comment, "Oxford is still news. . . ." Uneven coverage in the United States press, weighted heavily toward Oxford, has been due to fascination with the Rhodes scholarships and the subsequent zeal of those Americans who return from their Rhodes experience eager to bring a bit of Oxford back to the provinces. It is not by accident that we are apt to hear *Oxbridge*—rather than *Camford*—as the collective term for the British collegiate saga.[5]

The Oxbridge image is attractive because it suggests enduring and timeless forms and values. The danger is that we mistake "timeless" imagery for static history and frozen institutions, when such is not the case at all. The Oxbridge image testifies to the Universities' abilities to endure, yet is deceptive in that one does not gain readily a sense of the changes, fluctuations, and stances that accompanied endurance within each institution. How, for example, did the collegiate ideal come to be acquired, given the markedly different character of the medieval universities? What has been the interplay between universities and religious, political, and legal events? To what extent did British emigres transplant their collegiate arrangement to America and to other colonies and provinces?

Oxford and Cambridge have long commanded the attention of writers—of so many that one prominent academic library in the United States houses a special collection devoted solely to books dealing with the city and university of Oxford. The overwhelming abundance of commentaries and materials means that any attempt to deal comprehensively with Oxbridge history in a single chapter is destined to fall short. Hence, the limited task here will be to survey briefly centuries of institutional history with emphasis on additions and modifications in the images of Oxbridge students. The intent is to use these changing student images to identify changing social meanings of "going up to university," which will require attention to complexities of institutional change and to problems of ascertaining relations between schools and society.

THE SCHOOL AND SOCIETY ISSUE

Educators and lobbyists for school funding are fond of claiming that school systems have improved local and national life. Conversely, schools have been praised for their ability to preserve and hand down existing cultural values. A less complimentary view is that expansion of formal education has been inconsequential and ineffective as an agent of either social change or social conservation. The best resolution to these conflicting claims and circular arguments is to say that schools and society are not isolated from one another, although the nature and extent of connections are subject to variation according to time, place, and institution.

Official house histories of colleges and universities have been faulted for dwelling on *internal* events, oblivious to the larger world in which the institution is set. Bad as that fault might be, attempts to make higher education a part of social history have often been crude and unconvincing. The worst abuse has been the "paste-up" approach, in which an author presents a survey of national events and trends that parallel institutional events, leaving readers with the unwarranted impression that the connections between college and culture, school and society, are wholly congruent, consequential, and self-evident.

Historian Lawrence Stone, author and director of perceptive studies on higher education, has written directly to this point by noting that the school and society fallacy is the contention that "schools respond to societal needs." The flaw in such thinking, Stone argues, is "the assumption that there is a one-to-one correlation between what goes on in the university and the needs of the outside society." Rather, he points out that colleges and universities, as all social institutions, "are partly functional and partly antiquated, vestigial, or even frankly 'dysfunctional.' . . . All have a history and a life of their own, and their responses to outside pressure is consequently imperfect, stumbling, tardy, even reactive."[6]

How might Stone's warnings be heeded so as to promote a social study of colleges and universities which goes beyond parallel surveys of institutional events and national history? It is a perspective which reinforces Thorstein Veblen's concept of "lag"—the notion that a particular institution can be ahead of, behind, in step with, or oblivious to widespread ideas and practices. It is also congruent with sociologist Robert Merton's classic typology of groups and social structure. According to Merton, two important indicators of societal arrangement are whether a group aspires to socially approved goals and whether that group uses legitimate means to achieve those social goals.[7]

Following this scheme, a "pillar of society" is one who has done all the right things, played by the rules, and who is a winner and a success. Obviously, those who scorn both socially approved goals and conventional ways of doing things are designated outcasts or radicals. Categories become intriguing when we identify the retreatist or ritualist configuration, in which individuals go through the forms or motions of conventional aspiration, yet fail, or do not have their "hearts really in it." In contrast are those groups which use illicit means (vice, fraud, or other crime) to acquire wealth, status, legitimacy, and power for themselves or for their families.

If institutions possess corporate personalities, as the Cambridge alumnus noted in his discussion of subtle differences between Oxford and Cambridge, Merton's typology can be useful for describing how a particular school meshes or does not mesh with the larger social structure. This provides a coherent strategy for tracing institutional ascent and failure, for charting historical changes in the reputations and powers which colleges acquire and lose. The crucial consideration is that researchers must not only reconstruct some internal phenomenon (in this chapter, we shall focus on *who* were students at the universities), but also analyze *how* these educational and academic affiliations and activities were perceived and evaluated by various groups *outside* the colleges and universities.

Given Lawrence Stone's warnings, this requires attention to detail, as there is no guarantee that a particular campus will exhibit a consistent configuration in its policies and practices. What follows is not a total history; that is, we are not looking closely at the composition of the faculty, the arrangement of institutional finances, or the content of curricula. The attempt is to bridge social history and institutional history by showing how external national events and circumstances were related to reasons for "going up to university" and ways in which these historical changes contributed to the Oxbridge collegiate ideal which American educators have inherited.

THE CLERIC-SCHOLAR AND THE LAY SCHOLAR: DRASTIC CHANGE IN THE SIXTEENTH CENTURY

Oxford, followed by Cambridge, was founded in the Middle Ages and adhered to many of the patterns associated with the generic medieval university described earlier. One important deviation was that the British universities were not located in urban settings. Oxenford, site of the oldest university, was pastoral and provincial; it is plausible that the university might have acquired a different character and constituency had it been located in London.

For our purposes, it is important to note that Oxbridge students originally matched the profile of medieval cleric-scholars whose professional aspirations, beyond the hope for more study, usually consisted of church or state service in administration or canon law. Geoffrey Chaucer, himself a soldier and a diplomat, included a portrait of the English student during the late Middle Ages, the memorable "Clerke of Oxenford," in *The Canterbury Tales*, from which we glean the following features. He was thin, hardly overfed. The little money he had, often borrowed from friends or scrounged, went for books or to pay masters for courses. He read Aristotle and the ancient philosophers; he was happily immersed in a life of studies; and, to quote Chaucer, "gladly would he learn, and gladly teach."

It is difficult to associate the collegiate ideal with early Oxford and Cambridge, as the crucial internal units (which had disappeared by the

16th century) were called "halls." The legal and corporate entity of the university existed before the now famous colleges did. Although the cleric-scholar and the primacy of the university characterized Oxbridge in 1500, these images were drastically altered by 1600.

The structural change, starting in the 15th century and gaining momentum in the 16th and 17th centuries, was the practice of benefactors' and sponsors' founding *colleges* within the university. One could argue that the subsequent history of Oxbridge was the addition of new colleges; such generous patrons as bishops, monastic orders, or even the Crown would establish a college complete with elaborate provisions for fellowships, preparatory schools, stipulations on studies and curricula, living arrangements, and even rules regarding the geographical areas from which students must be selected. Oxford University in the 1500s came to be dominated by its member parts, the colleges. Today, Oxford consists of more than thirty colleges, each with its own traditions and emphases, ranging from All Souls (for graduate fellows) to Girton (for women). Even today, alumni loyalty and ties are strongest with the college, secondarily with the university.

Although institutional history requires attention to gradual change, one must also be alert for dramatic incidents which directly alter a campus. Such was the case with Oxbridge in the 16th century. The general external trend resulted from King Henry VIII's disputes with Rome and the church over his marriages. Here, university-educated scholars—canon lawyers—were influential and important in matters of church and state as advisers to the king as well as administrators of bureaucracy and legal affairs throughout the nation. The canon lawyers of the 16th century literally had their days in court, but fell from royal favor because they failed to provide the tight legal case which Henry VIII could fend off equally adept canon lawyers representing the papacy. When Henry VIII declared the Act of Supremacy and established the Church of England, the medieval profession of canon law and its place in the university came to an end.

Thus by 1540, the universities were dramatically changed by two events, both related to England's break with Rome. First, confiscation of monastic lands and dissolution of monastic orders meant that some of the most powerful colleges at Oxford and Cambridge were eliminated, since they had been founded by monastic orders. Second, prohibition of canon law and the awarding of canon-law degrees suddenly removed the most important and oldest course of study and professional preparation from Oxbridge. As Hugh Kearney has noted, "At one stroke a whole profession was abolished,'' and with it, a branch of university study.[8] What has been called the Tudor Revolution in church and state was equally dramatic for the complexion and composition of higher education.

These two dramatic events marked the passing of the medieval cleric-scholar. True, future clergy might still be educated at Oxford and Cambridge, but they would be parish clergy rather than canon lawyers or monastic leaders. A related consequence was that common law, a profession for which one was educated at the Inns of Court (not a part of the university), suddenly surpassed canon law as the most powerful career. As for the character of students, the consequence of the dissolution was that the university gained appeal with prosperous merchants, lawyers, and landowners who wished their sons to have a formal education. The shift, rather abrupt, was from the education of cleric-scholars to the education of lay gentlemen at Oxbridge.

Here, then, is the genesis of Oxbridge's association with the collegiate ideal and with the gentleman-scholar. Specifically, the Christian gentleman of the 16th and 17th centuries was often a Puritan gentleman. He was worldly in that he would inherit wealth, position, and contacts from his family in such areas as commerce, law, or politics, but he took his education and religion seriously and saw them as inseparable from national and local issues. Such students should be distinguished from gentleman-scholars whose families were the landed gentry. The distinction is important, as subsequent national struggles and disputes took place among this university group.

The important social change in the attraction and purpose of university education was that "going to university" ceased to have its medieval prospect for *professional* advancement in canon law, in the church. The new wrinkle was that gentlemen, both urban and rural, saw the university in terms of *social status* rather than professional power. A university degree did not make a gentleman, but for the first time, the academic experience and degree were perceived as fitting for gentlemen and as one of many useful steps toward high social rank. One indication of this change in social function and composition has been found in colleges' rolls and records, of the 16th and 17th centuries, in which registrars billed students according to social rank. Gentlemen were charged higher fees than plebes, who were also called "servitors" and "sizars." Hence, a young man entering the university had the freedom to identify himself, as a gentleman, but would have to weigh the benefits of paying additional costs to record this status officially.

Elimination of the colleges founded by religious orders did not curb growth of university enrollments. Instead, secular groups took increased interest in higher education. The Crown, for example, established regius professorships and founded such royal colleges as Trinity and Christ Church, which were called "academic palaces." These royal actions reflected not only interest in learning, but also a measure of self-protection as a means of monitoring and determining who would teach what subjects to which students. Although the university had shed much of its function of clerical education, religion, and orthodoxy remained important, as those who were not members of the Church of England were not allowed entrance.

THE UNIVERSITY AND SEVENTEENTH CENTURY CIVIL WAR

The problem for our institutional survey during the 17th century is to delineate the character and activities of Oxford and Cambridge in the midst of external conflict and almost a century of civil wars. Had the universities been unimportant or disinterested bystanders, the question would be moot. Such was not the case, however.

The national or external events from 1603 to 1688 included the ascension of the Stuarts to monarchy, attempts to restore Roman Catholicism to England, the execution of a king, the establishment of Oliver Cromwell's Protectorate and the Long Parliament, the restoration of Charles II, and finally, the Glorious Revolution of 1688, in which William and Mary were established on the throne in conjunction with parliamentary rule. The latter act was especially significant for American higher education, as the College of William and Mary was founded in the Virginia colony in 1693.

Keeping in mind the warning about the school and society platitude, one cannot automatically surmise university involvement in these national events. Tribute to the importance which the Crown and parliament attached to the universities, however, is the fact that between 1600 and 1660 there were at least five official visitations, involving governmental scrutiny of curricula, students, and faculty, with special attention to signs of loyalty, orthodoxy, and conformity. The issues with which university education was concerned—the proper study of theology, the training of future leaders, the granting of appointments and fellowships—were viewed by both sides of the civil and religious disputes as having real and symbolic importance. Civil wars did impede the daily and annual round of institutional life in that enrollments dropped to all-time low figures in 1640-1643. As the Oxford vice-chancellor lamented in his address to convocation on the impact of the war, "We will hang our harps on the willows and now at length bid a long farewell to learning."[9]

He had good cause for sorrow, as the city of Oxford had supported the victorious Parliament, while the university had remained loyal to the Crown. A logical expectation would have been for the university to receive a reprimand and punishment at the hands of Oliver Cromwell. Surprisingly, punishment and censorship were mild. The comparable incident of the forgiving of universities took place in 1660, when King Charles II ascended the throne, displacing the Puritan control. Leaders on both sides of the religious and political disputes smiled with favor on the universities, in part because many of these opponents shared the common bond of having graduated from Oxford and Cambridge. Elites and leaders did not share the populist view that the universities were "nurseries of wickedness" and "dens of mutton-tuggers."[10]

STUDENTS AND THE SPORTING LIFE: INSTITUTIONAL STAGNATION

The period after 1660, stretching well into the 19th century, has the dubious and uncontested reputation as the longest, lowest era in the academic and educational life of the universities. This stagnation at Oxford and Cambridge during the 18th century upsets any facile claim that academic greatness goes hand-in-hand with construction and architectural splendor. During this century, the campuses acquired the magnificent and picturesque visual image which has been celebrated and handed down to us, but the academic dimension of study and learning ceased to be important to fellows, dons, and students.

The emergence of the Christian gentleman or Puritan scholar in the 16th century indicated that the quest for high social standing was not inherently alien to serious study in classics, theology, and philosophy. The Puritan gentlemen in England (and, more familiar to Americans, in the New England colonies) were definitely an elite; but privilege and wealth were viewed as preludes to sober, learned service in national and commercial affairs. In the 1700s, the combination of high social standing and academic rigor among undergraduates broke down. Universities' pastoral settings, which appealed in the 16th century, to Puritan fathers' desire that their sons be spared the evils and temptations of city life, became havens for those same vices by the 18th century.

Anthony Wood, who provided an excellent account of the medieval

St. Scholastica's Day Riot at Oxford, has left the following complaint about the relaxation of manners and morals at Oxford of the 1700s:

> Before the war we had scholars that made a thorough search in scholastical and polemical divinity, in humane authors, and natural philosophy. But now scholars study these things not more than what is just necessary to carry them through the exercises of their respective Colleges and the University. Their aim is not to live as students ought to live, viz. temperate, abstemious, and plain and grave in their apparel, but to live like gentlemen, to keep dogs and horses, to turn their studies [and] coleholes into places to receive bottles, to swash it in apparel, to wear long periwigs; and the theologists to ride abroad in grey coats with swords by their sides.[11]

This strand of the Oxbridge saga is the conspicuous proliferation, even dominance, of the student as rake, or what might be termed the collegiate sport. Wood called them student courtiers, noting that they were "rude, rough whoremongers, vain, empty, careless." Worst of all, "the masters have lost their respect by being themselves scandalous and keeping company with undergraduates."[12]

Historians are still searching for conclusive evidence that any teaching or serious scholarship took place over a half-century period. Even the ritualistic pretense of academic duties seems to have been neglected by professors. The academic life had been usurped by the sporting life. Medieval statutes whose original intent was to endow colleges with provisions for scholarships for needy, able students were abused so that awards were handed down to relatives, friends, and neighbors, thus promoting insularity and provinciality within the colleges. As Felix Markman has noted, the drinking, gambling, and sloth within the universities were spectacular even by standards of 18th-century England—a period in which gin made drunkenness persistent and omnipresent. Serious scholars were in a marked minority, and Oxbridge would have provided 20th-century deans of admissions with nightmares. Samuel Johnson summarized the social gulf within the university with the observation, "We are men of wit and no fortune, and they are men of fortune and no wit."[13]

The significant social fact is that the stagnation and academic abuses at Oxford and Cambridge did not go unnoticed, either by satirists or by those concerned with scholarship and education. Although Oxford and Cambridge enjoyed a monopoly on granting degrees, thanks to their charters from the Crown, they were not the only organizational settings for advanced learning or higher education. Exciting and serious studies were taking place *outside* the universities, in the dissenting academies, the Inns of Court, the scientific research of the Royal Society, and in the Scottish universities and colonial colleges.[14]

REFORMING AND POLISHING THE COLLEGIATE IDEAL

The Oxbridge image circa 1800 is not especially flattering. If anything, present-day advocates of clean living, serious study, and hard play should cite Oxbridge's collegiate way as a model which should be avoided. On the other hand, 18th-century Oxbridge was an apt model for the excesses of F. Scott Fitzgerald's Princeton, or for the infamous contest between Yale College's classes of 1904 and 1905, in which the group with the lowest collective scholastic ranking was proclaimed victor.

The obvious sloth and educational waste within the universities were a national problem which resisted a solution. Governmental intervention in academic affairs risked violation of the colleges' custom of self-determination. Nonetheless, by the mid-19th century, a number of royal and parliamentary commissions started to investigate the universities. One consequence was that in 1871, universities repealed their religious test for loyalty to the Church of England. Yet reforms of undergraduate life moved slowly. The founder of Hertford College proposed that "every undergraduate had to do one written piece of work each week, and read it aloud before the whole college on Saturday." This innovation, along with plans to curb student spending and debts and to provide inexpensive living quarters, was rewarded with charges from within the university that the founder was "a crack-brained Man, being mad with Pride and Conceit."

The heroic figure in the formulation of Oxbridge's favorable collegiate image is Benjamin Jowett of Balliol College who, in cooperation with the Oxford Reform Act, initiated and/or elevated the tutorial system of instruction and the tripos (honors) examinations, and restored acceptability and honor to academic pursuits. Cambridge's nominee for greatness during the period of Victorian reform was Henry Sidgwick. The irony of this era, when Oxbridge's collegiate way regained and increased its stature, was that many advocates of reform within Oxford and Cambridge were looking *away* from the collegiate university plan. Despite the solid, confident Oxbridge image which we have inherited, there was considerable debate and confusion in the 1860s and 1870s over the idea of a college, especially over Oxbridge's peculiar tensions between the universities certification and professionalism functions and the colleges' residential and instructional purpose.

In contrast to the stagnant sporting life of the 18th-century undergraduate, the dominant ethos and image of Oxbridge students by the late Victorian period was that of the gentleman-scholar as public servant. This meant that Jowett's academic reforms had been fused with the idea and expectation that privilege incurred responsibility. The formal curriculum, weighted heavily toward the classics, was intended (among other things) to foster "character." This change in imagery and ideals was accompanied by a distinct career pattern: a large number of Oxbridge graduates assumed positions and pursued careers as civil servants in the imperial administration, serving as representatives in India, Burma, Africa, and hundreds of other distant colonies.

Another, related dimension of the late-19th-century undergraduate image came about via what has been called a revolution of the dons—the persistent and successful effort of university dons to salvage the place of Oxbridge in an increasingly industrial and commercial nation by reconciling the collegiate ideal with the business ideal. The dons' coup was to persuade wealthy, rising businessmen that "going up to university" was a good thing for their sons. The upshot was that the status and historical aura of the university were used to temper the business ethic with the collegiate ideal of national service. Henceforth, Oxbridge graduates were able and allowed to pursue business careers, since business was described as a profession. The corollary was that an inordinate number of sons from business families chose to enter nonbusiness careers (especially civil service, teaching, law, and science) after having attended university.[15]

FROM COLLEGIATE SURVEY TO COLLEGIATE SAGA

These reforms and campaigns of the mid and late 19th century rescued the Oxbridge collegiate ideal within the commercial culture. Although elements from earlier centuries contributed to the image, it is unlikely that Oxbridge would have had great appeal to American educators without the investigations and reforms of the Victorian era. The enduring image is what Abraham Flexner called the "ideal of the educated amateur": "the undergraduate who spends three to four years at Oxford or Cambridge and passes on, a charming and intelligent young person, but essentially an amateur, into parliament, the Civil Service, business, or a profession."[16]

Important to note are the *limits* of these educational reforms and collegiate ideals. Oxbridge did not—or was slow to—accommodate natural sciences, medicine, engineering, or law in the scheme of undergraduate education. The images which emerge from the 19th century are blurred, as the Oxbridge collegiate ideal is often mistaken for the invigorated public-school ideal of "muscular Christianity" developed by Thomas Arnold at Rugby and disseminated by Thomas Hughes in the popular classic *Tom Brown's School Days.* After all, the Duke of Wellington did *not* mention Oxbridge in his celebrated statement, "The Battle of Waterloo was won on the playing fields of Eton." On the other hand, the links between Rugby, Eton, Harrow, and the other great public schools and Oxford and Cambridge were strong and undeniable, as the "old school tie" was good assurance of admission to colleges in the universities.

Estimates of size and composition of student bodies are not wholly accurate. The best summary we can offer is this: the dominant "types" of students surveyed in this chapter were conspicuous and important, but they co-existed in some mix with earlier and other "types" of students. In terms of size, Oxford's enrollment grew in the 1500s and 1600s, suffered decline in the 1700s, and was marked by gradual increases in the 19th century. As for social composition, Lawrence Stone has documented and argued that in the 16th and 17th centuries, Oxford accomodated and was seen as an educational haven for bright boys from families of modest incomes—along with the university's appeal to the sons of wealth. In other words, there was considerable carry-over of the medieval tradition of patronage and educational mobility. We ought not over-estimate this "social access," yet it *was* much greater than the closed situation at the universities of the 18th and 19th centuries. Ironically, Oxford of the 16th and 17th centuries was attractive to *both* nobility and the poor; by the 19th century, those two groups were absent from the colleges—the poor were excluded, and the nobles went elsewhere for education. Social homogeneity was achieved within the British "upper middle class" at university.

Although one will never find "open access" or even "nation-wide representation" at Oxford and Cambridge, it is possible and important to delineate clogging and exclusion at their extremes. Such identifications suggest that the history of Western Civilization has *not* been the story of a linear extension of increasing educational opportunity. To the contrary, records of fluctuations in the size and social composition of the student bodies indicate declines in range of social class representation and a marked tightening of the socially exclusive character of life within the established universities of the 18th and 19th centuries.[17]

This leads to a sensitive issue for American expectations about democracy and educational opportunity: the persistence of social exclusion at Oxbridge. The preceding survey of undergraduate images has suggested significant changes in the student role and in the composition of the student body. These changes and related fluctuations in university respect and reputation in the nation have not implied great accommodation for either universal education or selection from a truly representative national pool. To look for that brand of egalitarianism invites frustration, for whether through stiff fees, religious tests, connections with the prestigious public schools, weaknesses in British secondary education, or popular indifference to university education, those students who have gone up to Oxbridge in 1600 and in 1900—have been essentially a social elite. That is neither a good thing, nor a bad thing, but it does suggest that one test for the societal and national purpose of these universities is as follows: During a given period, did Oxford and Cambridge succeed in educating a responsible and competent elite?

THE AMERICAN CONNECTION

We have noted that the late 19th century Oxbridge ideal of the "educated amateur" has had particular appeal for American liberal arts colleges. This curiosity and fascination is not without its myopia, since even the coveted Rhodes scholarships have tarnished spots within their image of excellence and success. When Cecil Rhodes (whose fortune was made through the very uncollegiate activity of mining diamonds in South Africa) applied to Oxford's Oriel College, the provost complained, "All the Colleges send me their failures."[18]

The connection between the Oxbridge ideal and American higher education precede the Rhodes scholarships and the 20th-century cluster-college enterprise. It is the 16th-century ideal of the educated Puritan gentleman which contributed to the shape of collegiate life in the New England colonies of the 17th century. In tracking down these roots of American colleges, we confront a perennial issue: how are educational institutions and ideas transplanted? Is the process one of distant emulation, or of direct contact and cooperation with the universities at Oxford and Cambridge? Given the stagnation we have observed in the 18th-century British universities, was Oxbridge an educational model to be embraced or avoided?

A debate among historians is over whether it was natural and inevitable that the American colonists should take the trouble to duplicate or follow the Oxford and Cambridge collegiate model. Frederick Rudolph, whose comprehensive history of the American college and university has become a classic of sound research and delightful writing, offers this account of the 17th-century colonial leaders:

Their purposes were complex, but among other things, they intended to recreate a little bit of old England in America. They did what people a long way from home often do, and certainly what Englishmen have often done. If it was the most natural thing in the world for an officer of the colonial service in the 19th century to dress for dinner in the jungle as if he were dining at his club in London, it was no less natural for the Englishmen of early Massachusetts to found themselves a college, an English college such as those they had known at Oxford, but particularly at Cambridge, where Puritan theology and Puritan aspiration had been especially nurtured.[19]

A contrasting argument by Oscar and Mary Handlin is that there was neither an imperative reason nor a precedent for colleges to be founded in the American colonies, that "higher education was not a usual feature of English colonies in other parts of the world."[20] The Massachusetts Puritans, far from imitating Oxbridge, wanted to create a new kind of college suited to carrying out their mission of creating a "city on a hill." Other historians have pointed out that features and practices of the American colonial colleges were often more like those of the Scottish universities than like Oxford and Cambridge.[21] Outside Massachusetts, especially at Virginia's College of William and Mary, historical records and charters indicate a significant departure from the Oxbridge curricula, as the colonial institutions had explicit provision for civil-service and professional education.

Drawing from Bernard Bailyn's hypothesis on education in the forming of American society, a plausible resolution of this debate might run as follows: The American colonists *thought* they were re-creating England—not just with colleges, but in the entire culture, family structure, and town government—but by the 18th century, they were surprised to find that they had developed their own style.[22] When the English ways and means were unavailable or unsuited to local conditions, colonists made improvisations, without being fully aware of their departures and uniqueness. The intent was for American colleges to be transplants of Oxford and Cambridge, but the colonial colleges acquired an increasingly American form, whether the colonists liked it or not.

THE PURPOSES OF THE COLONIAL COLLEGES: THE MINISTRY DEBATE

A related persistent issue concerns the fact that Harvard (founded in 1636) and subsequent early colleges were established as theological seminaries whose object was production of a ministry. An early pamphlet about Havard College, "New England's First Fruits," noted that the colony dreaded the notion of "leaving an illiterate Ministery to the Churches when our present Ministers shall lie in the Dust."

A clear understanding of American higher education requires that we recall the Oxbridge image of the Christian scholar and the Puritan gentleman of the 16th century, for this image appeared in the American colonies and at the American colleges. The Puritan tradition of a learned clergy was important, but there is a problem in historical conceptualization. We cannot apply our notions of clerical education and theological seminaries to the 17th-century colleges. As Richard Hofstadter and Wilson Smith noted,

> A theological seminary had no more meaning for them [17th century colonists] than an engineering school. They did not distinguish sharply between secular and theological learning. And they believed that the collegiate education proper for a minister should be the same as for an educated layman. They expected that the early colleges would produce not only ministers but Christian gentlemen who would be civic leaders.[23]

Perhaps a reasonable counterpart today is the tendency to perceive professional education as general education, that is, a number of people study for a law degree with little intention of practicing law, with the rationale that law is a good background to have for whatever field they enter.

One clear conclusion emerges from these arguments over collegiate forms and functions: the Puritan colonists displayed a remarkably strong sense of mission and order. Colleges may or may not have been a necessity, but once founded, they were not a peripheral or frivolous indulgence. In contrast to the sprawl, uncertainty, and conflicting purposes that can be identified in contemporary Amercian postsecondary education, Frederick Rudolph has noted, "At the beginning, higher education in American would be governed less by accident than by certain purpose, less by impulse than by design."[24] This extraordinary concern with colleges baffled the mother country; an attorney for the English Crown, tired of the colonial argument that a college would save souls, snapped back, "Souls! Damn your souls! Raise tobacco!"[25]

Weariness with the ministry debate and the stereotype of colonial colleges as hives of somber, tight-lipped scholars prompted Samuel Eliot Morison to investigate the history of Harvard College. His findings indicate that one must also see the colonial college as a place for the education of gentry and gentlemen, who were not as wealthy or as dissipated as their Oxbridge brothers, yet were hardly preoccupied with salvation in another world. As one wry journalist in 1897 commented, "One gets the impression from reading some of the old laws of Havard that in her early days her students devoted four-fifths of their time to pious works, and that butter rarely melted in their mouths. But laws are one thing and the observance of them is quite another.''[26] His revision is supported by the eyewitness account of two visitors from Holland at Harvard College in 1679, who found an unimpressive library, no professors, and ten students whose pipe-smoking led the visitors to believe they had stumbled upon a tavern, not a college. In fairness to the college, they happened upon Harvard at a poor time, when it suffered from the lack of a president, internal disputes, and low funding. Student riots over food during those years were fomented by the complaint that the former president's wife had been raking off profits by serving cheap food in dining commons, and that she had been caught putting lamb's dung in the pudding.[27]

To this one might add the revelry, gaming, and drinking of commencement excercises, which — against the wishes of college officials — had become a great popular holiday, a convenient excuse to crowd into Cambridge. Yet these anecdotes about student life do not diminish the claim that the Puritan ministers and leaders educated in the colonial colleges were capable and did constitute a learned and responsible leadership.

Provision for professional (clergy) education and general education in the same college raises the question of who was going to college in America and for what reasons. In the early 18th century, about half of Harvard's graduates went into the ministry, although an increasing number started to enter such learned professions as teaching, medicine, law, and commerce. It is important to note, however, that entry to most of these professions and vocations did not require a college degree. A liberal-arts education was seen as helpful, not necessary, for social and professional ascent. Consider the 1764 charter of the College of Rhode Island (later renamed Brown University):

> Institutions for liberal Education are highly beneficial to Society, by forming the rising Generation to Virtue, Knowledge and useful literature and thus preserving in the Community a Succession of Men duly qualified for discharging the Offices of Life with usefulness and reputation.

In a similar vein, John Witherspoon offered the following comments in 1772 concerning the College of New Jersey (Princeton):

> The children of persons in the higher ranks of life, and especially of those who by their own activity and diligence, rise to opulence, have of all others

the greatest need of an early, prudent and well conducted education. The wealth to which they are born becomes often a dangerous temptation, and the station in which they enter upon life, requires such duties, as those of the finest talents can scarcely be supposed capable of, unless they have been improved and cultivated with the utmost care. Experience shows the use of a liberal Education. . .to those who do not wish to live for themselves alone, but would apply their talents to the service of the public and the good of mankind.[28]

The American colleges were not "popular" institutions, as their aim was to educate a responsible elite. Supporters of Harvard in the 1670s summarized its importance to the commonwealth by noting, "The ruling class would have been subjected to mechanics, cobblers, and tailors. . . the laws would not have been made by *senatus consulta*, nor would we have rights, honors, or magisterial ordinance worthy of preservation, but plebiscites, appeals to base passions, and revolutionary rumblings, if these our fathers had not founded the University."[29]

Oxford's intellectual tradition of criticism, caution, and exposure of dubious claims carried over into the colonial colleges, as one prime purpose of the learned clergy was to guard the commonwealth from charlatans and religious zealots whose preachings departed from reason and order. The Harvard faculty of 1744, analogous to a consumer protection agency of the 20th century, warned citizens of the commonwealth that one preacher was suspect because he acted according to dreams and impulses and was charged with *enthusiasm*, which was considered a threat to the precarious social order which had been built in the wilderness of "Newe Englande."[30]

OXBRIDGE AND AMERICA: IMAGES AND IMITATIONS

All the preceding information suggests that the image of Oxbridge as a timeless pillar of British society is inaccurate, and that Oxbridge has not been without changes in the nature and reputation of undergraduate education. Furthermore, the various historically changing Oxbridge images of student roles—Puritan scholar, Christian gentleman, student athlete, and gentleman-scholar—have a long record of direct and indirect influence on American higher education. Looking beyond the colonial period into the 19th and 20th centuries, however, one can discern American patterns and practices which have curbed the extent to which the Oxbridge collegiate ideal has become the American collegiate reality.

One obstacle, noted at the start of this chapter, was the gulf in national philosophies of social mobility and educational opportunity.[31] It would be erroneous to accept at face value the American claim that theirs is a classless society void of schisms, differentiations, and syndromes of inequities in the social and economic order. American schools, however, at least have given lip service to and made some extensive provisions for the notion of "contest mobility," in which free public schooling has afforded numerous second chances to students. This contrasts with the ethos of "sponsored mobility," in which recruits into the British social elite have been carefully and consciously selected and guided through rigorous, prestigious institutions, including the famed public schools (which are private) and the universities of Oxford or Cambridge. And the absence of a nationalized, rigorous secondary school system in 19th-century America meant that few campuses were in a position to demand advanced scholastic preparation as an admission requirement.

The examples of Swarthmore, the Claremont Colleges, the University of California at Santa Cruz, and other Oxbridge-inspired programs have tended to promote selective admissions and/or honors courses and independent studies for American undergraduates, but these have usually been pursued within an American context; for instance, emulation of Oxbridge, no matter how strong, has prompted few campuses to switch from a four-year undergraduate curricula to the British three-year model. Electives, courses, cumulative degree requirements, mandatory attendance, and lectures have remained staples of the American liberal-arts colleges, which are reluctant to implement Oxford's and Cambridge's arrangement for collegiate tutorial instruction and university-wide syllabi examinations.

Several American institutions of the mid-20th century offered what was called the University College, but this was not a transplant of the decentralized "collegiate university" arrangement of the old British universities. Indicative of the lack of appeal which the Oxbridge administrative provisions have held for American colleges and universities has been the reception to the Claremont Colleges, perhaps the most enduring attempt to replicate the Oxford system. The prospect of a university without a president has been virtually beyond comprehension to Americans. When the trustees, faculty, and administrators initiated the Claremont Colleges in the mid-1920s, their plans included provision for a unique coordinating apparatus, an Oxford-inspired university. The resultant Claremont University Center has undergone no less than five name changes in fifty years, and its nature and functions are continually confused and misunderstood by outsiders, students, faculty, staff, and alumni associated with the member colleges. Although the Claremont Colleges have been academically sound and successful, it is not accurate to say that they have realized the Oxbridge ideal. It would be more accurate to see the Claremont Colleges as a federation of New England-style colleges rather than as "America's Oxford."[32]

Apart from social and philosophical differences between nations, the limits of the Oxbridge model in America are due to concrete reasons. American colleges and universities have accepted and adopted the Oxbridge penchant for the pastoral, picturesque campus. Yet Americans from the 17th to the 20th centuries have been either reluctant or unable to build those quadrangles which are the heart of the collegiate system at Oxford and Cambridge. The hilltop colleges of New England, especially Amherst and Williams in the early 19th century, had little provision for on-campus student housing. Students lived in the town, rented rooms, or scrounged for lodgings. True, American colleges in the 19th and 20th centuries built extensive dormitories, but a residential college hardly means that the tutorial instruction and collegiate living have been fused so as to promote close conference between student and don.

According to an elaborate memoir of student life at Yale in the 1870s, American colleges' eating arrangements were beyond the control of college officials and decidedly far from the Oxbridge ideals of dining commons and High Table. The Yale approach was that at the start of each academic year, groups of students formed clubs which hired cooks and stewards and rented off-campus kitchens and eating places.[33] Not until the late 1920s and early 1930s do we find concerted efforts on the part of American colleges and universities to build residential quadrangles which approximated the British model of the living unit as a locus of eating, instruction, counsel, and camaraderie. One reason was that construction was expensive and recruitment of dedicated residential instructors was difficult. Brown, for example, was unable to afford quadrangle construction in the 1930s (although the project was revived and completed twenty years later), opting instead for the novel and less expensive plan of organizing undergraduates around their fields of academic concentration.

Harvard's house plan and Yale's colleges are cited as the paramount American achievement in realizing the ideal of the collegiate university. What often escapes the formal record is that undergraduates and alumni resented and resisted the spanking new "model villages," as they were seen as an artificial intrusion on the historic student life of private dormitories, eating clubs, and independence in social affiliations.[34] Whether one looks at 1660 or 1960, the Oxbridge ideal has afforded American colleges and universities abundant inspiration and a difficult model for educational and institutional transplant.

4

Higher Education and National Development: Continental Universities, 1600 to 1900

UNIVERSITIES AND NATIONS: LOOKING FOR CONNECTIONS

Sorting through documents and records from the 19th century, one finds a tract within which appears the bold, alarming claim, "There is no higher education in France." Here is the kind of source material which threatens to end this chapter abruptly by providing an unexpected obituary for the history of universities. Although the brochure's assertion was misleading and not completely true, it does spur us to rethink our assumptions about the inevitable presence and durability of universities as a part of a nation's social, political, and economic fabric. Throughout the countries of Europe, from 1600 to 1900, there were recurrent and persistent campaigns to close or abolish universities. In some cases, these campaigns were successful.

These campaigns against universities are puzzling in that they point to both the solidity and the fragility of educational institutions. Had universities been completely fragile, they might have withered or died without external provocation. In fact, it was the *strength* of the universities to resist reform and accountability which kindled outside plans for their abolishment.

The abolitionist movements were also important in that they serve as a guard against our tendency to portray higher education as an unbroken success story of growth, expansion, and commitment to increased educational opportunity. One fallacy of institutional histories which this chapter hopes to correct may be termed as "follow the flag" syndrome in which an author tacks together a succession of institutional case studies drawn from various periods of time, the cumulative impact of which is presented as "evidence" of the "progressive sweep of history." Such narratives may kindle optimism and an exaggerated sense of manifest destiny, yet fail to reveal much about relations between higher education and a particular country. In this chapter, we will examine and question facile assertions and assumptions about national "progress" and the expansion of higher education.

There is, for example, a peculiar American belief that construction of new campuses, easing of entrance requirements, and increases in the percentage of eighteen- to 21-year-olds who attend postsecondary institutions have been interwined with national greatness. Possibly so—but one task for social and institutional analysts is to examine this claim and to pose with greater clarity and precision the connections and processes involved in the interplay between investment in higher education and a nation's distinctive character and development. Does "national development" connote economic growth, increased literacy, territorial expansion, mobility within the societal structure, political power, administrative competence, or cultural sophistication? How does funding a university contribute to national welfare or prosperity? Does expansion of higher education follow and merely ratify a nation's economic development?

To explore these questions, the cases and summaries covered in this chapter will at least entertain recent findings by economists, sociologists, and historians. Foremost, and disconcerting to conventional wisdom, has been the inability of social scientists to offer strong confirmation that there exist casual or correlational ties between higher education and numerous indices of national development.[1] Second, there is some evidence that the presence or absence of great universities ranks far behind other factors in explaining why particular countries emerged as strong nation-states. Availability of a skilled labor force or construction of a comprehensive railway system, rather than provisions for colleges and universities, might well be the keys to national greatness in the 19th century.

To explore these research revisions and to test hypotheses about higher education and national development, we shall consider briefly some incidents, trends, and vignettes dealing with Spain, Scotland, France, and the German states during the centuries from 1600 to 1900. A reasonable summary of higher education in Europe during those centuries follows: The universities established during the Middle Ages survived, and in the northern European countries university-building continued in the 16th and 17th centuries. But academic decline and university stagnation were a pervasive phenomenon which cut across regional and national borders during the 18th century, and were followed by concerted university reform programs in th 19th century. This is hardly the whole story, but it does provide a sound setting within which to examine complexities and ironies.

Chapters 2 and 3 noted that Oxford's and Cambridge's collegiate university model departed from the generic university associated with the Middle Ages. In this chapter, we pick up on that departure and resume observation of those universities on the European continent which evolved directly from the medieval universities. This distinction from the Oxbridge model includes the lack of appeal of the elaborate campus and residential scheme for those outside of the two English universities. The great European universities were usually located in cities, often in unspectacular settings. Academic affiliation on the continent emphasized the corporate association, not the construction of elaborate quadrangles and dormitories. Even in those institutions far from major cities, rectors and professors were uninterested in the logistics of housing, feeding, and policing students as a part of daily academic affairs.

Neither did there appear to be any requirement that a university stu· dent must first pass through a undergraduate liberal arts cirriculum prior to admission to advanced or professional studies, although such requirements varied from country to country. What we do find as a transnational trend in European countries between 1600 and 1900 is the appearance of a rigorous classical secondary educational system, based on the *gymnasium*, which selected and prepared a relative minority of schoolchildren for university studies.[2] It may well be that the secondary school, not higher education, was the crucial element of social and academic determination in the identification and preparation of leaders and elites. Certainly, in none of the European universities does one find espousal of the idea of mass higher education. There was, however, variance in *which* elites were pursuing which particular curriculum at a university. Lectures and syllabi rather than accumulation of course credits determined the instructional process. Degrees were awarded upon completion of comprehensive examinations and payment of a mandatory examinations fee. With this general introduction, let us turn to vignettes within European higher education.

UNIVERSITIES AND IMPERIAL SERVICE: SPAIN

Imperial Spain (Castile) supported expansion of higher education in two ways. The number of universities jumped from two in the mid-15th century to nineteen by the early 17th century. Records also indicate that student enrollments within these institutions increased steadily. One important point is that expansion was in large part due to the increased appeal which university studies and degrees held for the sons of Castilian nobility. The imperial bureaucracy thus enjoyed a situation in which it could select its officeholders and administrators from an educated nobility—a potentially "good thing" for affairs of church, state, and empire.

That prospect or generalization, however, fails to convey serious imbalances in composition of student bodies and distribution of academic rewards and resources within Castile's 19 universities. Richard Kagan's analysis of demographic trends, administrative records, and university archives suggests a more complicated profile of the place of higher education within the Hapsburg Empire.[3] First, Castile's three "imperial" universities (Alcala, Salamanca, and Valladolid) were the only universities which attracted students from all regions of the country. Most universities were local and regional in character and composition. Second, universities drew most of their students from relatively few urban areas, as students often attended the university located in the city where their families resided. So expansion of universities in Spain did not imply equal opportunity for or even distribution within or between regions.

The most severe imbalances were found in the inordinate attraction and prestige which the faculty of law held for aspiring students, to the neglect of Spain's historically strong and advanced studies in medicine, mathematics, and sciences. Furthermore, the three imperial universities held a virtual monopoly on routes to prestigious professional careers in law and in civil and canon administration. One consequence was that the new provincial universities held declining appeal to prospective students. Meanwhile, the three imperial universities were clogged with applicants.

Kagan's historical analysis revealed a related curricular pattern: relatively few students at the Spanish universities completed their studies and took degrees. The high attrition and incompletion rates were due in large measure to the high examination fees and to the corruption which came to be a part of faculty procedures in the awarding of degrees and licenses. Phillip IV even had to remind royal counselors in charge of patronage to consider graduates of universities other than Alcala, Valladolid, and Salamanca—but to little avail.

University education in Castile, then, narrowed to preoccupation with selection of and favoritism toward sons of nobles from among the ranks of thousands of students and office-seekers. Medicine, science, even theology took backseats to the primacy of law studies. As Kagan noted, Hapsburg Spain forfeited an opportunity to develop a broad-based university system in which access and rewards were oriented toward talent and achievement. Association of a university degree with competition for high office in the imperial service eventually led to increasing control of the universities by the Crown.

The smaller, newer, provincial universities attempted to attract students away from the prestigious imperial universities by offering students low examination and graduation fees, a survival tactic which turned the local and regional institutions into diploma mills. Nepotism and obsession with legal training and office-seeking contributed to the stagnation of the universities. Teaching and curricula were secondary to professional practice and collection of examination fees among professors. Although Spain had achieved a relatively high percentage of university attendance, the 18th-century universities had little in common with the academic excellence of their 16th-century counterparts. University education and certification had shifted from an academic elite to a social elite. Preoccupation with the prestige of law and legal careers eventually hurt the universities. When the profession of law declined in opportunities by the mid-18th century, the power and stature of the universities declined with it.

The argument that universities had contributed to the leadership and expansion of the empire is not very convincing in the case of Spain. A more realistic hypothesis is that the tight connections between university degree-granting and appointments to offices and the lure of positions in Madrid tended either to deny or to disappoint hundreds, even thousands, of able and ambitious students. (One irony is that administrative positions in the New World were perceived as leftovers for those office-seekers who could not gain appointments in Madrid, or for students from the less prestigious universities outside the favored circle of Alcala, Salamanca, and Valladolid.) It would not be inaccurate to say that the model of access, selection, finance, and certification which characterized the universities in imperial Spain ignored or thwarted talent which was a potential source of administrative expertise and service. Nor do we find evidence that the Crown, the nobility, or incumbents within the bureaucracy moved to support programs of advanced education in medicine, science, the arts, or other curricula which might have contributed to Spain's welfare in its economy, health, or manufacturing.

UNIVERSITIES IN SCOTLAND: EDINBURGH AS ATHENS

If Spain represents the extreme case of the European quest for imperial development, Scotland may well qualify as the opposite end of the spectrum: a small, economically underdeveloped country whose heritage and self-determination in matters of law, religion, and politics were precarious and shifting because of its proximity to England. Leaders and nobility in Scotland during the 17th century were forced to face the fact that political and economic divorce from England could not be pursued simultaneously. The goal of national greatness could not yet be reconciled with autonomy. Given these limits and compromises, how best could they foster nationalism in Scotland?

The 1707 Acts of Union brought Scotland's leaders (largely nobles) to London to take seats in the Parliament of Great Britain. Relocation of political acitivity from Edinburgh (heretofore Scotland's governmental center) to London was feared as a detriment to Scottish nationalism, since leadership would be drawn away from the local scene—a situation which might have reduced Scotland to a backwater whose elite was largely absent.

This was not the case, as universities in Scotland—Edinburgh, and to lesser extents Glasgow and Aberdeen—fostered the cultivation of a homegrown intelligentsia and an educated elite.[4] In the 17th and 18th centuries, the universities in Scotland did not follow the Oxford-Cambridge pattern of residential education for the sons of nobility and wealth. In Scotland, universities were urban in location and bourgeois in student composition. The academic life in Scotland remained closely tied to philosophy, mathematics, and religious studies. This latter tendency did not mean university withdrawal from national affairs; rather, the implication was the the clergy would remain active and potent in Scotland's politics and national issues. The universities in Scotland favored the pedagogical form of the lecture, in contrast to Oxbridge's tutorial sessions. Students lived in the city and tended to be academically serious. They were without hereditary title or great wealth and were upwardly mobile.

In the 18th century, one finds, Edinburgh students and alumni formed debating unions, political societies, and literary clubs which contributed to Scotland's national resources a lively, articulate, and intellectually disciplined group of young leaders, including such famous figures as Adam Smith and David Hume. Nicholas Phillopson's study, conducted under the auspices of Princeton University's Shelby Cullom Davis Center, argued that Edinburgh's relative isolation from London's political activity enabled this provincial city to host a generation of young university-educated men who established themselves in professions, launched political careers, and developed ideas and programs for national development and political economy in journals and debates.[4] Apart from the university's formal instruction, it was coffeehouses, clubs, and literary societies which promoted continuing intellectual and political endeavors. Perhaps this concentration of peripheral and informal resorces and facilities, which can attract and retain educated planners and thinkers, is one of the overlooked and unmeasurable services that universities can provide to national leadership. By this standard, Edinburgh is kin to the cluster of research organizations, publishing houses, bookstores, and consulting firms one finds in such American university cities as Cambridge, Berkeley, Iowa City, and Madison.

FRANCE: EDUCATION OUTSIDE THE UNIVERSITIES

At the start of this chapter we mentioned the claim "There is no higher education in France." The element of truth in that statement is that France's twenty-two historic universities were closed during the Revolution, and no university was reestablished until 1896. Many national and educational leaders argued that university abolition was no great loss, as these institutions had been inbred, stagnant, and impervious to reform for years. As Theodore Zeldin observed in his historical account of higher educatión in France:

> Many professors had abandoned lecturing altogether, and confined themselves to the lucrative task of issuing degrees. On one occasion the students of Bordeaux even used their professors to compel them to lecture, but this zeal was exceptional. . . . Examinations were more a financial than an academic matter, in fact the purchase of a privilege.[5]

The French universities followed a demographic trend which had appeared in Spain: the faculty of arts had become little more than a secondary school, as students' ages ranged from ten to seventeen years. According to Zeldin, this shift of the arts faculty toward secondary classical education impeded professor's involvement or interest in important scientific and scholarly investigations.

The closing of the universities did not mean that advanced and professional studies were abandoned in France. It does mean that those activities were pursued in new settings and arrangements *outside* the university structure and certification. In the United States, we now use the amorphous category, "postsecondary education" to link a variety of organizations which are not colleges or universities. In a similar vein, one finds in 19th-century France the flourishing of *ecoles normales* and *grandes ecoles*—institutions which were ostensibly committed to such specialized fields as teacher training, military education, and engineering, yet which were also sources of pedagogic innovation, seminars, advanced instruction, and research scholarship.

One remnant of the old universities which did survive in the 19th century were the so-called faculties, analogous to special colleges in such professional areas as medicine, law, theology, science, and pharmacy. Instead of a full-fledged university, a particular city held a cluster of faculties. But university reformers and rebuilders argued that these were fragmented institutional arrangements which could not—ought not—be accepted as permanent surrogates for a comprehensive university.

Universities were eventually restored in France, by 1896, and were accompanied by reforms in financial aid for students. The salient point is that reform within the old universities was unanimously regarded as impossible in 18th- and 19th-century France. Any experiments or expansion of national higher education had to take place outside the historic institutions. One curious phenomenon (by American standards) was the lack of professorial affiliation with the university. In contrast to the lóyalty and support from constituents, which the campus in America enjoyed, in France it was the faculty within a university which determined allegiance.

France's defeat in the war with Prussia in 1870 led to push for higher-education reform—namely, creation of a modern university. Their claim was that the German universities "had won the war."[6] Exactly *how* the German universities accomplished this military feat remained vague. This extreme statement characterized the overriding belief that higher education was of great importance for fulfillment of national destiny. In view of this admiration for universities in Germany, we will now turn to an examination of what all the shouting was about.

CREATING THE MODERN UNIVERSITY IN GERMANY

During the late 16th century, an itinerant scholar offered the following observation of academic life in Germany:

One thinge I cannot commend in the Germans, that for desyre of vayneglory, being yet without beardes and of smale knowledge, they make themselves knowne more than praysed, by untimely printing of books and verytoyes, published in theire names. Young students who have scarce layd theire lipps to taste the sweete fountaynes of the sciences, if they can wrest an elegy out of their empty brayne, it must presently be printed, yea if they can but make a wrangling disputation in the University, the questions they dispute upon, with the disputers names, must also be printed. Yea very grave men and doctors of the liberal professions are so forward to rush into these Olimpick games, for gayning the prise of others, as they seeme rather to affect the writing of many and great than judicious and succint bookes, so as theire riper yeares and second counsells (allways best) hardly suffice to correct the errours thereof, and change (as the Proverb is) quadrangles to round formes.[7]

The tendency toward academic Olympics which this observer satirized was a source of praise and envy among educators in the United States and Europe, especially when the German spirit was contrasted with the uninspiring examples of university stagnation in Spain, England, and France during the 18th and 19th centuries. German universities suffered comparable abuses in the 17th century, but although the historic universities at Heidelberg, Leipzig, and Vienna were stagnant, higher education in Germany was reformed and revitalized in the early 18th century by the founding of new universities at Gottingen, Halle, and Erlangen. In the aftermath of military and diplomatic defeats in the early 19th century (including Napolean's closing of the university at Halle), Germany rebuilt its political and educational systems, with the help of Baron von Humboldt's statutes for the founding of new universities at Berlin in 1810 and later at Bonn.

The image of devoted, painstaking, even plodding scholarships runs strong through the fiction, diaries, histories, and accounts of German life. The establishment of universities in Germany initially lagged behind that of medieval institutions of France and southern Europe (Heidelberg was not founded until 1386), yet German universities numbered 32 by 1700 and set the tone for what may be termed "organized scholarship." Looking at education below the university level, Carlo Cipolla concluded that in Germany, more than in other countries in Europe, statutes emphasized and enforced the notion of parental duty and obligation to send children to school.[8] Neglect of this scholastic responsibility was considered an offense against the prince and the state.

The new universities of the 18th and 19th centuries in Germany have been praised for the following contributions: the combination of teaching and research "as matters of educational principle"; two variants of academic freedom, including the student's right to attend lectures at several universities and the professor's right to pursue truth; "institutes" or provisions for advanced studies, more familiar to us as laboratories; and rigorous philosophical studies that were distinguished from technical and nonscholarly curricula.[9]

Some of the events and circumstances behind these attributes of German university life cloud the images with ironies and complexities. It is erroneous, for example, to assume that attempts at university reform were congruent with demands for modernization. In fact, curriculum at the "modern" university at Gottingen was decidedly reactionary in its composition. The university had been set up with the intent of appealing to sons of nobility and aristocracy, so its scholarly provisions for the study of classics and law existed alongside ample offerings in riding and dancing—ingredients suitable for the education of high-level civil servants. Nonetheless, by the 19th century, these unprogressive social features of the curriculum were forgotten, as Gottingen was the inspiration for the new, modern university at Berlin.[10]

Given the excitement and polemics surrounding Berlin, it is useful to reconstruct the size and setting of the university. Located in a relatively large city (population 150,000), the university opened with 256 students and 55 faculty members. Academic administration was combined with teaching and research responsibilities. Records suggest that one professor, who served as university rector, had a teaching load of three hours per day, with two days per week devoted to twelve hours of administrative duties. Faculty meetings were disastrous, as jealousies, quarrels between disciplines, and the arrogance of academic prestige led to inaction and stalling in matters of institutional self-governance.[11] Although American observers cited the maturity of German university students as a pleasant contrast to the immaturities of their own collegiate way, one reconstruction of the rector's duties at Berlin indicates that he had to deal daily with such offenses as smoking in the public gardens, insults, duels, and disturbance of the peace. Such records cast doubt on the contention that German universities were free of the petty concerns of acting *in loco parentis*.

How can we gauge the academic success of the modern university in Germany? Theodore Ziolkowski's study reminds us that the great scholar Fichte was insufferable in faculty meetings and often threatened to invoke the Ministry of Education if he was outvoted on an issue.

Humboldt, who had been commissioned by the Prussian government to set up the university, was exasperated by the professors' quarrels and resigned his position soon after the university opened.

Claims of academic freedom can be exaggerated, and one must look beyond lofty praises. Ziolkowski points out that during the post-Napoleonic years,

> the Prussian government sought to restrict the academic freedom under which the university had been founded, rightly suspecting in it a reminiscence of revolutionary ideas. 'The universities are not states within the state,' Education Minister Altenstein declared. 'Rather, the governments are the masters of the institutes.'

Nor did admirers of German higher education and national development write much about social and educational schisms within Germany during the 19th century. In fact, there was a serious gulf between industrialists and economic entrepreneurs on the one side and the highly educated professionals of law, medicine, academics, and the civil service on the other. If national development is defined in terms of economic growth, there is not much indication that the learned and academic professions made a significant contribution in that realm. A better case can be made for the university's contribution to Prussia's military victories; in 1813, most students at Berlin left the university to join the army, although that makes a dubious tribute to the importance of academic pursuits per se. Once again, Theodore Ziolkowski's portrait of Berlin deflates the grand images of academic sanctity, as he notes: "In 1813 Fichte requested a leave of absence in order to accompany the Prussian army as a sort of philosophical chaplain for the more highly educated soldiers. Other scholars exercised daily with the militia."[12]

As for certification, university degrees were relatively unimportant in 19th-century Gemany. The coveted prize or award was a high score on civil-service or state certification examinations. The subtlety, unnoticed by American observers, was that access to advanced professional training and high position was dependent on possession of a classical secondary-education diploma (the *abitur*). Entrance into that select secondary-education program was determined early in a child's scholastic career, and those chosen tended to be from affluent, highly educated families. A revised, accurate report on the German university would have noted that the university was the capstone of a complicated educational system and civil service.[13] The Prussian government and university were sponsoring a cultural elite, yet most of the mechanisms and agencies by which they did so were neither understood nor transplanted by American students who returned to the United States.

INNOCENTS ABROAD: AMERICANS OBSERVE THE GERMAN UNIVERSITY

From 1815 to 1900, a succession of American students, disenchanted with lack of libraries, laboratories, and provisions for serious study, traveled to Germany for study at such exemplary universities as Berlin, Marburg, Heidelburg, Vienna, and Leipzig. Starting with George Ticknor and George Bancroft in the period 1815-25, continued after the Civil War by James Morgan Hart, John Burgess, and Lincoln Steffens, and belatedly concluded in 1930 by Abraham Flexner, Americans wrote articles praising the scholarly life and university education found in Germany, which came to be a persistent feature in journals, discussions, and reform proposals.[14]

According to the observers and returning educational missionaries, the German university provided an antidote for the weaknesses and abuses of the American college. The favorable impressions of their experiences in Germany provided the model for campaigns for a truly modern American university. Despite such publicity, the serious question endures as to whether the German spirit, style, and structure of higher education truly transformed American higher education.

If we accept these commentators' reports that the German university was admirable, we are still left with the question and by their observations: Was the German university transplantable to American higher education? The usual response is to cite the growing interest in libraries, research, seminars, and graduate studies as testimony to the impact which these innocents abroad brought to the American campus in the late 19th century. Above all, the founding of the Johns Hopkins University in 1876 has been hailed by historians of education as the paramount transplant of the German scholarly ideal to the United States.

Accounts of the founding and early years of the Johns Hopkins University attest to the creation of a unique American institution. Yet by 1910, such perceptive analysts as Edwin Slosson noted, regrettably, that the Johns Hopkins University had not been able to sustain its program, which was designed to eliminate excesses of undergraduate studies and life and to expand provisions for advanced, serious, and graduate studies.[15] Nor is there evidence that many institutions, old or new, attempted to emulate the Johns Hopkins model. At best, some of the forms and nomenclature were pasted onto American campuses in haphazard fashion.

A revised view would argue that a dominant theme from this period was the failure of the German university model to disrupt the undergraduate collegiate arrangements found on American campuses. True, hundreds of institutions called themselves universities, but the bulk of these remained primarily concerned with the undergraduate education of students who had *not* received a systematic or comprehensive secondary education in the tradition of the German gymnasium. There is scant evidence that the new American universities broke the collegiate habit of building dormitories and hosting an elaborate (and juvenile) student culture. Perhaps the increased popularity of lectures and electives was a debt to the universities in Germany, although most American curricula did not eliminate mandatory attendance, weekly recitations and quizzes, and the practice of accumulating course credits. If foreign languages, sciences, laboratories, and libraries were added to American campuses, there was no assurance that they were integral parts of most students' campus experience.

One hallmark of the Germany university—commitment to advanced and specialized research—might be said to have transformed the American university and professoriat. But this influence is neither convincing nor clear, as much of the American university research effort was devoted to areas of utilitarian fields and applied sciences—very much the antithesis of the Germanic ideal. One would do as well to look at such American historical models as Transylvania University, the University of Pennsylvania, and Thomas Jefferson's University of Virginia for such research precedents as to cite Leipzig, Gottingen, and Berlin as the institutional inspirations. For all the talk of university change, most American professors devoted the majority of their time to teaching reluctant undergraduates. Nor did the American professoriat approximate the German arrangement, in which academic appointments were part of an elaborate civil-service structure. Coordination and centralization of secondary and higher education as part of a national educational ministry were conspicuously absent in efforts to remake the American university in the German academic image. The American campus, whether college or university, was very much a hybrid collection of inconsistent and conflicting educational plans. The creation of the American multiple-purpose university drew from numerous sources and influences, of which the German university was but one.

Regarding the limits which the continental university held for American educators and students, it is interesting to consult Abraham Flexner's 1930 study, *Universities: American, English, German*, in which the author provides an extended complaint that the American university had become a "dumping ground" for vocational courses, intercollegiate sports, preoccupation with fund-raising, and indifferent undergraduates who needed to be spoon-fed—all of which Flexner believed was deterring the university from the main, clear task, which the German university accepted so well: serious, advanced study in arts, sciences, and learned professions.[16]

PROBLEMS FOR SUBSEQUENT RESEARCH

It would not be appropriate to call this section a conclusion, since few universal or consistent truths or patterns have emerged in this survey of universities and national development. The cases—hardly comprehensive social histories—have indicated the varieties of arrangements and outcomes that respective countries have encountered in building, reforming, and supporting higher education. Commitment to identification and preparation of an educated, responsible elite appears to have been a frequent goal, yet in every case we find that this was diluted or compromised by nepotism, anticipatory socialization through the family, or selection based on nonmeritocratic factors.

Commentary on transplants of continental models to the United States has been subjected to critical scrutiny, because too many historical accounts assume, for example, that the German university was a good thing and an obvious influence on the American university-building movement of the late 19th century. American higher education faced a unique set of problems not encountered in European countries—namely, the lack of nationalized selective secondary-school system or government certification for professions, combined with some (but hardly ubiquitons pressure of extension of educational opportunity beyond 4 or 5 percent of the 18-year-old population.

Research on the role of higher education and national development might focus on the so-called knowledge industry—the proliferation of goods, services, and personnel engendered by expansion of postsecondary education. One problem with that topic is to delineate those items which were clearly and directly a part of higher education. By extension, one could argue that paper production or chain-link fence manufacture was stimulated by expansion of schooling; but that carries us far from the national consequences of having provided relatively open and inexpensive access to education.

The thorny problem will be to ascertain whether higher education in the United States has contributed to, discouraged, or been inconsequential in fostering social mobility. Christopher Jencks and David Riesman's discussion in *The Academic Revolution* has suggested that an overall rise in economic prosperity has tended to exaggerate the appearance that going to college has made a great difference in intergenerational social mobility.[17] Confirmation or rejection of that hypothesis is only the first step of the investigation. A striking feature of the American campus during the decades from 1890 to 1910 was that the ostensibly academic endeavor of going to college acquired status and appeal among those of America's sons and daughters who had precious little interest in the academic or intellectual aspects of the university ideal. And we find that colleges and universities accommodated, even encouraged this trend. In addition to prospects for having a "good time" in the elaborate undergraduate campus life, Americans acquired the belief that going to college was somehow related to success in adult business life. Tracking down *how* and *why* such beliefs emerged in association with the college and university presents a research problem equally as complex and important as identifying higher education's direct contribution to industrial and military efforts and production.

5

Institutional Roots: Identity Crises and Confusions in American Higher Education

THE HISTORICAL NAME GAME

Carlo Cipolla, an economist and historian who has taught at universities in both Italy and the United States, has noted that Italian academics delight in constructing elaborate regulations and bureaucracies—a delight matched only by their pleasure in subsequently working in and around the self-made labyrinths to carry out their personal scholarly interests and projects.[1] Perhaps a counterpart in American higher education is the indulgence of administrators and scholars in selectively invoking historical names and antecedents which conveniently make a case for some present and pragmatic institutional demand or interest.

Two key words in this vocabulary are *college* and *university*, institutions whose respective histories we have encountered in the preceding chapters on the Oxbridge legacy and the medieval and continental universities. When these are combined with the seemingly neutral, straightforward *public* and *private* categories, one has the potential for a complicated historical contest. In the course of any discussion of funding, support, curtailment, or expansion, these two variables are quickly laden and embellished with historical, or even moral, connotations. The names which an institution uses to describe itself, along with the categories and collectivities with which it chooses to align itself, are crucial for determination of institutional policies and corporate character. Thus, we step into *normative* contrasts, which include sequences of predictable adjectives; for example, the "small, private liberal arts college" is pitted against the "large, impersonal state multiversity.'' The natural rejoinder is to contrast the ''expensive, snob-bish, provincial college'' with the ''progressive, forward-looking, tuition-free state university.''

This ushers in point-counterpoint arguments in which symbols and innuendo are piled atop one another, far beyond the original categories and typologies. It is a strategy by which a single campus gains collective strength by seeing itself as part of some dominant or significant sphere or tradition: the public sector, the collegiate ideal, *ad infinitum*. The fact that there are large colleges and small universities tends to be ignored or regarded as a nuisance which impedes oratory on historical background in higher-education debates, pleas, and persuasions.

The Great Historical Name Game is hardly new to American policy-making, for we find as early as 1832 that Philip Lindsley, an innovative college president who sparred with numerous legislatures and boards of trustees, attempted to call a truce to the practice because he was tired of the abuse of names and categories. He pleaded:

> I care as little about names as any man. If the *name* of college or university be unsavoury in the ears of the people or of the people's guardians and conscience keepers, let it be cashiered. Let our colleges and universities be called academies, lyceums, gymnasia, common schools, or popular in-tellectual workshops—or by any other republican appelation, if any more or less invidious can be invented.[2]

Lindsley's logical and well-intentioned plea was ignored, of course, and this chapter does not intend to revive his campaign to rid American higher education of the historical name-dropping pastime. Rather, pro-fessional development ought to include some suggestions for expert par-ticipation in strategies for ''talking history'' in order to satisfy legislatures, win grants, and attract donors. We proceed from the premise that the maze of allusions, symbols, legacies, and categories which might confuse the uninitiated listener *does* proceed according to a peculiar logic of historical argument. Familiarity with the origins and connotations of historical categories (including *college, university, public,* and *private*) can assist the higher-education professional who wishes to deflate or counter the claims and precedents cited by an adversary. The supreme feat is to do some historical research on higher education so as to advance fresh precedents.

One novelist has argued that historical writing is comparable to animal husbandry in that both involve selective breeding. Whereas the husbandman breeds sheep or cows, the historian breeds assumed fact. Although the farmer uses his skills to ''enrich the future, [while] the historian uses his skills to enrich the past,'' there is a common feature (according to the novelist): both are usually up to their ankles in fertilizer.[3] Since a popular trend in managerial circles is to talk about research tools, it is fitting that this chapter provides a particular research and development tool suited to the novelist's observation—an analytical "shovel" by which higher-education participants can dig their way out of the historical refuse and verbiage which pervade discussions.

The approach will be to consider the categories of *public* and *private* in American higher education by tracking down institutional roots, tracing the etymology of the terms, and clarifying their uses and abuses in understanding the ways in which colleges and universities have arranged themselves. An important warning is that one must bear in mind two tendencies for change which complicate historical digging: *institutional* change and *terminological* change. Institutional change means that it is possible, even probable, that a given higher-educational institution may have at one time or another altered its name, location, endowment, curriculum, affiliation, size, mascots, official colors, charter, governance, support provisions, religious ties, or educational missions. Similarly, the legal and popular usage and the formal and informal connotations of crucial words and phrases (such as *professionalism, research, liberal arts*) have fluctuated over time and varied from one speaker to another.

Although we run the risk of jumping ahead of our story, a few case studies hint at these problems of institutional history. Consider the following items related to institutional and terminological change.

Item. In the late 1960s, when several branches of the California state system were granted university status, logos and letterheads were changed from "California State College at ____" to "California State University at ____." Along with that predictable and reasonable revision, alumni were notified that for a nominal fee, they could have their diplomas retroactively changed so as to bear the new *university* status.[4] Did this mean that they had attended a true university all along?

Item. To what extent does an institution's name directly reveal its affiliation? The University of Pittsburgh, for example, was not a city college, but a private, independent university for several decades, until the 1960s, when it became a state institution. If there is any trend in the association of a city's name with a college or university, it tends to indicate a Catholic institution; for example Boston College, Providence College, University of San Francisco, St. Louis University.

Item. Dartmouth, an institution which has gained considerable mileage from its historic reputation as *the* small college which was continually in danger of being harmed by courts, legislatures, and large universities, indicates the misleading permanence of institutional traditions. Consider the following summary of events, shifts, and changes which Dartmouth faced in the late 18th and early 19th centuries:

> It originated as a school for Indians located in Connecticut.
>
> It was chartered by the king and by the royal governor of New Hampshire after the colonial government in Connecticut showed no interest in the school.
>
> The founder and recipient of the charter appointed several relatives to the board of trustees.
>
> The founder attempted to persuade Vermont to adopt Dartmouth as its state college as part of an intricate (and unsuccessful) plan for western counties of Massachusetts to leave Massachusetts and become part of Vermont.
>
> The founder died and was succeeded by his son as president of Dartmouth.
>
> The president (the son) gained power in Vermont politics and acquired a land grant for Dartmouth. He threatened to leave New Hampshire. New Hampshire countered with a land grant of 42,000 acres to Dartmouth.
>
> Despite the fame of Daniel Webster's Supreme Court "small-college" plea, Dartmouth vacillated in calling itself a *college* or a *university* in the late 18th and early 19th centuries.
>
> In 1828 the president of Dartmouth defended the collegiate ideal and denounced "university" aspirations—failing to comment on the large enrollment of Dartmouth's medical department.[5]

Dartmouth's story became more intriguing and complicated in the mid and late nineteenth century because of matters of complicity with state funding, professional schools, and utilitarian education at an allegedly liberal arts college—but those specifics will be discussed later in the chapter. The preceding track record suffices to show that exaltation of the small-college saga glides over interesting and significant episodes of institutional history in which ivory-tower campuses are very much involved in real world affairs.

One strategy for circumventing these elusive and deceptive changes in college and university nomenclature is to look at institutional features and practices apart from rhetoric and terminology, that is, to reconstruct what was happening, what institutions were doing and offering, apart from what spokesmen or critics were saying about a particular campus's past or present. This strategy is comparable to the functional-analysis orientation developed by sociologists. Since the preceding case probed a cherished variant of the private college legend, it is only equitable that we apply the analytic strategy to the public higher-education saga.

CONFUSED CATEGORIES

Consider the features we associate with the historical development of public higher education in America—for instance, the archetypal state university whose visual and symbolic legacy is suggested by the monumental, ornate inscription on Hilgard Hall, the University of California at Berkeley's agriculture building: TO RESCUE FOR HUMAN SOCIETY THE NATIVE VALUES OF RURAL LIFE (Figure 4). Historian Frederick Rudolph links going down to state college with such agrarian American institutions as the state fair, Fourth of July picnic, church social, and Saturday night in town (Figure 5).

Conventional wisdom and popular belief tend to attribute the following practices and innovations to the state university:

> public service and community service
> state and community pride
> extension programs
> technical fields and professional education
> applied learning and research
> tax-supported funding
> low tuition or free tuition provisions
> secular education, free of denominational control
> popular access and open admission to higher education
> egalitarianism in student composition, as opposed to social
> privilege, snobbery, and exclusion

According to one careful historical study, all of these features were pioneered and/or developed in what we call *private* or *independent* campuses.[7] In fact, there was no strong, consistent connection during the nineteenth century among popular interest, public support, and state approval of proposals for a state university with educational mission in the areas of utilitarian studies and services. The state university has been celebrated for its capacity to promote popular education by accommodating large numbers of students. When this self-congratulation became warranted is not altogether clear.

Historian James Axtell, for example, checked enrollment figures during the 1880s—the height of the university-building vogue—and found that two-thirds of the largest twenty-six American campuses were private colleges.[8] Amherst College, for example, was as large as the state university of Wisconsin; Williams College enrolled more students than did Indiana University; Yale was far larger than such midwestern state universities as Michigan or Missouri. The 19th-century New England colleges also undermined the state university legend of popular access to higher education: the hilltop colleges founded by the 1820s (namely, Amherst, Williams, Middlebury, Bowdoin, and Waterville) were largely concerned with providing inexpensive education for students from poor, rural families.[9]

The intent here is not merely to deflate the state university saga and the small private college legend. The enduring implication is that neither the public nor the private sector has enjoyed a monopoly on educational integrity or innovation. Nor do the features we now tend to identify either as *collegiate* or *university* have smooth congruence with the historical record. If these present-day categories are incomplete and misleading for understanding trends and configurations in the history of higher education, how, when, and why did the terms *public* and *private* come into use?

CREATING THE PRIVATE AND PUBLIC SECTORS OF HIGHER EDUCATION

The distinctions between "public" and "private" educational institutions do not extend far back in American history. According to John Whitehead's splendid study, the terms were used and the categories were created in the late nineteenth century by two different sources.[10] After the Civil War, presidents of church-affiliated colleges in the Midwest described their institutions as private and free from government control, but only after these same denominational colleges had failed in bids to gain state support in Illinois and other states. The result was that the denominational colleges, fearing competition from new or future state universities, set themselves off by *creating* and *asserting* a categorical identity which had not existed previously and which might have appeal to potential donors and philanthropists. Whitehead attributes the idea of the eastern private university to a young president of Harvard, Charles W. Eliot, who from the 1870s into the 1890s carried on a vigorous campaign of speeches and articles which brought attention and praise to voluntarism in support of higher education as an antidote to real and imagined fears of abuse in government support and control of organizations, educational and otherwise. Eliot's appeal to this "tradition" of voluntarism was a curious revision of history in that it required glossing over Harvard's long record of complicated, varying relationships with Massachusetts and with government funding and regulation.

Such arguments were sufficiently pervasive and influential in shaping conceptions and discussions that by 1890, "knowledgeable commentators" on American higher education assumed that campuses fell into conspicuous types—old and private versus new and public.[11] Thus, the issues, writings, and rhetoric of the late 19th century imposed on American higher education the ill-fitting public-private dichotomy, accompanied by the erroneous implication that these were traditional, discernible, historic categories. This conceptualization ignored the multiplicity of alliances which had characterized college-state relations in the 17th and 18th centuries. Nor did the public-private, large-small stereotypes explain much about patterns and complications in institutional arrangements which were emerging among colleges and universities in the 19th and 20th centuries. So, although we have identified the sources of the public-private typology in the 1870s, we inherit another historical problem: How did institutions arrange themselves and describe themselves in the colonial and national periods before the *public* and *private* terminology was artificially imposed on the vocabulary of higher education?

THE COLONIAL COLLEGES

The generation of university-builders of the 1880s either forgot or ignored the historical fact that state assistance to higher education had a long tradition, although not a consistent policy or application, in this country. In the summary in Chapter 3 of the ministry debate and the purposes of the colonial colleges, we noted the danger of attributing modern conceptions to previous eras; for example, the fallacy of equating the education of colonial ministers with the education presented by a present-day theological seminary. In a similar vein, we ought to note that it did not occur to the colonists to distinguish an institution, especially a college, as either private or public.

In colonial America, the interests of college and government were mutual and interdependent, a congruence which was captured in the term *commonwealth*, still the official designation of Massachusetts. Note that the early colleges tended to be distributed one per colony. Brown, for example, was originally known as the College of Rhode Island and of Providence Plantations; Princeton, a name not widely used until the 1860s, was chartered as the College of New Jersey. Yale in those days was the college for Connecticut.

There is also evidence of government supervision to insure avoidance of institutional waste and competition. In 1762, Harvard petitioned the governor of Massachusetts Bay to oppose the founding of a new college in the western section of the colony (Hampshire County, later the site of Amherst College) with the following arguments:

> For, if such a college as is proposed were founded in Hampshire it cannot be thought that persons living in that part of the country, who might be favorers of it, in respect of its vicinity, or on any other account, would be willing to bear a part in endowing that at Cambridge, whether in a legislative or private capacity. It may naturally be concluded that they would rather endeavour to obstruct all schemes and proposals to this end; judging very justly, that the growth and flourishing of their own college depended in some measure upon the languishing and depression of the other.[12]

The petition went on to claim that the proposed new college would dilute the quality of education afforded clergy and civil leaders, as well as divide collegiate support along local and regional lines within the colony. The important dimension for our analysis is that Harvard College, which Eliot later hailed for its voluntarism tradition, recognized no conflict in the 1760s in making simultaneous use of governmental regulation and permission, private endowment, religious affiliation; and legislative arrangements. The strict "private" or "public" college was not a creation of the colonies.

Charters, an inheritance from the medieval university, indicate that the first American colleges were allied with their respective colonies (and later, with states) in varying manners of control and financial support. When the state granted an institution a charter, it acknowledged that institution's legal and formal existence and operation apart from the state. One implication was that the college, rather than the state, would grant degrees. The issuing of a charter suggested good relations between the government and the prospective institution. Within the cluster of American colonial colleges, there were several kinds of charters. Harvard and Yale, for example, were granted charters by the colonial governments—a daring move, as strict accordance with law and custom reserved that prerogative for the British Crown. Columbia (originally known as King' College) and Dartmouth adhered to the letter of the law, as both held royal charters which had been approved by the king of England.

After the Revolutionary War, relations between institutions and governments had to be either confirmed or reworked. Again, there was no uniform pattern in the nation, but, mixed arrangements which varied from college to college, state to state. There is evidence that in many instances, strong religious or denominational ties were questioned by legislators. The term *state-controlled college* could signify that a legislature and/or a governor constituted the ultimate authority in college matters and reserved rights of inspection and visitation. Such an arrangement might or might not have been combined with financial support from the state to the college. At Harvard, private philanthrophy was combined with grants of money from the state of Massachusetts. In post-Revolutiony New York, Columbia College (considered a Tory stronghold during the war) fell out of favor with the state assembly and was subjected to government vigilance without benefit of generous state financial support.

The forms of state financial aid to colleges varied, including proceeds from lotteries, revenues from land sales, toll taxes, outright monetary awards, or gifts of land. There is little evidence that these old, established colleges asserted private identity and attempted to absolve historic ties with the state. Nor does it follow that state support for new campuses meant state neglect of the older colleges.

FALSE STARTS AND FORGOTTEN EXPERIMENTS, 1800 to 1850

In place of the simplistic claim that the rise of the modern university meant the death of the private liberal-arts college, we advance the following explanation of higher-education trends in the first half of the 19th century. State governments made little effort to close down or break off alliances with old colleges. States *did* acquiesce and participate in the proliferation of new institutions by granting charters and/or providing some initial financial support for various campuses. One might argue that the founding of the University of Georgia, the College of South Carolina, and the Universities of Indiana, Michigan, Wisconsin, and Missouri hailed the emergence of state universities, but this is misleading.[13] In some of the southern and western states, state charters were not followed by continued or adequate funding; that is, legislatures might be persuaded to grant the charter, throw in cheap land, and consider their duty done. This could be carried out with little interest or understanding of curriculum or concern for advanced and utilitarian studies. And at the same time that states were founding state universities, they were chartering numerous small denominational colleges.

Between 1820 and 1850, most campuses, whether old or new, secular or denominational, suffered the fate of financial neglect and public indifference. John Whitehead has argued that battles for state funding took place not between state colleges and private colleges, but rather between schools and higher education. The old and new campuses exhibited no clear distinction in courses of study, as one finds within each institution a classical collegiate curriculum furtively mixed with hasty attempts at professional and "useful" studies. Contrary to the legend of the Morrill Act and the efficacy of applied education in a democracy, states were reluctant to subsidize agricultural and technical education.

Merle Borrowman has called the period from 1820 to 1850 the False Dawn of the State University, because there were a number of progressive, exciting experiments in higher education whose relatively brief spurts of expanded educational vision were not accompanied by public, community, or state support or loyalty.[14] Citing the cases of South Carolina College, the University of Nashville, and Lexington, Kentucky's, Transylvania University, Borrowman has identified campuses which pioneered medical education, applied research, secular learning, scientific laboratories and field studies, modern languages, and professional and technical education. Ironically, these anitdotes to an archaic, elitist classical college were sources of popular contempt and hostility. In terms of the functions, here was the genesis of the extended American university—but it was hardly an exclusive product of state or public demands or support.

By the mid-19th century, when state legislatures *did* exhibit sustained concern for provision of instruction in such professions as medicine, engineering, agriculture, and applied sciences, they more often than not looked at old colleges as likely sources for expansion and innovation. To complicate matters further, we find that technical and scientific schools were often started with bequests and donations from private donors. This hybrid curricular pattern within historic campuses is suggested by the following summary of colleges and affiliated schools in the mid-19th century:

> Harvard College, Bussey Institute (agriculture) and the Lawrence Scientific School
>
> Dartmouth College, medical department, the New Hampshire College of Agriculture, the Chandler Scientific School
>
> Yale College, the Sheffield Scientific School (which included the state of Connecticut's land-grant funds *and* private donations)
>
> Columbia College, college of physicians and surgeons, School of Mines
>
> Cornell University: college of arts and sciences, State of New York agricultural college, professional schools

Here we have old, private liberal-arts colleges acting like multipurpose universities whose historic heart, the undergraduate college, shared a campus with professional, utilitarian, and state facilities. The corollary is that the new state universities were remarkably persistent in their pursuit of the collegiate ideal, despite the rhetoric of applied and utilitarian studies associated with the Morrill Act of 1862 and the land-grant college movement.

THE STATE UNIVERSITY RECONSIDERED

In 1937, *Life* magazine's special issue on American higher education featured a photographic essay on the University of Missouri—"Big Mo"—as *the* large state university where agriculture and military science were predominant fields, a campus where students used "their hands as well as their heads."[15] A less conspicuous side of the land-grant campus emerges from the memories of economist John Kenneth Galbraith, who was a graduate student in agricultural economics at the University of California at Berkeley in the 1930s. Having encountered a discussion of radical politics and economics, Galbraith recalled:

> I listened to them eagerly and would have liked to have joined both the conversation and the [Communist] Party but here my agricultural background was a real handicap. It meant that, as a matter of formal Marxian doctrine, I was politically immature. Among the merits of capitalism to Marx was the fact that it rescued men from the idiocy of rural life. I had only very recently been retrieved. I sensed this bar and I knew also that my pride would be deeply hurt by rejection. So I kept outside. There was possibly one other factor. Although I recognized that the system could not and should not survive, I was enjoying it so much that, secretly, I was a little sorry.[16]

Galbraith's "confession" was not an isolated incident, as there is impressive evidence that one major, albeit latent, function of the state universities built in the late 19th century was to provide ambitious and bright young students with a route toward the liberal arts and the learned professions—away from agriculture. Ironically, Galbraith, the student who praised the university for having rescued him from "the idiocy of rural life," attended classes a short distance from Hilgard Hall and the inscription we noted earlier in the chapter, TO RESCUE FOR HUMAN SOCIETY THE NATIVE VALUES OF RURAL LIFE. That heroic offer did not enjoy unanimous consent among state university students.

Twenty years before Galbraith was a student at Berkeley, in 1913, James Thurber, later famous as a humorist and writer, entered the Ohio

State University and took six years to endure or evade such graduation requirements as swimming, military drill, and a laboratory course in the biological sciences. Mass education meant long lines and numerous forms, along with physical education requirements. Thurber recalled:

> Another thing I didn't like about gymnasium work was that they made you strip the day you registered. It is impossible for me to be happy when I am stripped and being asked a lot of questions. Still, I did better than a lanky agricultural student who was cross-examined just before I was. They asked each student what college he was in—that is, whether Arts, Engineering, Commerce, or Agriculture. 'What college are you in?' the instructor snapped at the youth in front of me. 'Ohio State University,' he said promptly.

The ideal of the land-grant campus did not always inspire or excite its students. According to Thurber, one undergraduate reporter on the campus newspaper who had been assigned to cover the College of Agriculture tried (in vain) to generate popular interest by filing a story whose opening line read "Who has noticed the sores on the tops of the horses in the animal-husbandry building?"

Life magazine's 1937 photographic essay may have celebrated the "A and M" (agriculture, mechanics, mining, and military) characteristics of the American state land grant university, but Thurber provides us with a dissenting view:

> Ohio State was a land-grant university and therefore two years of military drill was compulsory. We drilled with old Springfield rifles and studied the tactics of the Civil War even though the World War was going on at the time. At eleven o'clock each morning thousands of freshmen and sophomores used to deploy over the campus, moodily creeping up on the old chemistry building. It was good training for the kind of warfare that was waged at Shiloh, but it had no connection with what was going on in Europe. Some people used to think there was German money behind it, but they didn't dare say so or they would have been thrown in jail as German spies. It was a period of muddy thought and marked, I believe, the decline of higher education in the Middle West.

These numerous encounters and episodes led one instructor to snap at Thurber, "You are the main trouble with this university!" to which Thurber responded, "I think he meant that my type was the main trouble with this university, but he may have meant me individually."[17]

The anecdotal and good-natured recollections by Galbraith and Thurber exaggerate the excesses of popular higher education at the rural state universities. Yet there is an important kernel of fact and insight in such student memoirs, as the state universities of earlier decades (that is, of the late 19th century) were not unequivocally committed to the vocational and utilitarian studies with which they have been associated in the 20th century. What were some impediments to creation of true "A and M" institutions?

The study of agriculture as an applied field made slow headway for two reasons. First, farmers distrusted and resisted cooperation with the formal learning and programs of the state university. Second, when state universities of the mid and late nineteenth century *did* set up colleges of agriculture, these often included faculty members whose education emphasized the sciences and advanced research. Earl Cheit's study of professional schools has shown that allegedly vocational fields required heavy doses of the classical subjects pursued in the colleges of arts and sciences.[18] The implication is that in many instances, the public glorification of vocational studies was a partial facade to obtain funding for carrying on nonvocational projects and studies.

It appears that faculty, adminstrators, parents, and students were accomplices in these bootleg operations. One revisionist view of the state universities of the 19th century is that state and local elites created *de facto* liberal-arts college for their sons and daughters, or at least campuses which provided access to such learned and prestigious professions as law, medicine, architecture, and government, as well as providing extension services and vocational programs. As for popular education as an antidote to the social snobbishness of the eastern colleges, numerous memoirs and accounts attest to the elaborate social schisms within state universities, including the splits between Greek-letter fraternities and sororities and the "great unwashed."[19]

The truly modern state university had not replaced the old liberal-arts college. As often as not, it imitated the forms, the customs, and the revivalistic architecture of the supposedly archaic campuses. Advocates of applied and practical education in rural areas or western states underestimated the appeal which the traditional college held for the sons of farmers who were eager to *leave* the farm. Henry Seidel Canby, writing in the 1930s about American higher education of the 1880s and 1890s, observed that the "younger colleges, whether they were 'state' or 'privately endowed' institutions, modeled their life and aspirations upon the older colleges which were usually in the East and which drew heavily from the best schools or most cultivated classes."[20] Historian Allan Nevins recognized the element of imitation and emulation in the new state universities in their quests for academic legitimacy and campus character:

This requires time, sustained attention to cultural values, and the special beauties of landscape or architecture. It is the immemorial grace of towers and lawns, and recollections of great ideas and causes, the fame of eminent leaders, that makes the name of Oxford fall like a chime of music on the ears of men in Delhi and Melbourne. It is this which for generations has made men wake at night with memories of Old Nassau at Princeton or the Colonnade at Charlottesville, their warm brick and ivy, their atmosphere redolent with scholarship and principle. . . . This spiritual grace the state universities cannot quickly acquire, but they have been gaining it.[21]

Ironically, the land-grant institutions were exerting a less conspicuous yet significant and enduring influence on the content and conception of the liberal-arts college and curriculum. Economics, political science, history, and the social sciences, today regarded as established and traditional disciplines within liberal-arts colleges, were introduced into universities in the late 19th century as offerings restricted to the "second-class citizenship" of the scientifc schools.

THE "BOOSTER COLLEGE" AND CIVIC PRIDE

Despite the publicity and celebration associated with the university movement of the 19th century, the expansion of American higher education was dominated by literally hundreds of small, private, denominational colleges. The mortality rate of these campuses was high, yet the ridicule and contempt hurled at them by advocates of university-building underestimated the tenacity and popularity of the small, traditional campus. Philip Lindsley, a poor sport who was disappointed at the failure of his university plans to take root in Nashville, complained in 1829:

I am aware that as soon as any sect succeeds in obtaining a charter for *something* called a college, they become, all of a sudden, wondrously liberal and catholic. They forthwith proclaim to the public that their college is the best in the world—and withal, perfectly free from the odious taint of sectarianism. . . . They hold out false colours to allure and to deceive the incautious.[22]

Four decades later, spokesmen for universities and established campuses were still complaining about the money "wasted" on the founding of new colleges. Lyman Bagg of Yale bitterly observed in the 1870s:

The blessing to this country of having all such money sunk into the sea, could be only equaled by that other blessing of having all but a half dozen of all the American 'colleges' founded in the present century, blotted from existence, or turned into preparatory schools for the other ones.[23]

Harvard's spokesman, Professor Charles Eliot Norton, similarly commented:

> Whatever is generous in the object of the founders would be far more effectively promoted if the means required for the foundation and carrying on of the new institutions were concentrated and applied in an already existing school of learning. The lamentable waste involved in the needless duplication of the instruments of study, of buildings, libraries, and laboratories, would at least be avoided.[24]

The mortality rate of the new colleges was high, but as Daniel Boorstin has pointed out, every new town or city in the midwestern and Pacific Coast states aspired to civic respectability by including a college along with stores and municipal buildings and real-estate developments as a source of boosterism and local pride.[25] Charges of wastefulness, needless duplication, sectarianism, and anti-intellectualism, however, overlook voids and roles which these numerous "booster colleges" filled in the 19th century.

Denominational control was often a guise for ethnic identities. Consider the following correlations between demographic patterns in the church-college building:

Religion or Denomination	*Ethnic Group*
Lutheran	German and Scandinavian
Presbyterian	Scotch
Catholic	Irish
Congregationalist	Anglo (New England)

Given that settlement and migration in America tended to proceed along ethnic lines and clusters, it is reasonable that institution-building should follow a comparable pattern. Feelings of statewide loyalty, especially in new and large states, was undeveloped. Why, for example, should midwesterners who settled in the Los Angeles area feel devotion and attachment to a state university 500 miles away in Berkeley that did not serve local needs? Despite all the slurs directed at the "booster colleges," it is hard to deny that they were integral to town building and real-estate development. To use the example of southern California again, we note a pattern in which church-affiliated colleges founded in the late 19th and early 20th centuries took the name of the new city and described the college in terms of providing higher education for the local populace. Whittier, founded by Quakers from Indiana and the Midwest, was originally a Quaker town whose real-estate appeal was bolstered by provision for Whittier College. A comparable pattern was followed by Pomona, Redlands, La Verne, and Occidental. The University of Southern California, founded by Methodists, was a private institution which acted like an urban, public-service university, filling a void and seizing an opportunity caused by the failure to provide a state university for the most populous section of California.[26]

By these functional indices, the small church colleges were *de facto* community colleges, often praised by presidents of state campuses for having reached citizens, enriched the cultural life of towns, and educated sons and daughters of the state. Yet these debts tended to be forgotten when state university officials campaigned for expansion or extension. In fact, few states succeeded in fully consolidating state pride and support within a single campus. The duplication and proliferation of campuses which the university-builders deplored among the private colleges was shifted to the public sector in the 20th century, as sections and cities within a state lobbied for a campus, branch, or unit of the state's college and university system.

If competition between private and public institutions strikes us as fierce, we ought to observe the budget presentations to state legislatures concerning elimination or consolidation of graduate and professional schools, in which the following "state" campuses are rivals for support:

> University of Michigan versus Michigan State University
> University of Kentucky versus University of Louisville
> Texas A and M versus Texas Tech University
> University of California versus California State Colleges and
>   University System
> Indiana University versus Purdue University

On close inspection, the ideal of statewide cohesion seldom has been realized. Within each state, public-sector tensions attest to the tenacity of campus expansion and rivalry.

THE STANDARD AMERICAN UNIVERSITY, CIRCA 1910

By 1910, editor and journalist Edwin Slosson was confident that he could describe the features of the standard American University. In choosing campuses for inclusion in his anthology, *Great American Universities*, he noted, "The essential difference between a university and a college is the way they look. The university looks forward and the college looks backward." Throughout this chapter, we have attempted to show that such categorization was seldom subtle or satisfactory for understanding institutional character or origins. Slosson himself conceded that the dichotomy between college and university was not as clear as his phrase first suggested. Certainly, there was no clear delineation of great universities along the lines of public and private affiliations. Slosson's anthology may be broken down as follows:

Endowed Universities	*State Universities*
Harvard	Michigan
Columbia	Minnesota
Yale	Wisconsin
Chicago	California
Cornell	Illinois
Princeton	
Pennsylvania	
Stanford	
Johns Hopkins	

Slosson admitted that Princeton was "still a college in spirit," yet argued that no survey of great American educational institutions would be complete without Princeton. By this logic, omission of Dartmouth was conspicuous and curious; by 1890, Dartmouth was hosting a medical school, a scientific school, and New Hampshire's land-grant agricultural college, and it later added a business school to its undergraduate liberal-arts enrollment of more than 2000. Other institutional identities were confused, as Cornell did not seem like a state university at all, "but rather like Yale, Harvard, or Princeton." Such description was of scant pleasure to faculty and administrators at Cornell.

Thirty years later, Morris Bishop complained that the search for the truly "great" American university invariably led to the comment "Harvard, Princeton, and perhaps Cornell." After having reviewed Cornell's university-style innovations since its founding, Bishop took matters into his own hands (and pen), arguing: "Perhaps Cornell. It has always been the fate of our University to be Perhaps Cornell. . .it may be that foreign observers hunting the essentially American college will specify Cornell. And perhaps Harvard, Yale, and Princeton."[28] Lumping Yale and Harvard into the same category as "great universities" obscured years of institutional animosities during which editors cited Harvard and Yale as the polarities of the American philosophy of higher education.[29]

The pretensions to university status included overtures to research, advanced studies, and graduate degree programs. However, few (if any) of the universities in 1910 were shaped or dominated by their master's and doctoral programs. Professional schools, now a familiar source of status, funding, and research, enjoyed no sharp pattern of academic prestige or affiliation in the early 1900s. At the turn of the century, most medical schools were not part of an academic campus and had minimal admission or graduation requirements.[30] In those instances where medical schools were associated with a college or university, they tended to be viewed as havens for unambitious students and unscholarly athletes. George Santayana's *The Last Puritan* depicts Harvard Medical School as an easy option for the son of a patrician family after he had been expelled from Harvard College.

Most learned professions, especially law and medicine, have required applicants to hold a bachelor's degree only in recent decades. One official at Yale Law School, looking at the deluge of overqualified applicants for admission to the class of 1980, recalled the simple procedures of the 1930s when the admissions "problem" was to round up a sufficient number of academically able students to fill the class roster.[31] Perhaps the nonselective admissions of the 1930s had its rewards, as it enabled two former college football players (now Supreme Court Justice Byron White and former President Gerald Ford) to enter Yale Law School without benefit of sparkling undergraduate academic records.

How do Slosson's typology and "standard American university" designation fare when one looks at campuses outside the select fourteen which he studied in 1910? Once again, the *public* and *private, college* and *university* terms encounter repeated snags. An interesting case is the University of Kentucky, whose official name was adopted six years after Slosson's observations (1916). Working back through records and catalogs, we find a very interesting and complicated course of development and affiliation.

Prior to 1916, there appears to have been no University of Kentucky, although the state university claims to have been founded in 1865. What we do find is that from 1865 to 1878, Kentucky's land-grant Agricultural and Mechanical College existed as one of the colleges of Kentucky University. According to Kentucky University's official catalog of 1895-96, the university's organization included an academy and colleges of liberal arts, Bible, commerce, and music. Especially interesting for our *public* and *private* dichotomy is that Kentucky University summarizes its institutional history as follows: "Organized as Bacon College in 1836; united in 1865 with Transylvania University, which was established January 1, 1799." These records suggest that the state University of Kentucky has direct historical connections with two private institutions and two religious sects; it underwent three location changes, and had no fewer than four name changes—all of which was not straightened into familiar categories until 1916.

Despite these institutional complexities and confusions, Slosson's identification of the standard American university was important and timely in that it signaled the end of a half-century of incredible institutional innovation, combination, and experimentation. Lawrence Veysey has argued that this standardization meant the eclipse of several unique educational models, such as the Johns Hopkins University, Clark University, or Cornell University's early curricula.[32] The standard American university was an organizational hybrid and compromise in that many institutions ended up accommodating varied, even conflicting educational programs and philosophies. Campus presidents, avoiding hard choices in 1910, contributed to the overextension and diffusion which Clark Kerr attributed to the archetypal multiversity of the 1950s and 1960s. The danger of identifying the "standard American university" is that we forget that its development was neither inevitable nor planned. The college- and university-builders of the period from 1870 to 1910 were often wasteful, ruthless, insular, and uncooperative, and pursued their respective institutional dreams with little sense of the campus model which eventually emerged in the 1900s.

RECURRENT IMPLICATIONS AND COMPLICATIONS

The identity crises and confusions of the 19th-century colleges and universities are hardly a thing of the past. One interesting recent variation on bending institutional terminology has come about at the University of California at Berkeley, where alumni are asked to make donations to their alma mater because this state university is no longer tax-*supported* and prefers to describe itself as tax-*assisted*.[33] At the same time that the state university gets by with a little help from its friends, alumni, and public taxes, we find that private colleges and universities persist in asking state and local governments for tax exemptions on the grounds that the private campus is a civic resource which contributes to the local economy by providing jobs and by educating and preparing future citizens and professionals, along with providing nonprofit galleries, clinics, museums, and concerts.

From 1776 well into the middle of the 19th century, a number of advocates of higher education reform lobbied for creation of a national university, devoted to truly American needs, in which future national leaders would have access to research facilities and advanced curricula which drew from classical, professional, and applied fields. The proposals, whose authors range from Thomas Jefferson and Benjamin Rush to John Quincy Adams, make for fascinating reading; but the great hopes of these men met with little satisfaction in funding or sustained support. The closest approximation to a national university has been the federal grant universities of the post-World War II decades—a handful of large institutions whose budgets and professional activities have been shaped by government grants and projects. Once again, we have an example of a significant institutional category which has little correlation with the *state* and *private* typology.

Much of the preceding discussions has focused on curricula and affiliation as sources of institutional indentity within the public-private scheme. Present-day variations and implications might be found elsewhere—in the extracurriculum of athletics at a large state university, for example. In the 1920s, the United States Supreme Court ruled that major-league professional baseball was to be classified as entertainment, not business—a categorical distinction whose endurance has provided baseball-club owners with unique and financially benficial provisions. No less controversial are the distinctive categories attributed to intercollegiate athletics.

Varsity coaches often desc*r*ibe themselves as "educators," comparable to classroom teachers, whose concern is with the personal development and growth of player-students. "Personal growth," however, tends to be defined as "gain in weight" by assistant football coaches. Nonetheless, the case can be made that a 60,000-seat stadium is analogous to a lecture hall. Confusion, even contradiction, comes about when the same coaches justify large budgets and recruiting expenses on the grounds that after all, intercollegiate sports are "big business," in competition with professional teams (which are supposed to be entertainment) for fans' dollars. This argument has been used to prevent professional teams from playing in the same city or region as a college team.

At a number of state universities, the intercollegiate athletic program (which we shall call SUAA, which stands for State University Athletic Association) has been legally established as a *private* corporation within a *public* institution. Furthermore, the *private* corporation (SUAA) often is allowed to hold *public* performances in a civic or *public* arena or stadium, with exemptions from civic and public regulations. Ticket-scalping, for example, is often a criminal offense, yet the private SUAA is allowed to determine ticket and seat distribution on the basis of private donations beyond the face-value price of tickets.

Despite coaches' claims that intercollegiate athletics are an educational activity, the private corporations' training facilities and equipment are restricted; that is, they are not open to all registered students within a public university. However, this exclusion is partially tested by Title IX legislation, in which *federal* funds to the *state* institution require adherance to federal law by the *private* corporation within the *state* institution. No one has offered a sufficient explanation of the legal precedent which allows the SUAA to charge parking fees in parking lots which are university-owned and university-operated during the academic day. And at a number of campuses, academic budgets include funds for academic advisers whose services are restricted to those student-athletes under the provisions of the private SUAA.

These protective precedents and arguments constructed by spokesmen for the intercollegiate athletics programs are designed, of course, to maintain the programs' autonomy within the public institution—the best of several worlds. It has not been an infallible strategy. In the 1960s, a football coach at a state university sued *The Saturday Evening Post* because that magazine had run articles which implied that the coach had been associated with possible abuses, including gambling and game-fixing. The coach's suit contended that he was an employee of a *private* corporation, the university's athletic association (which had its own payroll apart from the university's faculty and staff), and hence he ought not to be subjected to *public* libel and slander. The effective counterargument was that the coach, although an employee of a private corporation, was a public figure. The latter interpretation was fitting since winning coaches have a long history of claiming that a victory by the state university's team is a victory for all the people of the state.

The cases and categories of institutional history and identity, then, are subject to variation and manipulation. If historical analysis of the rhetoric and symbols of institutional identities seems to have made a shambles of familiar college and university categories and names, it also suggests a measure of tribute for the creativity of higher-education professionals in light of Oscar Wilde's quip that "consistency is the last refuge of the unimaginative."

FIGURE 4

Going to College in America: The State University Legacy United States Post Office Commemorative Envelope (1962) in honor of the Centennial Celebration of the Morrill Act for support of "Land Grant" campuses.

Courtesy of personal collection of J.A. Wolfgang Tatsch.

FIGURE 5

Going to College in America: The State University Legacy—Variations on a Theme: "TO RESCUE FOR HUMAN SOCIETY THE NATIVE VALUES OF RURAL LIFE." Inscription on Hilgard Hall, The University of California, Berkeley, circa 1920.

Courtesy, University of California Archives, The Bancroft Library.

6

The Sporting Life: Higher Education and Athletics

ADMINISTRATORS, AMERICANISMS, AND ATHLETICS

Chapter 5 concluded with a brief discussion of athletics as a source of complication in the public-private identities of educational institutions. The topic of intercollegiate athletics is too important and too interesting to leave there. The historical precedent or inspiration for administrative concern with athletics as part of the higher-education structure and enterprise can be found in the following comments made by the president of the Carnegie Foundation for the Advancement of Teaching almost a half-century ago. He noted:

> . . . that final responsibility for the effective administration of college sport belongs not to the alumnus, the down-town business man, or the newspaper writer, but to university or college officers.
> The principle has long been recognized but not always acted upon. The result has been much adminstrative confusion and—still more unfortunately for our nation—a serious impairment of the product of our secondary and higher education. This impairment affects directly the contribution and graduates of our colleges and universities have been able to make to our national life.[1]

The danger is that American educators mistake American accommodation of college sports as the global norm, which is not the case at all. Most countries have devised provisions for support and development of amateur organized sports teams. France, for example, is singled out for a remarkable job placement program in which members of the national ski team pursue careers as customs inspectors—at alpine border stations, of course. Several years ago, the Olympic rosters for several Eastern

European countries were filled with athletes who displayed inordinate aptitude for engineering or military service. Within the United States, there are factory and company teams, city youth foundations, or religious-affiliated teams (Athletes in Action) in which allegedly amatuer athletics are pursued. The unique American contribution, however, has been the accommodation of high-caliber competitive athletic programs within the college and university campus. Anyone who has spent time on an American campus cannot help but be awed by the resources, facilities, publicity, and homage which varsity sports command.

Elsewhere, university officials have not promoted or supported extensive formalization of students' interinstitutional competition. Apart from the Saint Scholastica's Day Riot in medieval Paris, described in Chapter II, physical endeavors and contests did not play a large part in academic life. The German schools and universities of the 19th century developed extraordinary programs for physical fitness, but these were not fused with the sports ethos of intercollegiate competition. In fact, looking back to the 15th-century German universities, we find the following document, which suggests attempts by the Heidelberg rector to control and curb student athletics:

> The rector of the university, to the members of our university, all and single, we enjoin, strictly commanding, that no one of you shall presume to attend fencing schools or participate in their exercises, nor attempt to practice the art of fencing publicly or secretly, at least so far as teaching others and introducing them to this sort of art is concerned, under the penalty of two florins and the greater penalty which the university may decide to establish for the future for transgressors of this sort. Given in the year of the Lord 1415.[2]

In 1874, student teams from McGill and Harvard played a series of matches which have been hailed as the birth of intercollegiate football, as distinguished from soccer—a distinction in names which still escapes most of the world.[3] What has happened in the hundred years since the McGill team traveled from Canada to visit Cambridge, Massachusetts? Has American higher education cultivated its own version of the "playing fields of Eton" rhetoric? What is the educational and structural status of athletics in contemporary American higher education? This chapter will attempt to ferret out some of the distinctive connections which Americans make among collegiate sports, educational opportunity, and social mobility, and how these are arranged and administered by oficials in colleges and universities.

In 1975, several football coaches from major American universities testified before a United States subcommittee that enforcement of the Title IX guidelines prohibiting sex discrimination in educational programs threatened to destroy "college sports as we know it."[4] The coaches were shocked that President Gerald Ford had betrayed his own college football heritage by having approved the proposed legislation. Amid press coverage and arguments, there was scant comment by college and university faculty or presidents. Given present tensions over lean budgets and educational priorities in an era of institutional "steady-state growth," one would have expected American educators to have an interest in athletic programs sponsored by academic institutions. To the contrary, presidents, deans, and professors seemed to be intent on removing themselves from intervention into such matters.

Why the conspiracy of silence? Consider that in the past five years, parents in Philadelphia and San Francisco have been indifferent to budget cuts in secondary-school music, art, and foreign-language programs. The one thing which elicited public outrage and intervention by state legislators was city school-board announcements that varsity sports were to be eliminated. Clearly, no one concerned with the serious study and administration of American education can deny that significant numbers of Americans do consider varsity sports to be an integral part of the *educational* program.

Nor does it follow that the topic is boring or obvious. One premise of this chapter is that a college's or university's athletic policy can tell much about that institution's educational ideals. Frederick Rudolph's essay on "The Rise of Football" in the 1880s and 1890s provides an excellent introduction to the topic, but ought to be seen as a stimulus to investigation, not the final word on the subject.[5] Sports in American higher education have spawned a prodigious legacy of clichés, heroes, slogans, and stories. Despite the familiarity of much of this oratory and literature, the American collegiate sports ethos has not been described and understood once and for all. The nostalgia which pervades sports history is selective and obscures important incidents, issues, and characters of earlier decades. This is an area where sound historical research could contribute to formulation of educational policy.

LOOKING BACKWARD: FORGOTTEN HEROES

In 1973, the National Collegiate Athletic Association (NCAA) celebrated college football's one-hundredth anniversary with numerous posters and television spots which depicted the present-day game as heir to the traditions of the late 19th century. Here was a curious abuse of history, in that the NCAA capitalized on the patina of heritage, legitimacy, and longevity without truly acknowledging the code and ethos of the early collegiate game. A thorough and accurate account of college football in the early 1900s would have conflicted with the NCAA's contemporary glorification of college athletics as part of "the American way" of social mobility. Amid all the celebration, the NCAA paid no tribute to the greatest college sportsman of the pre-World War I generation. We know where Joe DiMaggio has gone (to advertise and endorse coffee makers), but our sense of sports history is shallow. Today, the mention of the name Hobey Baker brings the response, "Hobey *who?*"

It was not always so. Hobey Baker of Princeton (Figure 6) was a versatile athlete, an All-American in football, and the greatest American hockey player of his day. He was the inspiration for collegiate heroism in the stories of F. Scott Fitzgerald and was popular with both fans and his college classmates. He scrupulously shunned payment and cheap publicity. When he was killed in France during his stint as an ace pilot and hero in World War I, he was genuinely mourned by thousands of collegians.[6] All this matters little to contemporary football promoters. Hobey Baker has been ignored because he is an embarrassment, a liability to the present interpretation of the American collegiate sports ethos. He is an unsound hero for today's youth because he never viewed sports as a way to get ahead. The gentleman's code to which he ascribed is neither understood nor appreciated today. After all, Baker was a WASP, attended a boarding school, and graduated from Princeton. Instead of receiving rightful historic recognition as an All-Amerrican, Hobey Baker has been neglected or dismissed as un-American, not quite right for egalitarian adulation.

The case of Hobey Baker suggests it is time, then, to review the roots of the collegiate sports hero—this tradition which is now used to justify and embellish nationally televised college football games. in the 1890s, when campuses were attracting the attention of magazines and feature writers, the collegiate hero emerged as a dominant character in popular journalism and fiction. The stories of campus life, characterized by romanticized accounts and inflated prose, emphasized themes of courage, character, grit, and strength in the face of problems and adversity. An inordinate number of stories were set at Yale, with such titles as *Boltwood of Yale*, *Sons of Eli*, *Boys and Men: A Story of Life at Yale*. Of all the heroes, none could match the fictional "Frank Merriwell of Yale." From 1896 to 1915, his adventures appeared in the *Tip-Top Weekly* for 986 consecutive weeks and in 415 paperbound novels.[7]

The fictional "Frank Merriwell," along with the *real* Yale, created what strikes us today as an anomaly: popular admiration for an elite hero and institution. George Santayana, upon returning from a visit to Yale in 1892, exclaimed: "The place is sacred to the national ideal. . . . No wonder that all America loves Yale, where American traditions are vigorous, American instincts are unchecked, and young men are trained and made eager for the keen struggles of American life."[8] The huge white varsity "Y" on a blue sweater, along with other Yale symbols, had tremendous popular appeal. Yale had more than winning teams: the New Haven campus was the messianic center of the football tradition. Old Blues were hired as football coaches throughout the nation, and thus spread the Yale football gospel to colleges from coast to coast. (Figure 7)

The important social fact was that the collegiate hero, the ideal college athlete, was a *gentleman*. College experiences and athletic contests were raised to lofty heights as the core of a gentleman's education. Yale's Walter Camp, the "Father of American Football," preached to American boys, "Be each, pray God, a gentleman! It is an easy word, and a pleasant one. I don't doubt but that you all pronounce it trippingly enough, and have each one his own high ideal of what a gentleman should be. Do you live up to it?" According to Camp, a gentleman playing against a gentleman always played to win; a gentleman did not make his living from his athletic prowess, and gained only glory and satisfaction from his victories. Nor were gentlemen physical or mental cowards. Camp's sermon concluded:

> Now, my young college friend, it is your turn. Remember, it is upon you that the younger brother looks for example, and whatever you do in your four years' course, you will see magnified by the boys who come after you. Support your class and your college in every way compatible with your position.[9]

Hobey Baker, whose Princeton teams competed against Yale, realized and fulfilled the collegiate ideal which Walter Camp extolled. The problem is that we erroneously assume that the collegiate ideal circa 1900 implied great wealth, snobbey, or withdrawal from participation in the active life. This was not the case. By 1937, editors of *Life* magazine noted that Eastern collegians were "clinging to a steadily dwindling share of athletic supremacy." The article explained:

> In the past two decades, athletic reputation has largely moved West and South. A host of high school athletes, graduating into the elaborate sports arenas of the State universities, have rudely trampled the belief of an older generation that Harvard, Yale, Princeton, Cornell, and Pennsylvania symbolize greatness at football, crew, and track.[10]

With that change in the geographical and institutional locus of athletic victories, the collegiate hero was modified to embrace the legends (real and embellished) of the egalitarian state university. The modern, revised version of Walter Camp's collegiate hero was Horatio Alger, who now went down to State U. rather than tend the stove in a countinghouse as a strategy for socioeconomic mobility. According to this version, athletic scholarships were a key to helping poor but determined boys gain a college education and proceed on to adult success, often measured by such indicators as a professional sports contract or election to political office. Countless variations on this theme have provided the heroic model which attracts poor youth to college for the wrong reasons.

Americans have become so enamored with college sports as a route to success that they conveniently overlook inconsistencies in and departures from the formula. First, an athletic scholarship has always been a risky means of achieving a college degree. Second, athletic scholarships are not awarded on the basis of financial need. This latter feature has been protected by university coaches, even though most academic scholarships for undergraduates are awarded to students only if they can demonstrate need for financial assistance. Third, a college education has never been necessary for a professional sports career. Consider how the collegiate-hero formula was scrambled by two famous, world-champion boxers: heavyweight Gene Tunney was a Yale man, and flyweight Fidel LaBarba graduated from Stanford. Both were popular athletic heroes and both were truly American in their recognition that a college education could bestow social status, learning, and respectability. But they upset the conventional notion of mobility because they chose to attend college *after* having achieved sports fame and wealth. The alternative route, seldom mentioned in collegiate literature or by college coaches, warrants reconsideration now that a bachelor's degree is no longer mistaken as a guarantee of the proverbial "good job."

In recent years, college and university coaches have learned to make fine distinctions between a young man's educational development and his financial opportunities, as the professional basketball league's "hardship rule" has permitted teams to sign a college athlete to a professional contract before that athlete has exhausted his collegiate playing eligibility, *if* the student athlete can demonstrate great financial hardship. Naturally, this has not pleased college coaches, whose star sophomore and junior players leave school for a professional contract. The stock response is for the concerned coach to bemoan the intrusion on the athlete's scholastic achievement. Such expressions of educational concern are not convincing, especially when one bears in mind a recurrent syndrome among students on athletic scholarship: dropping out of school *after* completion of varsity playing eligibility, yet *before* completion of degree requirements.

DIFFICULTIES OF RESEARCH AND REFORM

Perhaps contemporary faculty and administrators shy away from the past and future of college sports because the topic has eluded those few scholars and researchers who have attempted analysis and intervention since the turn of the century. Consider the case of Edwin Slosson, editor of *The Independent* in the early 1900s, who wrote perceptive accounts of higher education during the formative years of the American university. His numerous campus profiles were laced with frequent commentary on the extraordinary place which sports were acquiring in colleges and universities. Slosson identified an important topic, yet his predictions were sorely off the mark.

After having visited the Pacific Coast in 1909, Slosson argued that California colleges would not imitate the sports programs of the older eastern institutions. The abundance of hills and sunshine made hiking and other outdoor recreation far more enjoyable and healthful than the confined drudgery of indoor sports. Slosson was so confident on this point that he claimed there was no need to rebuild the Stanford University gymnasium, which had been leveled by an earthquake. Given this projection for the future of Pacific Coast basketball, it is well that Slosson did not live to see the popularity and national championships of UCLA basketball in the 1960s and 1970s.

California's geographical isolation was supposed to have minimized football's collegiate appeal. At the time of Slosson's campus tours, both Stanford and the University of California had dropped football in favor of rugby. The experiment seemed to please students and led Slosson to assume that the change would be permanent. Most important, Slosson was impressed by the open fields, amphitheaters, and warm climate, and predicted that California students would opt for Grecian-style outdoor festivals rather than the passive role of spectators to the grunts and groans of combative football.[11] We know that this has not been so.

Slosson's campus profiles are important because most of his insights on the course of American higher education were correct. As indicated by his poor track record in the preceding examples, the study and reform of intercollegiate athletics has not been simple. Nor have other investigators fared well. In 1929, the Carnegie Foundation for the Advancement of Teaching published Howard Savage's *American College Athletics*, a study which included hundreds of examples of flagrant commercialism in the supposedly amateur world of college sports.[12] Again, the scholar's recommendations and findings had negligible reform impact. Most disturbing about Savage's 1929 study and the Carnegie Foundation's 1931 sequel is the tone of naiveté and false optimism. The 1931 report, for example, predicted that public and student interest in spectator sports was waning, and offered the confident projection that intramural contests and physical education would modify or replace the abuses of promotion and commercialism in big-time sports. Perhaps the protocol of a committee report curbed publication of penetrating analyses or drastic indictments—and that may well be an inherent limitation of committee reports.

At the same time that Howard Savage was carrying out the Carnegie Foundation study, Abraham Flexner's critical study of American universities cited the University of Chicago's use of billboards for advertising the football schedule as a prime example of the abuses of sports in American higher education. A year later, Chicago underwent a wholesale transformation of athletic policy, as Robert Maynard Hutchins de-emphasized intercollegiate sports (Figure 8). According to a 1931 brochure written by Hutchins:

> College is *not* "a great athletic association and social club, in which provision is made, merely incidentally, for intellectual activity on the part of the physically and socially unfit." College *is* an association of scholars in which provision is made for the development of traits and powers which must be cultivated, in addition to those which are purely intellectual, if one is to become a well-balanced and useful member of any community.[13]

Hutchins may have been successful in altering the athletic and academic atmosphere at the University of Chicago, yet his model was not the source of great emulation elsewhere in American higher education. It would be more accurate to say that his definition and prescription provided a model to avoid for most American campuses. It is sad but true that reform recommendations and experiments have had negligible impact, and certainly misinterpreted the public attitude toward intercollegiate sports in the mid-twentieth century.

The major consequence of investigations, foundation surveys, and commission reports has been to increase and consolidate the regulatory power of the National Collegiate Athletic Association. It has not meant that expensive sports budgets and dependencies on spectators, box-office receipts, and broadcasting have been tapered down. *Amateurism* has been redefined and altered numerous times so as to bear little resemblance to its original meaning, ''competition without financial gain or payment.'' In the 1970s, the NCAA allowed students who were professional athletes in one sport to compete as amateur collegiate players in another sport.

Similarly, it is not clear that NCAA regulations and reforms have supported the educational and academic protection of student athletes. For years, freshmen were ineligible for varsity play on the grounds that the first year of college should be devoted to academic adjustments, without the pressures and demands of competition with older, more experienced players. By 1971, the NCAA allowed conferences to change this rule so that student athletes were allowed four years of varsity eligibility, including the freshman year. The benefit of the rule change was that universities no longer had to field freshman squads; they gained an extra year of play from students on athletic scholarships, and the change minimized the problem of academic ineligibility which had faced numerous athletes after freshman-year grades were released. One irony is that this movement away from an academic waiting period came to a time when academic indicators of entering freshman (SAT scores, course entrance requirements) were declining. Furthermore, the conference with the least worry about the academic standing and preparation of its freshmen athletes, the Ivy League, opted to maintain freshman squads and the historic three-year varsity eligibility rule.

NCAA ''reform'' has followed a pattern of concession to commercial and quasi-professional practices, usually to the benefit of those large institutions with big-time teams in football and basketball. From 1976 to 1978, when delegates to the NCAA annual conventions proposed limits on the number of scholarships and assistant coaches any college or university might have, a handful of universities with national-caliber programs complained that the pursuit of excellence and individual autonomy was being threatened, a charge that conveniently overlooked the cumulative privileges and corporate strength (and televisions rights) which the NCAA had made possible for them. Any measure designed to curb overemphasis has led to a proposal that twenty to fifty of the major universities secede from the NCAA ''tyranny'' and form a new ''super-conference.'' But even though the NCAA is a voluntary association, it is doubtful that the large universities will follow through on their dramatic threat, simply because the NCAA has assisted and promoted the consolidation and extension of elaborate, expensive varsity programs for male student athletes.

One consequence of the ineffective investigations and reports is that a number of educators have concluded that preoccupation with sports is so strong on the American campus that academic administrators and faculty members should transplant the forms and spirit of football to the academic realm. Looking back through the records before World War I, one finds that Edwin Slosson provided readers with a futuristic account of intellectual competition between Cornell and Columbia in New York City:

> Park Row is packed with upturned faces watching the bulletin boards. . . . A shout from a thousand throats is heard when the street sees that Dr. Haas of Columbia has translated the Dararupa of Dhanmaja until the applause is checked by the announcement of Dr. McKelvey's study of the groups of birational transformations of algebraic curves of Genus.[14]

According to Slosson's 1910 projection, contest results were to be telegraphed all over the country, and newspapers were to feature photographs of winning scholars and box-score summaries of championship dissertations.

This reform proposal was wishful thinking, as academic all-stars and the champions of grantsmanship have never been able to match the publicity and color of varsity athletics. The closest approximation of Slosson's reform fantasy came in the early 1960s, when General Electric sponsored a weekly, nationally televised "College Bowl" program, complete with rival teams, varsity scholars, brain coaches, half-time breaks, and toss-up questions. The program's popularity dwindled after a few seasons. Intense academic competitoin was hopelessly incongruent with the ideals of open admissions which were gaining favor in colleges and universities throughout the United States.

One additional source of reform initiative has come from the popular press. Sportswriters have kept readers well stocked with exposés of abuses in college sports, and recruiting scandals, slush funds, point-shaving investigations, cheating rings, and exploitative coaches have become hardy perennials of American journalism.[15] But these become predictable and boring incidents that constitute an ineffectual "dirty history" which coaches and athletic directors can usually deny or dismiss because writers have relied heavily on anonymous tips, off-the-record quotes, or accusations by disgranted players and losing (fired) coaches. Instead of exposés, other ways must be found to document and analyze changes in the American collegiate sports ethos.

GAUGING CHANGES IN THE AMERICAN COLLEGIATE SPORTS ETHOS

Taking a cue from Robert Bellah's discussion of civil religion in America, we define and justify our activities in terms of historical and noble purposes through public statements. The rhetoric and oratory of testimonial speeches and press conferences are the means through which spokesmen for intercollegiate sports reveal that which they consider to be sacred and safe for public consumption. What follows is a number of recent "Americanisms" on college sports which indicate shifting thresholds of public acquiscence and acceptability. The approach, then, is to consider what coaches and athletic directors have had to say to the public and to government officials about justification for existing university athletic practices.

During the 1975 government hearings on the Title IX legislation, the athletic director of the University of Maryland complained that the Department of Health, Education and Welfare did not understand intercollegiate athletics. He generously assumed the task of reeducating the inquiring officials and pointed out that implementation of the Title IX provision for equal opportunity for women's sports would destroy established activities. He said, "To me, this is poor business and poor management," and noted that the university was "in competition with professional sports and other entertainment for the consumer's money" and "did not want a lesser product to market."[16] In the same spirit, the football coach at another large state university explained to reporters that a losing season and bad publicity hurt his program, saying, "We're in the entertainment business and are susceptible to the whims of fans who may get upset with our performance."

In late 1974, the University of Pittsburgh's athletic officials proudly told *Time* magazine reporters that their football program included the following expenses: $600,000 for operating the program; $350,000 for scholarships (140 players at $2500 each); and $30,000 for the head coach's salary. Furthermore, the head coach received a weekly television show and a blank check for recruitment. In less than a two-year period, alumni donated $181,000 for the athletic program, none of which went for general university or educational use. Specifically, the donations paid for enlarging locker rooms and installing carpeting, a lounge, and a stereo system. The coach's comment was, "Carpeting floors doesn't win ball games for you, but it sure makes things more comfortable."[17]

The hazards of the coaching field can be eased. In the mid-1970s, alumni at Florida State University bought up the contract of a losing coach, which meant that the ex-coach received two years' termination pay, totaling more than $90,000. If that does not strike one as sound, efficient financial management, consider alternative strategies for athletic administration. In 1978, the University of Texas board of regents adopted a policy under which coaches will receive an 8 percent bonus if their teams appear in postseason games. According to the news release, the bonus is aimed at rewarding coaches who ''have assumed more than normal mental, physical and time loads and who achieve outstanding team performance.''[18]

All this is neither new nor startling, unless one's involvement with higher education has been outside the United States. For decades, critics and muckrakers have exposed the large budgets, slush funds, and expenses of intercollegiate sports, along with the ''up or out'' syndrome in which a few institutions drop varsity sports each season while the big and rich get bigger and richer. An important change in the 1970s is the *source* and the *tone* of the recent comments quoted above. The figures and statements do not come from clandestine documents, interviews, confessions, or rumors; there has been no digging through departmental files or illegal reproduction of confidential records. Information which would have once been presented as a scandal is now presented as a matter-of-fact, even proud, description of institutional practice by the advocates of intercollegiate sports programs.

Conspicuously absent is the tired cliche that football is an educational activity. Herein lies the seed of a potentially dramatic revision in the American collegiate sports ethos: a departure from celebration of college sports as a means to some other end. Ike Balbus, a political scientist at the City University of New York, has written a perceptive analysis of the sports metaphor in American life and suggested that sports have been a prelude, an excuse, and analogy for American politics and institutions.[19] Now we might conclude that sports are sufficiently important in themselves to take on a new identity.

The most worn-out aspect of the American collegiate sports ethos has been glorification of sports as a training ground for some future reward beyond athletics—income, job, or national leadership. At one time, colleges and universities claimed that a big-time sports program boosted the overall *academic* reputation and resources of the university. If this spin-off effect was in operation today, the University of Oklahoma might be continually confused with the University of Chicago—an insult to Oklahoma's football program which might bring about a taxpayers' revolt in that state. Traditional wisdom held that a successful coach at a state university was in good position to cultivate local political ties and build a base for election to the state legislature, the governorship, or the United States Senate. This is not so today. To go from a position as a successful coach to a position in politics would probably mean a loss of publicity, popular acclaim, local and regional influence, and income. Governors and presidents now *envy* coaches.

There is a slim possibility that the current autonomy and arrogance of intercollegiate athletic programs will eventually degenerate into hubris. If coaches and athletic directors continue to describe their programs with such terms as "entertainment," "superior products," "marketing," and "competition for consumers' dollars," they might cut inter-collegiate sports from the protective moorings and special exemptions which the government bestows upon nonprofit and educational ac-tivities. College and university athletic budgets are large, yet fragile; fickle fans, stingy alumni, and a limited number of television broadcast opportunities make all but a handful of collegiate programs subject to a precarious fiscal fitness.

One interesting—and startling—interpretation of varsity sports as an educational pursuit was offered in 1978 by a head football coach who told reporters that people who go to college to play football ought be able to major in football as a field of study. His discourse on the philosophy of education went as follows:

> Look, a person who's a woodworker and is in school to learn to carve isn't interested in the guy working on computers in the engineering depart-ment. And the saxophone player who wants to become a music teacher couldn't care less about the law classes. If a kid wants to play football, with the idea of turning professional, then he ought to be allowed to earn a degree in tollege football.[20]

One winces because the university's public-relations office did not brief the coach on some problems his candor might raise. It publicly confirm-ed persistent complaints which have been raised about overemphasis on college football, namely that college football demands so much time and energy that a student athlete cannot properly attend to academic studies, and that professional sports teams have freely benefited from college athletic programs which behave as if they were *de facto* minor-league training teams—with bills paid by the colleges and universities.

Apart from the coach's obvious ignorance of degree requirements and curricula which promote general education and exposure to several fields of learning, he is on dangerous grounds. If degree programs were monitored according to productivity and job placement, the football major would have difficulty passing faculty review. Using the figures cited for the 1974 University of Pittsburgh team, let us assume that a major college team has 140 players on football scholarships, likely candidates for a football major. Assuming also that we limit our sample to one hundred universities, this means that each summer, roughly 3500 graduating seniors with football majors would be applying for the 350 vacancies for rookies which the professional football leagues have on their rosters. The "B.Fb." degree surplus would make the Ph.D. glut appear to be a minor problem in the gap between higher education and jobs.

In fact, intercollegiate sports will have an increasingly difficult time explaining themselves as educationally and academically legitimate programs. Years ago, the stereotype of the dumb athlete who majored in P.E. was widespread. This is not necessarily the case today, as departments of physical education at many American universities have acquired a strong, independent indentity as areas of research, development, professional training, and graduate education, and have little to do with varsity sports programs and personnel. There is only an accidental connection between the training and teaching practices of varsity coaches and the research findings of the physical-education discipline. There is no provision in varsity-sports hiring practices to assure that a coach is knowledgeable in such areas as nutrition, health, motor development, sociology of sport, pedagogy, or physiology. One obvious example of varsity sports' isolation from rigorous research and development in physical education is the tradition of the pregame training meal—the big, rare beefsteak. For years, researchers in nutrition and diet have pointed out that this is about the worst meal one can eat prior to vigorous physical activity. Nonetheless, the tradition had died out slowly at varsity training tables. Above all, physical education departments have been making major contributions to development of programs and facilities which promote lifelong participation in health and recreation. Intercollegiate sports have no coordination with and may be contradictory to these goals.

Discussions and proposals for investigation and reform of intercollegiate athletics run the risk of moral indignation and the unwarranted assumption that there is consensus as to the direction and content of reformed sports programs. The preceding section has focused on contradictions and inconsistencies within the ranks of varsity coaches and athletic directors, in their respective explanations of the proper relationship between athletics and curriculum. But a plea for consistency and logic does not carry the imperative that varsity sports be eliminated. This distinction and warning serves to remind educators and administrators that there are several variations in the dissatisfactions with intercollegiate athletic programs. The demand for de-emphasis is markedly different from the campaign for extension and expansion of existing practices, although both constitute reform movements. Consider the complexities of sports reform and the higher education of women.

It is not by accident, hardly an oversight, that this chapter has been confined to analysis of men's varsity sports. It is an accurate reflection of the NCAA's scope and the separate policies practiced at most colleges and universities. Significantly, Title IX says nothing about trimming big-time spectator sports as a necessary step in accommodating athletic demands of women students. It is plausible that the solution is to elevate women's intercollegiate sports to the level of competition and commercialism associated with the NCAA.

One social-historical critique of women's colleges advertises itself with a dustjacket which proclaims, "Adam's Rib versus the New Feminism: Can the Seven Sisters change to meet the needs of women in a changing society?"[21] On the one hand, the author criticizes women's colleges for having constructed an academic curriculum which has been a pale imitation of that offered by men's liberal-arts colleges—a prelude to an argument for creation of a distinctive model of education for women. Yet this polemic runs into reverse complications in the area of collegiate sports. From roughly 1880 to 1910, the women's colleges developed unique and distinctive instructional, recreational, and intramural programs which emphasized lifelong health, hygiene and nutrition, and such sports as crew, field hockey, and tennis, in marked contrast to the varsity programs for men. And these women's athletic programs were a continual source of ridicule and satire, probably because they were far ahead of their time.

If the reform impulse in American higher education had favored an end to the expensive, spectator-oriented contests in major sports, the women's college sports programs might well have provided a sound historical model for revision. Such does not appear to be the case; the feminist author of the book mentioned above indicts the Seven Sisters for havng stayed "out of the business of athletic scholarships, with its indecorous, unladylike pressures and potentials for corruption, a decision that may in time further reduce competitive sports opportunities for nonparticipants."[22]

The disturbing implication of this critique is that adequate funding and support for athletics on campus must or ought to be carried out through athletic scholarships, alumni fund-raising, and spectator-oriented contests. If so, that wish has started to come true for women's intercollegiate sports programs in the late 1970s. The Association for Intercollegiate Athletics for Women (AIAW)—without ties to the NCAA—now has to deal with charges of sports recruitment abuse, overemphasis, coaches' raids, and financial-aid irregularities: truly a microcosm of the overemphasis associated with the NCAA. Hence, "reform" in women's intercollegiate athletics has followed a pattern of extension and expansion of existing practices and attitudes in men's varsity sports.

The social fact might be that the American public's dissatisfaction with intercollegiate competition is that it does not go far enough. Coaches and citizens in Oklahoma were upset a few years ago when the NCAA denied permission to substitute the traditional spring practice intrasquad scrimmages with full-scale games against conference teams. Perhaps there is in all aspects of American life an incipient "jockism" which cuts across lines of sex, class, and vocation. Locker-room slogans (once confined to locker rooms, of course) have power to sell newspapers. A *Wall Street Journal* advertisement of 1977 featured executives in pin-striped, vested suits and horn-rimmed glasses gramacing as they raced over hurdles; the caption read, "When the competition in business gets tough. . . *The Wall Street Journal* can help."

Meanwhile, many American colleges and universities are susceptible to being caught in the embarrassing situation of sponsoring intercollegiate athletics but no longer taking the trouble to go through rituals or formalities of deference to educational purposes. One solution might be to portray intercollegiate sports as a public service to the state or local community, a rationale not unlike that used in the early 1900s to create and fund agricultural extension programs. The agriculture school analogy is especially useful here, as university presidents and athletic directors might wade through the heritage of American public higher education to resurrect the old "A and M" label. Whereas a century ago this designated an institution committed to agriculture and mining, agriculture and military, or agriculture and mechanics, American higher education in the 1980s demands a new wrinkle. "A and M" could stand for "athletics and money," an appropriate public symbol and a terminology which would bring university identity and activities into congruence with the contemporary American collegiate sports ethos.

MASCOTS AND SYMBOLS: A RESEARCH STRATEGY FOR INSTITUTIONAL AFFILIATION

If we accept, or at least entertain, the argument that intercollegiate sports constitute an integral part of a campus's public-service activities, how might this influence institutional planning? One approach which would bring collegiate sports into the mainstream of higher-education research and development is to recognize that corporate icons and symbols are a potent source of organizational affiliation and loyalty. For colleges and universities, the mascots and colors associated with varsity teams have been an obvious yet underappreciated source of institutional information. There is little indication that institutional researchers have fully acknowledged that campus constituents *do* consider these symbols to be serious matters.

A few analysts, such as Stephen Novak, have gone so far as to contend that intercollegiate football has become America's "regional religion." One journalist, who grew up in Arkansas, affirmed this perspective and offered the following comments to the national intellegentsia:

> You probably have seen us on television and, football fan or not, have been bemused, puzzled or even angered by our peculiar and irrational zeal. By 'us' I mean hog callers, razorbackers, adepts of the red-swine cult; fanatic followers of the University of Arkansas' teams. Of course, I could just as well mean Nebraskans, Oklahomans, or Alabamians, for the football bowl season is upon us: a time for pilgrimages and for the wearing of colors.

For skeptics who underestimate the pervasiveness of these college symbols and mementos, he noted:

> Other persons in the stands will wear Razorback jackets, lapel pins, sweaters, overalls, even underwear. If there is an item of clothing that one cannot purchase somewhere in Arkansas with a pig on it, I suspect it is available only from Frederick's of Hollywood. At home they may have left Razorback clocks, rugs, plaques, wallhangings, toilet-seat covers, wallpaper and even telephones. Possibly they even do their barbequing on a currently-popular cast-iron grill shaped as a rampant swine, with ducts for escaping smoke located appropriately at the nostrils and anus.[23]

For one who seeks ties between campus and community, the varsity sports of the state university provide one very good answer. The columnist concluded, "As for the sheer, vulgar spectacle of the thing, cheerleaders, pom-pom girls, marching band, imprisoned mascot and all, I find it exhilarating. We might well be living in medieval London."

One implication is that college and university presidents ought to use caution before tampering with a campus's mascot or colors. In Lexington, Kentucky, architects and planners—outsiders, of course—demonstrated ignorance of state priorities when they used "good taste" instead of "local color" in painting the logo on the civic arena, which was to be the home court for the national championship University of Kentucky basketball team. The designers rejected "Kentucky blue" in favor of burnt orange for the structure's logo, overlooking the fact that orange was the color of Kentucky's archrival, the University of Tennessee.[24] The ensuing local outrage confirmed Mark Twain's observation that one may break laws, but must always observe customs.

Mascots are no laughing matter. At Scottsdale Community College in Arizona, students united to oppose local community demands for a strong varsity football team by voting official approval to a satirical mascot, the name "Fightin' Artichokes," and official colors of pink and white. This ushered in prolonged disputes with administrators and townspeople against students and faculty, and eventually led to the president's resignation.[25] And mascot loyalty has financial consequences: in 1974, the regents of the University of Texas at Austin were unable to convince a donor that $50,000 ought to go for academic scholarships, instead of his proposal for designing, sculpting, and erecting a statue of Bevo, the University of Texas's Longhorn mascot.[26]

A number of colleges and universities have felt uncomfortable with the mascots and logos they have inherited. In 1976, one vice-president at Michigan State University sponsored a contest for a revised drawing of the Spartan mascot. In attempting to do away with the brutish, grimacing Spartan face which had adorned souvenirs and mementos for over a half-century, the university administrator commented, "I think it was done originally to frighten children into eating their lima beans."[27] Whereas Michigan State officials wanted to move away from ferocity, some campuses during the 1970s abolished mascots which might carry connotations of social slurs; and here we find a decline in use of the Indian as a collegiate symbol of athletic prowess. The University of Massachusetts shed its Redmen mascot tradition and became the Minutemen, although the process of change was not very rapid. In fact, the transition took several years, during which time one student group lobbied for a mascot which paid homage to a distinctive New England creature—the clam.[28] Given the tendency for the university to be in a period of "steady-state growth," the inactivity connoted by the clam suggests that it was an appropriate symbol.

Stanford University, whose teams were originally known as the Cardinals (the color, not the bird, Stanford officials are quick to note), adopted the "Indians" nomenclature for decades, then returned to the "Cardinal" designation in 1972. Five years later, a petition signed by 225 athletes from 18 varsity sports was presented to the Stanford president, urging designation of the griffin as the new Stanford mascot.[29] Herein lies a problem: there are over 2000 colleges and universities in the United States, yet there are a finite number of colors and mascots, which impedes institutional originality. The irony (and perhaps an unexpected development) was that Stanford, with its national reputation for scholarship and academic excellence and numerous national, international, and Olympic-caliber teams and athletes in its varsity sports program, was edging toward a mascot already associated with a college whose sports program was markedly different: Reed College.

Reed College, home of a distinctive liberal-arts curriculum and a rigorous academic environment, has not pursued a program of big-time varsity and spectator sports. In one year, Reed's moment of intercollegiate athletic glory consisted of a victory in a darts match against the University of Oregon Dental School in Portland. Yet Reed, not Stanford, had first claim to the griffin mascot (Figure 9). According to the Reed alumni magazine, the college identified with the mythical creature for the following reasons:

> The legendary Griffin is part lion, part eagle and emits solar rays. The Griffin, as guardian of the earth's treasure, signifies supra-solar light, or the highest degree of intellectual insight and awareness. The opposite of this light is chaos, a Greek word meaning darkness. An Associate of the Griffin is a friend of Apollo and furthers order and intellectual attainments.[30]

Few colleges have chosen mascots with such careful attention to intellectual and cerebral characteristics. The intercollegiate landscape is dotted with predictable and oft-repeated ferocious beasts: lions, tigers, bears. Yet if one looks beyond this obvious mascot menagerie, one finds a number of institutions whose symbols and logos do attest to state or local history and heritage. We have already encountered Arkansas's tribute to the area's razorbacks, to which we might add the following:

Institution	Mascot
Indiana	Hoosiers
Oklahoma	Sooners
Oklahoma State	Cowboys
Nebraska	Cornhuskers

| North Carolina | Tarheels |
| Mississippi | Rebels |

Another strategy is for the mascot to represent the school's particular curriculum or educational mission. Here the Purdue Boilermakers, the MIT Engineers, or the Cal Tech Beavers celebrate the applied and engineering functions. A few campuses, especially Catholic colleges, allude to ethnic roots (Notre Dame Fighting Irish, St. Mary's Gaels), even though this has scant correlation with the ethnic composition of Notre Dame's starting lineup.

One problem is that a handful of large-university teams which dominate NCAA championships and sports-page coverage obscure the colorful and imaginative mascots and nicknames which lesser-known colleges have acquired—a body of lore which constitutes a neglected part of our higher-educational heritage. Robert Strauss, a graduate student and campus journalist at the University of California at Berkeley in 1974, picked his way through the archives and backwaters of American higher education to assemble an interesting roster of institutional mascots whose selection suggests admirable humor and originality. Strauss noted:

> But, O muse, there are gems for the lightheaded among us to savor. Specks of creativity, microns of uniqueness, sands of musicality lie in the naming of some mascots of academia. Chimes ring at the mention of the St. Louis U. Billikens, the Oberlin Yeomen, the Southern Illinois Salukis. Visions of treachery, abandon, and fiber appear at the calling of the U. of Alaska Nanooks, the Idaho Vandals, the Furman Paladins, the Western Illinois Leathernecks. Myth heightens man's incarnate incandescence when he hears of the Canisius Golden Griffins, the UC San Diego Tritons, the California State (Pa.) Vulcans, the Los Angeles State Diablos.[31]

A significant number of colleges and universities have honored either the founder or the person for whom the institution was named:

Aquinas	Tommies
Bernard Baruch	Statesmen
Vanderbilt	Commodores
Franklin and Marshall	Diplomats
Washington and Jefferson	Presidents
Washington and Lee	Generals
Amherst	Lord Jeffs
Brandeis	Judges

This approach has snags; one doubts the physical strength and athletic prowess of teams at Whittier College, where students celebrated John Greenleaf Whittier by adopting the nickname of the Poets. On the other hand, this name is less contradictory than the one which Whittier College carried in the early 1900s and which the University of Pennsylvania teams carry today, the Fighting Quakers.

Since intercollegiate athletics bring to mind institutional rivalries, it is worthwhile to propose appropriate contests. Robert Strauss, for example, looked forward to a football season which included the following schedule of games:

> Heidelberg Student Princes versus Glassboro State Profs
> Wake Forest Demon Deacons versus Ohio Wesleyan Battling Bishops
> Tufts Jumbos versus Yeshiva Mighty Mites
> Centre College Praying Colonels versus Duke Blue Devils

Higher-education administrators are warned that configurations and associations among mascots and institutions have followed no simple pattern or logic. In some cases, the mascots tend to distort, not celebrate, institutional realities. How to explain the Austin, Texas, Kangaroos or a Pennsylvania college which identifies itself with gators? Nor do the mascots always lend themselves to graphic depiction. Harvard has long been famous as the Crimson, although in the 1870s, the campus official color was magenta. This leads to a peculiar facing those colleges which call themselves by a color variant for instance, the Crimson, Big Blue, or Great Grey. At games, Harvard is represented by a bigger-than-life Puritan, supposedly a tribute to John Harvard. Cornell's Big Red brings to mind an amorphous scarlet blob, although at one time an imaginative public-relations artist personified Big Red as an 1890s Irish ward politician. The University of Oregon teams, popularly known as the Ducks, were officially the Webfoots; neither name was sufficiently intimidating, so the campus now calls its team the Big Green. Although Williams College is officially the Ephmen, its mascot is a purple cow.

Again, logic has its limits in explaining or creating appropriate institutional mascots. Administrators must pay attention to the historical accidents, legends, and figures which surround a campus, and any attempt to alter mascots and symbols requires careful monitoring of institutional character and mission. The preceding cases hardly exhaust the interesting developments in mascot possibilities or etymology, but they do suggest the difficulties involved in understanding the connections between campus character and lore and relations with community, region, and state.

FIGURE 6

Forgotten Hero. Hobey Baker, Class of 1913, Princeton. Embodiment of the Collegiate Ideal before World War I, and described by John Davies as follows:

"Hobey Baker was different. A Philadelphia aristocrat and product of St. Paul's, looking like something out of the pages of Charles Dana Gibson or the Arrow collar ads, to the public during his career at Princeton and St. Nick's he was the *college* athlete supreme: the gentleman sportsman, the amateur in the pure sense playing the game *pour le sport,* who never fouled, despised publicity, and refused professional offers."

Courtesy, The Seeley G. Mudd Manuscript Library of Princeton University.

FIGURE 7A

"Tradition and Change in the Collegiate Sports Rituals: Team Captain Photo, 1931."

Courtesy of Yale University Department of Athletics.

FIGURE 7B

"Tradition and Change in the Collegiate Sports Rituals: Team Captain Photo, 1979."

Courtesy of S. Frinzi.

FIGURE 8

The Roar of the Crowd and Reform of Intercollegiate Sports: The University of Chicago's Amos Alonzo Staff Field after varsity intercollegiate football was dropped in 1939. In the final game of the 1939 season, the visiting Harvard team defeated the University of Chicago by a score of 62-0. By the late 1970s, however, Chicago revived varsity football.

Courtesy, Department of Special Collections, University of Chicago Library.

FIGURE 9

Institutional Identity and the House of Intellect: Reed College's "Griffin"—one of the few mascots in the menagerie of American colleges and universities which represents cerebral, as well as athletic, prowess. The Griffin, part lion and part eagle, is a legendary creature who was guardian of the earth's treasure, and symbolizes the light of insight—and is the enemy of Chaos (darkness).

Courtesy, Reed College Archives.

7

Gatekeepers and Headhunters: Admissions, Exclusion, and Sorting in Higher Education

HOW BAD WERE THE GOOD OLD DAYS?

In 1911, Robert Benchley gained a prominent place in Harvard College lore by his deft handling of an examination question on international relations. Confronted with an essay question which dealt with maritime policy and Canadian fisheries, he asked if anyone had considered the point of view of the fish.[1] The topic of the history of admissions and access to colleges and universities over the past century is no less difficult, and leads one to ask, "Has anyone considered the point of view of the dean?"

That question deserves to be asked because reconstruction of a college's admissions practices and results is not easy; nor are many conventional indicators a valid source of enduring social and institutional information. As Bruce C. Vladeck, professor of public health and political science at Columbia University, has observed:

> The competition for students and faculty is closely interwoven with the general drive for institutional prestige. Like most people, administrators and trustees are generally eager to do a good job and to appear to be doing a good job. But in higher education, as in most nonprofit services, it is extremely difficult to tell what a good job is, since it is so extraordinarily difficult to evaluate the quality of the "product."[2]

Evaluation difficulties are compounded when one adds an historical dimension to the study of admissions. A comparison of institutions and eras elicits ambiguities and vagaries when one attempts to reconstruct nor are there today many surviving samples of application forms or quantitative data from which to assemble an accurate, comprehensive picture of what was going on in matters of college selection and differentiation. There persists a strong temptation to see the history of admissions as a story of steady improvement, in which obstacles to access have been gradually, though not painlessly, removed. True, the expansion and extension of higher education in terms of numbers and categories of students has been an obvious theme in American social history of the 20th century. Yet expansion and extension hardly offer wholly satisfactory explanations of the differentiations and admissions decisions within the unwieldy corpus we call higher education.

Just as retiring college presidents find it convenient to cite building construction as an indicator of institutional progress, so we are quick to applaud coeducation, integration, financial aid programs, open admissions, and selective academic admissions as gains. The danger is that we write off colleges and universities of past eras as "snobbish" and "elitist," epithets which are incomplete and possibly incorrect. To restate a theme noted earlier: there has been little consistency in practices, priorities, or values which social groups or institutions espouse over time.

In the mid-19th century, for example, there were occasions when a college rushed ahead of national norms by offering admission to women and to men—an early example of coeducation. Although this might bring nods of approval by the standards of the 1970s, its "enlightened" impact is dulled by a closer check, which reveals that women were not permitted unrestricted access to college's curricula and facilities once they were admitted. Partial gains, fluctuations, and inconsistencies, rather than heroes and villains, characterized the study of admissions.

As noted in chapters 2, 3, and 4, medieval and continental universities, including Oxford and Cambridge, often had definite exclusionary policies which shaped the composition of their student bodies. One important question to raise is, what were contemporary responses to a particular code or practice? Religious tests, which remained at Oxford until late in the 19th century, did provoke resentment. We can readily document that significant numbers of students who were denied admission on religious grounds perceived the policy as unjust, and this led to creation of dissenting academies and concerted campaigns to change policy at the ancient university. Historical materials on objection to (or acceptance of) women's exclusion from the universities are less abundant; until documents and records are assembled, that issue will be left in the realm of conjecture, without grounding in historical fact.

Let us turn to the perennial charge of snobbery and exclusion at America's historic colleges. Historians have amply documented cases of discrimination and ethnic and religious intolerance at America's old East Coast colleges. Examples include Yale College students who jeered William Jennings Bryan's campus visit and populist speech in 1896; remarks about the "Jewish problem" by Dean Keppel of Columbia and President Lowell of Harvard in the 1910s and 1920s; the misuse of character references and photographs in selective admissions procedures adopted in the 1920s and 1930s; and charges of anti-Semitism and quotas at Dartmouth College in 1946.[3] Certainly these incidents call for critical institutional analysis. Lawrence Stone was quite correct in 1971 when he scolded historians who spent their time "defending the Oxbridge and Ivy League of the past, crammed as they were with wellborn, lazy, and often rather stupid 'gentleman C's,' passing comfortably through on their way to inheriting elite positions in the outside world."[4]

If we assume that Stone's reconstruction is accurate, we are still left without clear guidelines as to which goals or practices would constitute desirable policy by which to redress the grievances and correct the situations Stone found odious. Is there consensus that a college would be in good health if it were crammed with energetic stupid students? Or would "poor-born," lazy, rather stupid students represent educational progress? A student body with "A" averages might—or might not—draw from a broad socioeconomic base. Although these queries are overstated, they are not out of line with the differences in reform proposals and varieties of campuses one can now find in the United States.

One strength of recent research is that historians have not been content simply to dismiss the historic colleges as "just elite" institutions. We must be wary of the tendency to exalt either equality or meritocracy as admissions goals. A number of recent studies have brought attention to the limits in which colleges or universities have operated as well as to the unexpected consequences and unforeseen problems which have come with alterations in college admissions policies. And there has been increasing scrutiny of the distinction between exclusion at college entrance and discrimination within a campus's student body.

Institutional stereotypes, however, do persist. Hugh Kearney's *Scholars and Gentlemen*, a history of universities and the advent of industrial society, closes with some harsh comments on late-19th-century American colleges. Kearney argues that

in a sea of rising democracy, the colleges were "citadels of privilege." . . .

Harvard was the only Eastern college to go any way towards adapting itself to the new conditions of social revolution. The *elitist* traditions of Princeton and Yale remained unchanged well into the twentieth century.[5]

The composite portrait of wealthy decadence does not hold up against recent analyses of family and income backgrounds of undergraduates at Dartmouth, Amherst, Wesleyan, and Williams. Whatever prestige and social exclusion came to be associated with these colleges in the 20th century, in the 1880s most students were the sons of farmers, clerks, ministers, and teachers. It is erroneous to extend the real and imagined worlds of F. Scott Fitzgerald beyond the Princeton campus and back into the 19th century. We now have an excellent case study of the development of connections among Harvard College, the Boston elite, and preparatory schools during the period from 1800 to 1870.[6] But if Kearney is correct in singling out Harvard for its "adaptations" to social revolution in the late 19th century, we are left with an intriguing question: How did this institutional transformation take place? Nor is Kearney's indictment of Yale College of that period wholly convincing. Yale was an institution which prided itself on the geographical and economic diversity of its student body, its large number of "self-help" students, and other features of democracy which led editors and commentators to call Yale the American college.

In calling the eastern colleges "citadels of privilege," we must also consider why going to college had limited appeal. Perhaps formal education was of meager interest to restless youth intent on making a fortune. Christopher Jencks's *Inequality* (published in 1973) argues that access to schooling has had relatively little consequence for socioeconomic mobility in the United States. If this is plausible in the mid-20th century, why should hindsight fault 19th-century colleges for failing to be open, egalitarian institutions? Often the private eastern colleges are accused of being wary of diplomas from public high schools in distant regions, even though such wariness is a legitimate concern sometimes. Furthermore, proponents of the land-grant universities admitted and complained that many public high schools in western and midwestern states were so weak that state and private colleges often had to devote considerable time and resources to noncredit remedial instruction.

Discussion of the exclusionary role of private colleges in the late 19th century ought make clear how much responsibility the eastern colleges had for altering or compensating for external factors which determined the applicant pool. Were New England colleges under social or moral obligation to send recruiters to, say, California or Texas in 1900? Is there anything sinister or suspect about the historical fact that numerous graduates of a given boarding school chose to apply and were admitted to a nearby college? Rather, localism and a college's confidence in a nearby school whose teachers and curriculum are familiar to college officials make sense.

EXCLUSION AND DISCRIMINATION: A CLOSER LOOK

One revised interpretation is that the eastern colleges faced a very different situation in 1910 than they did in 1890. Along with changes in the size and composition of entering classes, going to college had gained increased appeal as a source of "polish" and "contacts" and as a real or imagined social elevator. This increased popularity and subsequent strains of size and assimilation within institutions led deans and college officials to monitor and intervene in the admissions process.

What was the inspiration for the old colleges' intervention? Nativism and fear of a "Catholic peril" or a "Jewish problem" were a large part. However, one also notes that these concerns were not confined to the old private colleges. Many states constructed multiple institutions, segregated by race and by sex; whether this was right or wrong, the practice seems to have been pervasive. Instead of the ideal of the comprehensive campus, American higher education tended to follow a pattern of decentralization in which disparate groups, whether defined by religious denomination, race, ethnicity, sex, or field of study, had their respective turf.

A far more persistent problem which faced all-male, predominantly white Protestant eastern colleges was the fear of a given college that it was losing students to neighboring rivals, which created a circular pattern of institutional malaise. Also, colleges were concerned about the large and growing number of students who were the idle sons of new business wealth. This latter topic came up time and time again in faculty meetings, official reports, presidential addresses, and even in novels written by students. This problem did not go away, leading a number of colleges in the 1920s to initiate selective admissions procedures and to place a limit on the size of entering classes. One spokesman explained:

> It may be said that this method produces an aristocracy of culture. But we must have an aristocracy if we would have the highest'culture, and it will be no less, rather a gain to the nation and to the world if some of the colleges will be content to remain small, to drop the unworthy and the hopeless, and devote themselves to training for scholarship and leadership.[7]

Between 1910 and 1930, then, we have some evidence of the genesis and hammering out of the selective admissions which are familiar to the post-World War II "university college." Again, the extent and precision of early attempts ought not be overestimated; first bouts with brochures and school publicity were limited, and in many cases unauthorized alumni efforts outstripped the college officials' strategies and budgets. By the 1920s, however, Dartmouth had coordinated an elaborate system of alumni interviews, reference letters, secondary-school grades, and College Entrance Examination Board (CEEB) to guide admissions decisions. The selective admissions criteria used at Dartmouth and elsewhere present historians with a problem: they were increasingly both meritocratic and proscriptive. Academic standards had risen, but at the same time there was more room for screening on the basis of race, religion, and ethnicity. "Character," for example, has been criticized as a guise for favoring those of Anglo-Saxon, Christian background. Letters of reference from principals, headmasters, ministers (as opposed to priests and rabbis), and teachers might be used to identify the "unassimilables."

No rationalization or dodge can dispel the fact that quotas and systematic exclusion of minorities occurred between 1910 and 1930. A balanced account of this increasingly elaborate admissions machinery acknowledges that it was in large measure a concerted, earnest effort of college deans and presidents to root out the fast set, the philistines, the aimless and indulgent students. Above all, exclusion at the admissions stage paled in comparison to the intolerance, discrimination, residential segregation, jokes, and ostracism which ethnic, racial, and religious minorities suffered *within* the student body. In addition to looking at screening and collusion at the admissions office, one ought focus on the schisms in the student culture, clubs, organizations, and housing. One could reasonably argue that in the 1920s, when Jews constituted over 20 percent of the undergraduate enrollment at both Harvard and Columbia, many of the old private colleges had become far more accessible than most institutions in American life. The limit of that claim, however, is that the abuses of nativism, racism, and snobbery existed within the institutions and in any number of associations which overlapped with college and university life.

If this is the avenue which one chooses to probe, there must be careful distinction among administrations and among colleges. Was a given college president reluctant to intervene in student life, or were attempts at reform ineffective? President Eliot of Harvard may be lauded for having promoted a diverse and cosmopolitan student body, but his laissez-faire policy toward student life raises an important issue: By what assumptions and standards do historians judge a college's official attitude toward alterations within the walls of social and residential arrangements which would not be altered in society at large?

To illustrate the comparative and relative nature of this question, it is useful to consider racial discrimination and segregation in American institutions. Black students certainly were not served well by the elitist private colleges at the turn of the century and there after, even though formal exclusion might have been eliminated. But were colleges more or less unjust than American organizations elsewhere? The sports field, which seems to have supplanted the schoolroom in the American mythology of mobility, was not an open door or a melting pot: integration in major-league baseball did not take place until after World War II. In a similar vein, integration of many public, state campuses was achieved only in the 1960s. Given these chronological differences, coupled with *de facto* separation of groups into special-interest organizations, the quest for a short, simple appraisal of the colleges' accommodation of minorities remains futile.

A PORTRAIT OF THE DEAN

What is the composite portrait of the dean of admissions which emerges during the twentieth century, when expansion of higher education and formulation of selective admissions policies took place? Was he a WASP gatekeeper? Was he sometimes a well-intentioned yet ineffective meritocrat? There is evidence which suggests that the office was sometimes held by a dedicated reformer whose innovations were repeatedly thwarted or restricted by the limits of institutional inertia, traditions, finances, and scattered campus groups.

At one Ivy League campus of the 1930s, we find a former history professor who accepted the position of dean of admissions and inherited a difficult assignment: to refute the college's reputation for academic indifference and enthusiasm for football and drinking.[8] To alter this reputation, the dean attempted to curb alumni boosterism and gain editorial control over pamphlets and brochures used to recruit students. He did succeed in attracting a larger pool of academically outstanding applicants, but this was only a partial triumph of talent, as the college did not have resources to sponsor the generous scholarship and need-based financial aid programs we associate with the 1960s and 1970s. In 1934, this dean told an alumni group, ''For the maintenance of its financial resources, the University desires a large number of applicants for admission who can meet their college expenses without financial aid from the University.''[8] This was lamentable, but it was a fact of institutional life and suggests the limits of institutional transformation.

Rather than fulfilling the functions of WASP gatekeepers, it is important to note, most deans of admission at public and private campuses—even during the 1950s and 1960s—have had to worry about filling the entering class with reasonably sound students. Recruitment and survival, rather than selectivity, have been the norm of American collegiate admissions. At one state university, the charter was amended so as to insure that brochures and recruitment materials would be distributed to students in secondary schools throughout the state. The provision read as follows:

> The president shall, on or before the first day of July of each year, have printed and mailed to each county superintendent of common schools of this state at least as many circulars of information relative to said college as there are common school districts in said respective counties. Said circulars shall set forth in full the benefits of, methods of admission into, and the probable cost of beneficiaries of said college. The county superintendent of common schools shall have at least one of said circulars posted in the schoolhouse of each common school district in their respective counties during the term of the free school thereof.[9]

This task was not taken lightly, as the charter of the university explicitly noted that any superintendent who failed to carry out this mandate would be charged with neglect of duty and subjected to a fine of as much as $50.00—which by the standards of 1893 was a substantial sum. Elsewhere, deans wrestled with the problems of propriety and taste in recruitment brochures and campaigns. Limited travel budgets, small staff size, and lack of extensive writing and design expertise meant that recruitment was essentially local or regional.

There were also statements about recruitment and institutional image which were not intended for the public eye. Here is an excerpt from a limited circulation handbook for alumni interviewers, prepared by the Yale Admissions Office in the early 1940s, in which alumni were instructed to avoid criticism of other schools and above all to dispel popular misconceptions about Yale:

> Outside Connecticut and the neighboring states, Yale is assumed to be a rich man's college. The real cost of four years at Yale is exaggerated. Nothing is known of the enormous sums expended each year for the aid of the student body. It is generally assumed that, even with a scholarship, the poor boy entering Yale will be handicapped socially unless he happens to

be an athletic star. He is assumed to have no chance successfully with the graduates of Eastern preparatory schools for anything except scholastic honors. Outside of New England and the suburban schools of New York and a few other cities, the school principals and their students may assume that the College Board examinations constitute an impassable barrier to admission to Yale.

This kind of internal document does suggest that the admissions office was disturbed when public misconceptions of the college hampered attempts to recruit able students from outside the traditional clientele. Similarly, at Harvard in the late 1940s, officials complained that attainment of a geographically diverse student body was accompanied by a tendency for many high schools to believe that they should send only eggheads to Harvard. The celebrated phrase of the 1950s and 1960s was "balance in the college," in such areas as geography, school, ethnicity, race, father's occupation, areas of study, and special talents.[10] Yet here was a built-in source of tension and conflict, as diversity and balance were not the same as the ideal of admission on the basis of academic merit. These problems of abundance and oversupply of outstanding students, however, infrequently beset admissions offices at most American colleges and universities.

WOMEN AND ACCESS TO HIGHER EDUCATION

In the 1860s, a discussion of women and colleges would probably have been dominated by argument over whether women should be allowed to pursue higher education at all. By 1890, the question was not whether but which institutions would admit women students. The usual impulse is to associate coeducation with western, public campuses, whereas the founding of separate women's colleges (or "coordinate colleges") characterized the East. These patterns, however, were not all-inclusive, since we find a number of states creating state colleges for women, just as private campuses such as Mills, Scripps, and Colorado College for Women flourished in the western states.

It is the private women's college, an institution which plays havoc with our contemporary attempts at generalization, which has attracted considerable revisionist historical attention in the 1970s. A number of works have pursued a sensationalistic tack by citing the declining appeal of single-sex campuses, allegedly confirmed by a drop in number from 259 to 193 colleges during the 1960s and early 1970s. One author concerned with the historical "failure" of women's education, asked, "Can the Seven Sisters change to meet the needs of women in a changing society?"[11]

In Chapter 1, we noted the use and abuse of period-piece photographs which "tell" about college life in the past. Just as Yale College imagery has been shaped by stylized team pictures, the history of the Seven Sisters and women's colleges in general tends to be indelibly linked with photographs of daisy chains, hoop-rolling, basketball in bloomers, and May Day festivals. These also become facile sources of evidence that the education and orientation provided at the women's colleges were tantamount to those of finishing schools. Such stereotypes are incorrect and misleading, as there is sound indication that many of the women's colleges founded in the 1880s and 1890s enabled students and graduates to compete well in learned professions. In many cases, the laboratories, medical schools, libraries, and scholarly offerings at the new women's colleges surpassed those offered by older, established men's colleges. Follow-up data on women in law and medicine suggest that the generations of students who graduated from women's colleges in the 1880s and 1890s constituted a greater percentage of those in professional practice than did women who graduated from college in the 1920s and 1930s.

The point is that revisionist history of the women's colleges ought to consider fluctuations and changes within the institutions. It is possible that the timidity, the avoidance of career, and the second-class citizenship associated with the finishing colleges were not features intended or instilled when the women's colleges were first opened, but rather, characteristics of later decades. The distinction is important. Is the complaint that the Seven Sisters have wallowed in anachronistic practices, clinging to a century-old style, or is the indictment that these colleges have departed from their original and laudable mission?

A residual issue concerns the relative merits of coeducation and separate women's colleges. The Betty Coed image and syndrome of state universities in the 1930s and 1940s hardly suggests that women were afforded full encouragement in or access to various fields of study. In fact, a disproportionate number of women educated at the "open" coeducational campuses entered curricula and programs in elementary education, librarianship, and nursing, instead of opting for those careers and fields associated with main avenues of status and influence in American public life. There exists no obvious or clear evidence as to which institutional arrangements have best served women.

That riddle remains unresolved today. In the 1970s, numerous women's colleges either merged with men's campuses or went coeducational—a move which did not guarantee either rising enrollments or rising academic standards. One could argue that the decision to become coeducational cost many women's colleges an opportunity to assert a distinctive collegiate setting for women.

Perhaps one of the most intriguing aspects of access and selection in higher education is the differential representation of women in undergraduate and graduate education. If one looks at figures for college attendance and award of the bachelor's degree, women have gained parity in access to higher education in the United States. Yet this breaks down drastically in graduate programs and advanced degrees. How should we approach investigation of the problem?

The study of graduate-school admissions is difficult in that most decisions on candidates are made by individual departments, with little centralization of records. One intriguing study at the University of California at Berkeley in 1973-74 tackled this problem by looking at aggregate data on admissions to the graduate programs both as a whole and department by department.[12] The aggregate data indicated that women were grossly underrepresented in both entrance into graduate programs and completion of advanced degrees, leading to the hypothesis that women were facing discrimination at the admissions level. However, a program-by-program analysis suggested that within a given department, there was no great schism in acceptance rates of men and women applicants. How can we explain the disparity? The authors noted that women were tending to apply in disproportionate numbers to master's and doctoral programs which had relatively few places for large numbers of candidates, programs which had relatively high noncompletion or lengthy completion rates. One tentative conclusion was that anticipatory socialization (the tendency to enter some fields and to avoid other fields), rather than overt admissions discrimination, contributed to the maldistribution of women in graduate study. Increases in the number and percentage of women entering medicine and law schools during the mid and late 1970s may have adjusted that imbalance. The enduring message is that formal policies and practices of the college or university can seldom offer total control or reform of underlying social or cultural phenomenom.

ADMISSIONS AND THE "BLOODY MONDAY" RITUAL IN AMERICAN LIFE

Undergraduate admissions occupies a special place in the literature of higher education because it regularly surfaces into public scrutiny as a predictable source of expose and outrage. Since no admissions policies will ever seem equitable to all groups in American society, there has been a market for a variety of books and articles, including shocking revelations, replies by knowledgeable deans, and the ubiquitous guides "So You Want To Go To College. . ."). Indicative of this was the situation in the late 1950s and early 1960s, when a series of articles appeared in national news magazines in which parents demanded that the selective colleges publicly explain the admissions decision process. These were followed, predictably, by a book, *How an Ivy League College Decides on Admissions*, along with spin-off reports from faculty committees.[13]

Whereas many articles in the late 1950s were complaining that indices of merit (SAT scores and high-school grades) were being played down in favor of geographical diversity, athletics, and alumni favoritism, by the late 1960s and 1970s, the recurrent theme was that most predictors of academic potential were culturally and racially biased. Here was the potential fulfillment of Michael Young's prophecy for the 21st century in *The Rise of the Meritocracy*: that an educational system whose rewards and advancements were based wholly on merit would end up offending the poor and those who are wealthy but not so bright.

One important variant of the admissions exposé is the thesis that the process of grooming, coaching, and competing associated with college admissions has become a rite of passage in American life which scars its participants whether they are admitted to or excluded from college. One book published in 1978, *Hurdles: The Admissions Dilemma in American Higher Education*, assembles an anthology of laments from deans, headmasters, campus psychiatrists, and officials from the Educational Testing Service, the gist of which is to criticize the SAT examinations and selective admissions for causing traumas.[14] The irony is that these critics are in large measure the architects and managers of the very system which they chastise. If *they* are unable to initiate reforms within the institutions where they occupy leadership positions, prospects for policy changes are slim. Furthermore, all of the authors are winners in the hurdling competition, which has bestowed upon them the benefits of expertise. This illustrates a situation in which an alleged problem in higher education probably will not be solved, since too many people stand to lose from wholesale reform.

Although a number of articles and essays deal with open-door and nonselective institutions, works such as *Hurdles* are concerned primarily with access to prestigious colleges and medical and law schools. A paradox which makes reform elusive is that at any given time, certain institutions cannot accommodate all the qualified, motivated applicants. No change in selection procedures can alter the harshness which accompanies the prestige of scarcity and certification.

It is important to note that institutional reputation has not been static, but fluctuates with student and parental demand. One could enter Harvard Medical School without a bachelor's degree in the 1880s—hardly the case today. One dean at Yale Law School recalled the 1930s as a period when the admissions problem was finding a sufficient number of academically able students to fill the class. By the 1970s, the situation was that a number of once-selective liberal-arts colleges were seeking good, motivated students, yet these same applicants were scrambling for admission to the Ivy League schools, the Little Three, and a handful of other campuses which enjoy perverse abundance while most colleges and universities face declining numbers of quality of applicants. The dilemma is that Americans continue to endure the pleasure-pain which accompanies entry into the hurdles race. For all the complaints about ''Bloody Monday''—the day in April when acceptance and rejection letters are mailed by colleges—the ritual of collegiate hurdling has retained strong fascination in education-minded families. It does not, however, describe the normal experience of most American high-school seniors, since most postsecondary programs have either open admissions policies or minimal entrance requirements.

HEADHUNTERS AND COLLEGE MARKETING

Popular conceptions of college admissions offices have been dominated by two conflicting stereotypes fostered by articles in the national press. At one extreme, there has been dramatic focus on the gatekeeper, the person in American higher education whose exclusions and arbitrary practices have sullied selective admissions. In the late 1970s, journalists have also exposed the abuses of ''headhunters'' and the admissions ''industry,'' whose hard-sell, arm-twisting practices and flashy brochures are cited as an indication that many colleges have ceased to be concerned with scholastic qualifications and professional ethics in the panic to fill classrooms and dormitories during what demographers have called a dwindling college market.[15] Few articles address or reconcile the contradictions between the two stereotypes.

Articles in professional higher-education journals argue that to survive the crunch, liberal-arts colleges need a marketing approach, an advocacy which has led to a proliferation of external firms, promoters, and publishers which seek colleges as clients.[16] The proposed formula is for colleges to ''borrow a page from the corporate book and learn how to market their products.'' According to the director of public relations at one college, the admissions staff becomes the ''sales force'' of the college.

Many of these proposals are of limited worth since it is difficult to measure if such campaigns and marketing approaches work. The most accurate appraisal is that they provide business for the external firms and enable admissions personnel to look busy. There is also the risk that adoption of promotional measures and new curricula can cause a college to alienate and forfeit its traditional clientele. Or, if students are attracted to a campus on the basis of slick publications, the disillusionment of campus reality may create a future problem for the admissions office: a high attrition or transfer rate.

The preoccupation with admissions marketing is another example in which higher education risks degeneration into a belated and pale imitation of business and industry, with little guarantee of gain in the deal. For all the fears of college mortality, an indication of the understated solidity of higher education is that it is still news when a campus does fold. Nor is it clear that other organizations competing for 18 to 21 year olds are more attractive than colleges. As of 1979, the United States Army was concerned that its five-year plan for massive advertisement to attract enlistees had not met quotas or expectations. Here was an organization which often competed with colleges for high-school seniors, and which had the benefit of extensive budgets for television spots and full-page advertisement in national circulation magazines, yet was unable to meet its marketing targets.

A corollary of college marketing has been student consumerism, a movement which includes the demand that educational institutions avoid making false claims in catalogs and brochures for prospective applicants. In some states, legislatures composed bills which would require schools and colleges to publish elaborate reports on student retention and attrition and on the job placement and employment of graduates. A number of colleges and universities perceived such legislation as hostile attempts to penalize nonvocational or nonprofessional institutions which could not demonstrate that there was a job payoff associated with a diploma. In fact, much of the legislation was directed toward proprietary schools. Colleges and universities which were accredited by a national or regional agency were considered to have complied with the state regulations. What was originally feared as a punitive measure by the colleges was really a vote of confidence in established nonprofit higher-education institutions.[17]

Colleges which saw themselves as declining in appeal and selectivity during the 1970s were unwitting victims of their own press releases from the 1950s and 1960s. First, the abundance of college-bound students after World War II was mistaken for the usual state of affairs, when it was an anomaly in comparison to preceding and subsequent decades. Second, even during the peak years, the number of applicants to a college was often inflated. A college might have had six applicants per place, but each applicant might have applied to several other colleges. Valid assessment of gains and losses in institutional stature and admissions success from one era to another was difficult, since the underlying cultural phenomenon of going to college had changed; that is, the practice of multiple applications was relatively unknown until the 1950s. The question for the 1980s is this: Has a college suffered a significant decline if its applicant pool drops from, say, 4 to 3 per student place?

PROBLEMS OF INSTITUTIONAL RESEARCH AND EVALUATION IN ADMISSIONS POLICY

The preceding historical sketches and cases have served to illustrate various ways in which admissions efforts and results resist precise or significant study. It is an important consideration when, as is the situation in the 1970s and 1980s, federal and state regulations require colleges and universities to comply with directives and goals. Court decisions and legislation dealing with access to higher education, however, have not said much about the processes by which broad, nationwide goals are expected to filter down to institutional practice. Governors, judges and congressmen have given scant indication that they are familiar with the settings in which admissions staffs must work, yet the vague assumption persists that each college will be able to comply with and implement reform mandates. This chapter concludes with samples of research and evaluation issues which might be faced by a college's admissions office in reports to external agencies and to authorities within the college.[18]

Applied research in college admissions is distinguished from research in access and differentiation in higher education conducted at such centers as the Educational Testing Service (ETS), American College Testing (ACT), regional consortia, or statewide councils. Whereas transinstitutional agencies are concerned with nationwide trends and large samplings, the research effort within an admissions office deals with specific implications for institutional reputation and programs, and its whose findings must be digested so as to guide annual plans for recruitment and service activities. Popular "Golden Fleece awards" for extravagant research projects conjure images of large-scale facilities in staff. In fact, most colleges have lean provisions for applied research, often only a marginal supplement to the office's ongoing service functions. Apart from in-house information, a college admissions office might subscribe to profiles and data banks offered by a consortium or by ETS and ACT. In the course of an academic year, a selective college's admissions office will attempt to compile and analyze data in such areas as enrollment trends, composition of the student body, attrition and retention patterns, correlations between SAT scores and high-school grades, efficacy of school visits, and perceptions of the college of those admitted. There are, however, no clear guides to either analysis or policy alteration, as the following discussion of school visits and student diversity illustrates.

Mandates for reform in access to postsecondary education often emphasize the importance of student exposure to and familiarity with college and university programs and options. Hence, college staff visits to secondary schools can be a significant link in the socialization and self-selection process students undergo. College admissions officers visit secondary schools buoyed by the assumption that there is some positive connection between visits and subsequent student applications and counselor cooperation. An external agency might suggest that a college could increase its visibility (and applicants) in underrepresented groups by visiting schools in the relevant locales. However, such a plan would require either staff expansion by the college or cutbacks and redirection of visits to other schools.

Admissions staffs are caught in a logical bind. Neglect of those schools from which the college has a tradition of receiving applicants could cause longtime ties to be broken or weakened. A strict cost-benefit approach would dictate that a college staff ought restrict visits only to proven schools. On the other hand, that brand of trimming glosses over the idea that venture, risk, and exploration might promote diversity within the student body. The enduring social fact is that admissions reform, if it is to promote expansion, access, and visibility, is essentially inefficient. And the costs of inefficiency are usually born by the college.

Admissions directors recognize, even accept, low yields and modest returns as a fact of life. What is disconcerting to admissions staff is externally proposed remedies which do not recognize the patience, custom, and time investment which school visits and informational activities require. In the aftermath of a 1978 court decision, for example, one governor cited the image of college officials sitting with their "feet are on the desk, smoking cigars, and drinking brandy,'' and commented, ''They've got to put more energy into finding people and letting them know they truly want their school or profession to reflect the population at large.''[19] Such comments evade serious issues. First, it is not evident that college admissions staffs have been idle; it is equally plausible that they have been too active in the recruiting process. Second, the urge for putting ''more energy into finding people'' presupposes unlimited budgets within admissions offices and does not address itself to the potential abuses of hard-sell recruitment tactics. Above all, there is little recognition of the limits to which a college can intervene in the college-choice process. There are push and pull factors in which both the college and its potential applicants play integral roles. This is a dimension of the admissions pattern which emerges when one looks at a college's records on final college decisions made by applicants who were offered admission.

Earlier we discussed ''Bloody Monday,'' that traumatic April day for high-school seniors who receive thick and thin envelopes from college admissions offices. Often overlooked is the fact that admissions officers face their own annual day of reckoning (usually in early May), when applicants notify admissions offices of their choices. The phenomenon of multiple applications obstructs clear analysis of the relationship between high-school students and access to higher education, as there is little coordination of applications or related data. Each college is left to wait and see who among its accepted applicants plans to enroll, and to find out the reasons why they are (or are not) choosing a particular college.

In an era of multiple applications, a crucial measure is that of *yield*—the percentage of applicants who were offered admission and who did in fact accept that offer. A truly selective college would be one with a high number of academically strong applicants per college place and a high yield. The yield figures are especially important for external auditors who wish to gain a measure of a college's efforts to attract and encourage minority applicants. In fact, one might argue that it is a more valid indicator of the admissions office's activities than the eventual composition of the entering freshman class. Assuming that an educational goal is for access to a college to be on a par with a group's percentage representation in the national population of high-school graduates, let us consider comparative data on minority recruitment and admissions at two colleges which see themselves as having similar academic standards and educational purposes:

Minority Group	College A	College B
Percentage of national population of high-school graduates (the goal)	15	15
Percentage of total applicant pool	20	10
Percentage of admissions offers	25	20
Percentage of enrolled class	10	18

To an external auditor, one conclusion is that College A has lagged in fulfilling the goal of proportionate educational representation, whereas College B has surpassed that goal. This is hardly the whole story, as the data suggest that College A's admissions office succeeded in reaching and encouraging a large number of minority-group students to consider college and to complete application forms and procedures. Above all, the admissions office at College A followed through on its recruitment and informational efforts with offers of admissions which surpassed those of College B. The problem which faces College A (compared to College B and to national goals) is that of *low yield*.

One implication is that we can distinguish an *admissions* problem from what might be termed a *campus* or *institutional* problem. By this we mean that College A's weaknesses do not appear to be in areas of recruitment, visibility, or contact with students. Rather, some factors are influencing admitted students to *choose* to go elsewhere, even though the admissions office has pursued a course of encouragement rather than exclusion. It may well be that enrollment of students will depend less on marketing and more time and energy spent on recruitment than on attention to conditions elsewhere in the college, beyond the admissions office. A college which finds itself turned down systematically by a discernible group of admitted applicants cannot say that the problem is mere lack of image or visibility. To the contrary, the abundance of serious and qualified applicants suggests that mythical College A is known, is visible—and that student rejection of admissions offers may well be based on accurate information. An attempt to rectify this situation by putting more time and money into public relations and recruitment indicates a college's refusal to face and correct enduring, difficult structural and internal problems.

This latter response within a college is not implausible, as leaders within organizations can (and often do) ignore bad news. The reports and patterns compiled by the admissions office can constitute a reasonably accurate profile of institutional health, yet there is no guarantee that the admissions research effort will guide college policy. If the college's faculty, president, and trustees see the admissions staff as divorced from the educational life of the institution, they probably will be reluctant to listen to such reports. Equally frustrating is the recognition that knowledge of negative factors does not insure sound or possible corrections. The admissions office may be able to document conclusively that admitted applicants are repelled by the college's architectural and geographical settings, yet it does not follow that a college can or ought to build a new campus or move to a more pleasant locale. Most admissions officers are limited to talking about (and accepting) the college's existing conditions.

Earlier in this section, we noted that push and pull factors between applicants and the college exert influence on the eventual character and composition of the campus. The limits of control which the college has over the situation can be best illustrated by the situation found at a selective campus, Stanford Univeristy, in 1978-79, when the dean of admissions enjoyed the support, cooperation, and agreement of the university's faculty and president in having identified a problem among applicants and those admitted: weaknesses in the secondary-school preparation. The dean of admissions's report noted:

> We focused on the question of whether or not our entering students, and the larger number of applicants for admission from whom they are annually selected, are as well prepared as they ought to be if, once given the opportunity, they are to gain the most from the unusually rich academic programs and resources offered them by Stanford. That program and those resources are costly to provide.[20]

The dean and faculty acknowledged that Stanford had been fortunate in being able to attract students with good academic records, a luxury experiences by relatively few colleges, especially in the 1970s. Nonetheless, there was cause for concern:

> The Stanford faculty generally find their students to be exceptionally bright. But it is also the case that there are occasions on which they find them suprisingly lacking in one or another area of preparation. For example, it is not just a matter of observing that too few of them appear able to write well. Rather, upon closer inquiry, we have found that all too few appear to have been required to write much at all prior to entering college. And even for those who did do a good deal of writing in secondary school, too few report they were ever afforded the kind of sustained criticism which nurtures improvement.[21]

Here is an example of a situation in which external conditions (namely, a pervasive dilution of secondary-school curricula and teaching) are beyond the control or solution of the admissions office. The "solution" is not merely to deny admission to those applicants who are ill prepared, since this college is already dealing with an admittedly select pool. It would be reasonable to estimate that the problem of poor secondary-school preparation gets worse as one looks at colleges and postsecondary institutions less selective than Stanford. If the problem cannot be ignored by Mt. Olympus, it must be widespread throughout the fabric of American secondary schools.

THE LIFE OF COLLEGES

One commentator has argued that the admissions office is umbilical cord of a college. Possibly so, but that lifeline can be severed by external institutions or by decision-makers within the campus, leaving a dean of admissions with the message that information and insights do not necessarily guide policies or reforms. College admissions staffs are often caught between two forces, the American cliché that all problems, including access to higher education, have solutions, and the impediments of institutional inertia, lag, and limited staff, time, energy, and influence.

The conflict is further compounded by demographic and attitudinal circumstances: a declining birth rate indicates fewer 18-year olds; most perplexing to college officials, there are signs that "going to college" has declining attraction within that shrinking pool of high school graduates. For a generation of college and university administrators who believed in and worked for expansion of college-going opportunities, such indifference and disinterest undermine the ethos and machinery of the campus. It is a problem which defies technical solution.

The harsh irony is that for decades, conventional wisdom was that the shifts from elite to mass to universal participation in higher education would be achieved if only sufficient institutions and resources were constructed and made affordable. Indeed, those have been achieved—yet are only intermediate structures which have limited use if not linked to a secondary school system and cultural patterns which ascribe to college education as an important, desirable activity.

8

Alma Mater, Inside and Out: Studying the College and University Campus

AN APPROACH TO THE PROPER STUDY OF COLLEGE LIFE

More than a century ago, a young alumnus of Yale College grew weary of popular stereotypes about American campuses and proceeded to write a lengthy, clinical reconstruction of life within a college. He explained the need for such a work with the following introductory comments:

> The erroneous and absurd ideas which very many intelligent people who have not chanced to experience it, entertain upon the subject of college life, have led me to believe that a minute account of affairs as they exist to-day at one of the chief American colleges would not be without value to the general public, nor without interest to the alumni and undergraduates of other colleges as well as the one described.[1]

The author, Lyman Bagg, was correct in identifying an enduring public interest in American colleges. And we remain indebted to him for his monumental detailed account, *Four Years at Yale*, in which he set out to look "at things from the undergraduate in distinction from the official stand-point," and in which he gave "as little attention as possible [to that] which a formal historian would render prominent," and went "into the smallest details in cases which he would take no notice of." This example, however, did little to impede journalists' fascination with campus fads or the eagerness with which American reading audiences have received these accounts.

To see the distance we have come since Lyman Bagg's campaign against facile depictions of college life, let us consider the editorial comments of an issue of *Glamour* magazine: "Before putting together this College Issue '76, we did a survey of 400 campuses to find out what are

the prime things that college students want to do better. For instance—how jeans are worn. . . ." Partial consolation to Bagg would
have been the following response by a disgruntled undergraduate:

> As a Yale senior, I am, of course, concerned about the jeans issue, but I
> feel tht the Shetland sweater question is of more widespread importance to
> today's college youth. Why must America believe that there is any consen-
> sus among college students on anything, from foreign policy to aerosol
> sprays? In trying to establish just who and what the undergraduate set is in
> the mood to buy, politicians, merchandisers, . . . magazines and film
> studios have created a false impression of universal student agreement.[2]

The Yale student proceeded to comment that he was grateful he had not
gone to Havard ("where," according to one journalist,
"undergraduates bear sole responsibility for the fate of the nation"), as
he probably would have been exhausted by continually filling out questionnaires for magazine polls:

> Thank God I go to Yale, so all I have to worry about is getting my tuxedo
> pressed, as I may have to re-create the Jazz Age at any moment. Maybe
> I'll have time after I finish studying, since somehow I have also become in-
> volved in bitter pre-professionalism. Somewhere along the line I'll sneak
> in a return to the '50s; only yesterday I had to refuse a needle full of
> heroin, since I have switched to beer and cheap wine (who am I to con-
> tradict *Newsweek*?). Then, while I'm indulging in the casual sex resulting
> from coed dorms, I'll have to phone for tickets to the Prom since formal
> courtship is back.

The undergraduate's comments provide both a catalog of stereotypes
loosely attributed to college students of the 1970s and insight into
problems which confront researchers in higher education. Serious
research ought not ignore the collegiate fads—these deserve to be
recognized as significant *social* facts. The task is to devise a balanced,
comprehensive research effort which does not mistake the popular images and fads as either the major or the enduring facet of the college experience.

There now exists a sizable body of professional literature devoted to
the social-psychological study of students' values.[3] One important
dimension of this research has been inclusion of numerous attempts to
discover the impact of the college experience or campus environment by
measuring changes in students' attitudes and personalities. This genre
of higher-education research is sufficiently prominent (and discussed
and funded) elsewhere that we can afford it only brief and indirect com-

ment in this chapter. Instead, we shall concentrate on a related issue which requires a shift in research strategy and emphasis, giving primary attention on the distinctive features of the campus and collegiate setting, and secondary attention to lasting changes in attitudes and values of those who have attended college. Before we turn to this latter area, in which historians have made potentially significant contributions, it is important to note a characteristic of the social-psychological research on students.

In fairness to the maligned editors of popular magazines, it is difficult to escape the impression that many works and studies devoted to bringing the behavorial sciences to bear on analysis of students' values and attitudes have contributed to preoccupation with drastic yet transient features of student life. In the late 1960s, numerous scholars and academic researchers rushed to publish works and reports on student radicalism and activism that often carried the implication that these may well have constituted an enduring transformation in student values. Note that interest in and funding for studies of student activism were rather short-lived and elicit little research attention in the 1970s.

Susceptibility to vacillations and dramatizations about ''generations'' of students is recurrent in the professional literature. In 1960, for example, Nevitt Sanford's comments in an anthology, *Impact of College*, gave credence to hackneyed portrayals of college life and contemporary events:

> We are not now experiencing anything like the excitement, the mobility, the ferment of the Jazz Age, or the Depression, or World War II. Correspondingly, there is relative quietude on the intellectual and ideological fronts. In the early years of the century we had the movement toward greater freedom for women; in the twenties we had Freud and the revolution in morals; in the thirties we had the Depression, social change, and the influence of socialist economic theory; in the forties the war, fervent democratic idealism, imaginative postwar plans. What are the big ideas of the fifties? The automatic anticommunism of recent years has not been exactly inspiring. Efforts to bring about a return to religion or to evolve a new religious outlook have been rather feeble—in some cases, perhaps even phony. One does not hear much intellectual discussion on the campus for the simple reason that there is not very much to discuss. Times will undoubtedly change, and new ideas will appear, but for the time being we are in cultural and intellectual doldrums. This I would posit as a major source of student lethargy.[4]

Historical studies of various periods or decades modify Sanford's condensed images by revealing that, for example, the collegiate life of the 1920s did include the so-called Jazz Age—and much more! Similarly, one finds that the phrase "apathetic students of the 1950s" is an incomplete and simplistic description of those in college during the post-World War II years. The need is for studies which acknowledge continuities as well as the changes in college life.

This dimension—continuity—can be discerned in part if one looks away from aggregate student responses to questionnaires, and turns instead to the distinctive patterns, symbols, and norms which some campuses transmit to newcomers. This is related to the notion of saga which was introduced in the final section of Chapter 1. The collegiate culture, then, can be understood as the collective and historic ways of doing things to which one ascribes as a member of a campus. Such institutional culture is essentially stable and conservative in that it provides guidelines for behavior, dress, play, and work while one is within the campus walls. It may well be that this campus culture has little enduring hold on students once they leave the campus (although this is not necessarily so), but despite the permanence or transience of that culture with departed alumni, an important point remains: campuses are special places, "total institutions," which are able to host command distinctive patterns and rounds of daily and annual life for constituents.

To illustrate the shift in emphasis away from student attitudinal research and toward the study of institutional structure and culture, it is useful to consider a recent applied-research problem encountered at a selective residential college. The dean of students was concerned that the rate of undergraduate attrition had increased, and contracted with an educational psychologist to investigate the matter. The research strategy upon which the consultant and the dean agreed was to have a large sampling of students take a personality inventory. Then, results were to be analyzed to see if dropouts had exhibited some discernibly different pattern of responses. The findings would be used to anticipate and identify potential student dropouts.

Useful as that strategy might have been, we would suggest inclusion of additional or alternative research designs. First, one might look at the campus environment to see if structural or social situations might indicate that a student's decision to leave was a reasonable response to a bad or undesirable campus. Inquiries could clarify the condition and location of dormitories, provisions for activities, the social or intellectual character of the place. Or one might suspend the idea that dropping out is a problem. In Chapter 4, we cited the continental practice of wandering students; in the 1960s, the appearance of multicampus state university systems and the trimester or quarter plan facilitated "easy in, easy out." The situation which the dean viewed as a breakdown or problem may well have been the fulfillment of Clark Kerr's vision of the campus as an academic service station. Or it may well be that the *student* culture of the college endorsed or encouraged "stopping out." In any event, the issue is more complicated than assumption of student attitudinal differences implies. Investigation of educational policies and campus environment might be a more fruitful approach than identification and counsel through the dean of students' office.

Behavorial scientists, of course, have shown some interest in the study of campus environments. One memorable example was in 1963, when a psychologist attempted to describe the measured differences among campuses by means of student responses to questionnaires about their campus's character. The instrument, called CUES (College and University Environment Scales) included the following dimensions of institutional climate: practicality, community, awareness, propriety, and scholarship. [5] Accepting the proposition that these dimensions are integral to gaining an understanding of an institution's character, let us also impose an obstacle: we cannot rely on student questionnaire data for formulation of our reports. (We could argue, for example, that a shortage of number 2 lead pencils led to cancellation of the survey-administration session). Herein lies an opportunity to review the findings and methods which historians have used to probe patterns of life and activity within American campuses.

Discussion of campus architecture, college subcultures, and collegiate fiction in the following sections will not constitute a definitive or complete historical study. The chapter is intended to serve as a primer and stimulus for incorporating these kinds of materials and sources into problems encountered as part of campus planning and reevaluation of such offices as student services.

CONSTRUCTION AND EVOLUTION OF THE CAMPUS

In 1953, recently elected President of the United States Dwight Eisenhower visited Dartmouth College and exclaimed, "This is the way I always thought a college should look."[6] Not everyone will agree with his particular campus choice; nonetheless, the salient point is that we have come to a reasonable consensus as to which features and images one expects to find on an American campus (Figure 10). Just as the game board for Monopoly delineates the components of a modern metropolis, a number of components (Memorial Stadium, Saint Grottlesex Library, Founders Hall, *ad infinitum*) can be identified that define a more-or-less standard institutional environment. As one college president wryly told entering freshmen, "Every campus has a lake. . .except ours."

If architecture is the indicator by which one surveys and analyzes developments within the life of a college or university, one must look for the social context and events which have accompanied construction and use of the building. At some campuses, for example, libraries (intended for serious study) have become recognized unofficially yet pervasively by students as a place for serious socializing and play. This is the brand of *latent function* which resists prediction or official control. One implication is that an analyst may have to look elsewhere than the library to find the setting where serious study does take place. Tom Wolfe, for example, has argued that the proliferation of scholarly conferences throughout the nation has turned Chicago's O'Hare airport waiting rooms into the academic forum of the 1970s. That hypothesis is both extreme and intriguing, and certainly gives substance to the notion of the extended campus.

Even though we may agree on the essential features of an American college or university campus, we must guard against the historical illogic that acquisition or evolution of the arrangement and design was inevitable. In Chapters 1 through 4, for example, we already encountered discussion of differences among such institutional arrangements as medieval universities, the colleges which constitute the universities of Oxford, Cambridge, and the nonresidential, urban, continental universities. To review briefly, the American colonial colleges did *not* replicate a pure model from any one of these historical institutions. Elaborate dormitories and landscaped, monumental campuses were not characteristic of the 19th-century American colleges and universities.

To understand alterations in college and university life, it is useful to see how one's particular campus has added (or avoided) the following structures: library, stadium, student unions, commons or dining halls, co-op housing, off-campus fraternity and sorority houses, Quonset huts. To understand these buildings is to understand the social history of higher education. Student unions, for example, were brick-and-mortar testimonials to the university's accommodation of commuting students during the early 1900s. Establishment of commons or dining halls in the late 19th century often represented an attempt by college officials to break down social schisms within a diffused student body as well as to provide students of modest means with regular meals at low prices. In some cases, the dining-hall solution created new problesm for administrators; students were united in a common dislike for institutional food, which often resulted in infamous food riots. Social cohesion within the campus was obtained at the price of recurrent insurrections, which were harmless, yet expensive.

Quonset huts and barracks buildings, constructed in the late 1940s, still survive today on many campuses, an artifact of the post-World War II influx of students, many of whom were married, had children, and were veterans. An intriguing study of the lack of status within academia would be to identify which departments or programs inherited these structures after the flood of postwar students and families subsided. A linguistics department, for example, which is reassigned to the corrugated aluminum quarters of Building T-3 probably will feel threatened and slighted when the university's vice-president for planning is busy across the campus at dedication ceremonies for the new astrophysics laboratory and research center. On the other hand, the modest and nearly invisible basement facilities for atomic research at the University of Chicago in the 1940s provide a warning that if one wishes to infer relative status, structural appearances can be deceiving.

Before we leave the 1940s Quonset huts, let us consider a generalization about the changes in the composition of student bodies associated with the accommodation of veterans into American higher education after World War II. A recurrent interpretation has been that this was a good thing for colleges and universities because it represented a qualitative and quantitative change in the character of student life. According to this version, the veterans were serious, academically able, and not prone to immature collegiate pranks and traditional activities. This was possibly so, but in a number of memoirs, articles, and short stories, there is a persistent mild dissent which argues that the seriousness with studies often meant impatience and anti-intellectualism; and a number of professors and traditionally younger students complained that veterans of the early 1950s tended staunchly to promote McCarthyism. These two extreme views, both weighted with bias and personal impression, are not subject to quick resolution or reconciliation. Rather, the views do illustrate the need for careful study of the impact of such legislation as the G.I. Bill.[7]

Anyone who has spent time on an American campus will point out that unofficial buildings are in fact central to the life and personality of a particular college or university. The examples which come to mind are restaurants, bookstores, coffeehouses, and bars which acquire a loyal following among some configuration of students, faculty, and alumni. Along with places that provide food and books, one historically important structure which was both apart from and a part of the American campus from the late 19th century onward was the YMCA.[8] Here was an organization which attracted the energy and support of thousands of students throughout the nation, usually with the blessings and encouragement of college presidents and deans. Yet this alliance and cooperation did not make the "Y" a formal part of the college structure. In the period from 1890 to 1910, the so-called Settlement House Movement—involving student participation in social work, tutorials, religious education, and community services—was under the auspices of the YMCA and may well have been the most popular, significant student activity of the era. Decades later, during the controversial Free Speech Movement at the University of California at Berkeley in 1964-65, the YMCA building played a pivotal role in student campaigns and planning; since it was technically off campus and not an official part of the university jurisdiction, the YMCA became the *de facto* host and haven for student meetings. This example of off-campus facilities' serving an integral role for students provides a good point from which to consider some of the conventional assumptions and ideals about student life and the college or university.

PATTERNS OF STUDENT SUBCULTURES

College brochures often attempt to enhance institutional appeal by reassuring applicants (and applicants' parents) that *this* college avoids impersonality, does not treat students "like numbers," and does offer a close relationship among students and faculty. We cite this latter stock phrase in the lexicon of American education as one which gains widespread support in public statements, yet much less support or enthusiasm (from both students and faculty) in practice. This does not necessarily mean that college brochures are misleading, or that college professors are shirking their responsibilities. There is sound historical evidence that suggests that students and faculty, on large and small campuses, find segregation to be mutually beneficial and enjoyable. The codicil is that both groups welcome and accept fraternization when necessary or beneficial, but that such interaction is subject to stern (albeit upspoken) ground rules.

This hypothesis is not offered as a venture in academic heresy.

Rather, we cite it to illustrate the complexities and subtleties of liturgy, ritual, rhetoric, and behavior which contribute to the stability, harmony, and effectiveness of living and working within a campus community. During the past twenty years, a number of historical studies of American higher education have independently suggested or attested to a certain pattern of student life: students pursue an activity outside the official regulations or curricula of the college; college officials unsuccessfully attempt to root out or abolish the activity; the activity (not unlike strains of disease which have survived penicillin) continues to be supported by students; college officials eventually allow or even give official support to the activity. In some cases, the final chapter is that students lose interest in the activity once it does gain college acceptance. Another variation on this theme is that the college's official support for an activity does not diminish student interest or participation, but does promote loss of student control over the enterprise or activity.

This historical model helps fit such familiar aspects of college life libraries, literary magazines, dining halls, varsity athletics, foreign-language study, journalism, fine arts, and performing arts into the evolution of the American campus. It is an important observation in that it suggests that students do influence policy and institutional character and that college and university presidents make accommodations and concessions to student behavior, if not to student campaigns and demands. One irony occurs in the case of intercollegiate athletics, where undergraduates are allotted only a few hundred tickets to student sports contests held in stadiums which seat thousands.

Another quirk which upsets conventional wisdom about student subcultures and values is that there is no consistent alignment in the support of scholarly or intellectual activities. Howard Miller's study of Presbyterian colleges and universities in the late 18th and early 19th centuries indicates that at one time, Princeton's students and students' parents were united in opposition to the college's president in complaining that the curriculum was not sufficiently academic or rigorous. James McLachlan's and Frederick Rudolph's respective accounts of 19th-century colleges argue that the pursuit of advanced and serious study in undergraduate literary societies with libraries and book collections was perceived as detrimental to the college's official mission.[9]

Historical investigation of campuses continually reaffirms the contention that students and subcultures within the student body were remarkably powerful in "voting with their feet" to shape both the content and the structure of the institutions. Two works worthy of special note on this topic are Henry Seidel Canby's *Alma Mater: The Gothic Age of the American College* (1936) and Laurence Veysey's discussion of the gulf between students and faculty in his classic, *The Emergence of the American University* (1965).[10] Both Canby's memoir (he was a student in the 1890s and a faculty member for several decades) and Veysey's brilliant exhumation of miscellaneous student accounts and university records from the period from 1890 to 1910 describe the ways in which pranks, taboos, punishments, rewards, rituals, and comparable normative phenomena enabled undergraduates to create a world according to their own terms. Instructors, for example, ascribed (willingly or not) to a student-imposed code on class recitations. Canby also points out that from time to time, a student would forget the code and offer an earnest interpretation or opinion, an offense which was promptly reprimanded.

One searches in vain for cases where programs designed to promote proximity among students and faculty achieved enduring success. Accounts of faculty teas for students at eastern colleges in the 1890s and early 1900s focus on the discomfort experienced by both students and instructors. In the 1930s, Brown University attempted to promote student-faculty cohesion by having undergraduates pursue social affiliations through their departmental major—an endeavor which quickly jointed the category of experiments which were canceled owing to lack of student interest. An important aside on that episode is that Brown's president and deans proposed the departmental plan as an inexpensive alternative to a proposal that the university should build residential quadrangles comparable to Yale's colleges and Harvard's house plan.

During the late 1950s and 1960s, a number of selective colleges and universities were able to offer honors programs, advanced courses, seminars, and tutorials in which undergraduates did work closely with professors. Yet this apprenticeship format was unusual, and tended to work only in those instances where very able and motivated students perceived themselves as incipient professional scholars and planned to pursue advanced degrees. This certainly was not a reasonable or representative model or ideal for most undergraduates in American higher education.

This discussion of the historic split between students and the official organization of a college or university suggests that subsequent research would do well to seek information beyond the official records of the institution. To promote and assist that pursuit, we turn to consideration of the characteristics and peculiarities of the fiction, memoirs, journalism, and ephemeral literature associated with going to college.[11]

COLLEGIATE FICTION AND MEMOIRS

Several publishing houses have enjoyed steady sales for decades by specializing in the preparation and distribution of plot summaries, chapter outlines, and answers to sample examination questions on "great books" and classics of literature. Along with *Classics* comic books, such material has rescued thousands of procrastinating students from having to read original (and lengthy) versions of works by the Brontes, Dickens, Henry James, and so on. This section, however, will not serve a comparable function for those who want condensed versions and plot summaries of novels, memoirs, and essays about college life. A more correct description of this section is of an invitation for higher-education professionals to read collegiate fiction as a part of the professional literature in the field. This is one area of professional development which can be enjoyable and, if accompanied by some guides and supplementary warnings, an invaluable source of information about the impact of the college experience on participants and observers.

One excellent anthology of short stories, articles, memoirs, songs, poetry, cartoons, and photographs about colleges and universities is *The College Years* (1958), edited by A. C. Spectorsky. The selections defy brief description since the range of institutions, experiences, roles, and tones collected in this single volume is wide. It is a work whose importance and depth ought qualify it for recognition as higher education's equivalent to medicine's *Gray's Anatomy;* that is, it is a massive work whose contents are integral to subsequent study in the field and to which one can refer year after year.

Given Lyman Bagg's 1871 complaint about popular images of colleges, it is noteworthy that campus profiles have been regular and recurrent features in American magazines (at many levels of reader sophistication) since the late 19th century.[12] During the 1950s and 1960s, *Holiday* magazine commissioned several writers to visit and report on their respective alma maters, a series which included Stephen Birmingham on the Little Three of Amherst, Williams, and Wesleyan, Budd Schulberg on Dartmouth, Cleveland Amory on Harvard, Alfred Bester on the University of Pennsylvania, John Knowles on Yale, and Henry Morton Robinson on Columbia. These peaks in journalistic profiles, of course, share company with a prodigious number of feature stories on the college scene.

Apart from essays, journalism, memoirs, and historical fiction, one study indicates that between 1890 and 1960, more than two hundred novels about college life were published in the United States.[13] (These selections did not include novels published for juvenile audiences, a genre which was popular). What themes and recurrent features characterize the collegiate novel? On the matter of campus setting, one finds that a handful of historic, prestigious colleges dominate, with Harvard, Yale, and Princeton running far ahead of other campus locales. If an author did not choose a well-known college, the tendency was to create a fictional campus, an option which ushered in such names as Sanford College, Siwash U., the ubiquitous State University, or (recalling a short-lived television series of 1964) Channing College. Why the preference for Harvard and Yale? One explanations for this phenomenon is that reading audiences tend to be attracted to and curious about the old, presitigious, and allegedly exclusive campuses; another is that certain colleges (namely Harvard, Yale, and Princeton) have educated a disproportionate number of writers and novelists. An interesting variation on the latter comment is the observation that a large number of Yale graduates have pursued careers in the publishing industry and hence have been hospitable to manuscripts submitted by alumni and/or about their alma mater. The number of stories, novels, and memoirs is so large that one literary historian in 1958 published a bibliography 135 pages in length devoted to Harvard Fiction. A few years earlier, Harvard University Press published a select anthology of previously published memoirs about Harvard by Harvard alumni.[14]

Collegiate fiction often represents first books by young authors. The campus years are often depicted overdramatically as a series of intense episodes in which a student goes through four years of initiation, fall from innocence, recovery, and maturity, and parts on good terms with Alma Mater.[15] Many of the selections in Spectorsky's anthology, *The College Years*, are refreshing and subtle in that they do manage to avoid this obvious formula. On other other hand, the overly dramatic tones might be taken as historical and social index of the intensity of student life within the walls.

There seems to be little indication that popular curiosity about scandal at elite colleges and universities will ever be satisfied. In the 1970s, the succession of "memoir-expose" works about higher education have included inside accounts of Harvard Law School, Harvard Business School, the United States Military Academy, and the football program at the University of Texas. An interesting trend (which may be short-lived) is that several of these recent exposés deal with professional schools. Historically, it has been the undergraduate student and subculture which have captured the fancy of both authors and readers. As admission to medical, law, and business school become increasingly difficult and prestigious, these selective graduate programs may acquire the ability to titillate readers. *The Paper Chase*, a novel-cum-movie, managed to inject a sense of drama into Harvard Law School's introductory course in contracts—no easy feat, as you will know if you have ever looked at law texts (and their grim effects on first-year law students).

Despite the recent charisma of law and medical schools, few authors have argued that a novel about graduate school can hold great interest. To the contrary, journalistic Tom Wolfe (veteran of graduate school at Yale and holder of a Ph.D. in American Studies) has contended that there is a conspiracy of silence among graduate students and former graduate students. The extended, dismal suffering of the perennial graduate student is allegedly so painful and boring that no one dares to use graduate school as the setting for the Great American Novel.[16]

Whether the collegiate novels deal with undergraduate, graduate, or faculty experiences, the memoir-exposé genre can assist research in higher education by airing an institution's "dirty little secrets," previously known only to those inside the classroom, dormitories, or faculty club. Reading the inside memoirs is a first step in solving the institutional research problems of penetrating the platitudes of public-relations releases and the edited information provided by formal reports. Autobiographical fiction—and here, Owen Johnson's *Stover at Yale* (1912) stands as an excellent example—is often filled with reconstruction of the customs, jargon, daily life, and annual cycle of groups within a campus community. The warning is that such reconstructions cannot be taken as historically accurate unless validated by checking and counter-checking with such achival sources as student yearbooks, class reports, college newspapers, and other remnants of personal history.

The prodigious quantity of stories, autobiographies, memoirs, and essays on college life impede nomination of "best" works. Several novels by F. Scott Fitzgerald come to mind, since he displayed an exceptional ability to capture the atmosphere of pre-World War I Princeton—although one critic has reminded us that Fitzgerald's *This Side of Paradise* was rejected by many publishers before it was eventually accepted. One "sleeper" novel, George Anthony Weller's *Not to Eat, Not for Love* (1933), seems to have attracted a loyal following over the years and is continually being rediscovered by new generations of serious college-fiction readers.[17]

To promote the reading habit, let us consider some features which make Weller's novel memorable and significant. *Not to Eat, Not for Love* is hardly original in its setting—Harvard. And the story starts out in predictable fashion by focusing on the Harvard College experiences of a freshman, "Epes Todd." The unique quality of the novel is that undergraduate Epes does not dominate the tale. Rather, one encounters a series of vignettes about disparate campus figures whose activities and destinies seldom converge. One is treated to perceptive, graphic accounts of graduate students, professors, research assistants, bored sportswriters assigned to the college teams, tourists who visit the campus, and poor but bright commuting students. If unity is given to this motley crowd, it is through the author's ability to look at them through the eyes of a bemused, traditional undergraduate who has fleeting curiosity about these invaders of the historic college, which has grown to be a large university by the late 1920s.

One exemplary character who is presented as part of the university pageant is the alumnus who has stayed on as a young dean in the academic bureaucracy:

> He was a slim middle-sized man of twenty-eight who was usually dressed in dark blue, with brown hair smoothly parted in the middle and a decent oval face. He had been a baseball manager and third marshal of his class, and there was a place waiting for him in the Dean's Office when he came back from his year at Cambridge. They had made him Dean of Records, which meant days of writing letters like: "I regret to inform you that the Committee has not found it possible to grant your petition to retake the midyear examination in Geography 12." . . . Sometimes he said, "Please feel free to call at my office," or "If at any time I can be. . . ." And he always said, "It has not been found possible," because there was still for him in the word "impossible" something too much like a knell. He knew the Catalogue and the past decisions of the Committee. . . . When queries came to him he did not answer directly if he could help it. He reached for the Catalogue of Courses, and with a lean hand, he passed over the book, open at the solving page.[18]

Such perceptive, observant sketches of college and university characters provide those in higher education with shocks of recognition. The preceding profile might stimulate critical thought on the changes in academic leadership which have accompanied university growth. Weller, the novelist as institutional analyst, prompts us to ask, "Is the depiction valid?" As with all worthy research projects, this functional equivalent of a pilot study has encouraged subsequent research and investigation. George Anthony Weller's ability to capture the sense of several Harvards was accompanied by portrayal of the modern university as both an insular world with its own logic and norms and an institution which intertwined with the surrounding city. This is the dimension which leads to a proposal for incorporation of institutional history into the realm of urban studies; that is, analysis of colleges and universities as factors in local and regional development.

CAMPUS AND COMMUNITY: LOCAL HISTORY

Almost a half-century ago, Henry Seidel Canby wrote, "Surely it is amazing that neither history, nor sociology, nor even fiction has given more than passing attention to the American college town." To encourage the remedy of that neglect, Canby offered his own portrait of the archetypal clean, neat, small-town setting for colleges in the late 19th century:

> As trading or industrial centers their life might be indistinguishable from towns or cities of a like size, but in their social consciousness there was always some recognition of peculiarity. For the heart of the community was a college. Its subtle influences were as pervasive if less noticeable than the quite unsubtle symbols of college life—playing fields, cafés, and collegiate clothing. . . . The campus and the college buildings dominated its architecture like the temple and citadel of a Greek city-state, a difficult relationship since there was always some doubt in the minds of the town folk whether the college was an asset or a parasite. The town with its college was like a woman's club committee with a celebrity in tow, a credit to them but also an embarrassment and sometimes a nuisance.[19]

Canby's portrait, combined with Daniel Boorstin's account of the booster college, provides an adequate introduction to the 19th-century college town. It is not clear as to how this portrait should be revised to include 20th-century changes in higher education. Can we delineate a composite university town of the 1950s or 1960s?

To update Canby's college-town portrait, researchers will have to discern the clustering tendencies of colleges, universities, and peripheral service organizations of the so-called knowledge industry. One urban model might be Palo Alto in northern California, where Stanford University has altered the population and economy of the area by attracting numerous consulting firms, private research institutes, and para-academic enterprises. Princeton, New Jersey, suggests a comparable pattern: its historic heart, Princeton University and the surrounding community, has since the 1930s been joined by the Institute for Advanced Study and since the late 1940s by the large Educational Testing Service. The size and budgets of Harvard and the

Massachusetts Institute of Technology have blurred the functional distinctions between Cambridge and Boston, and these institutions have exerted influence in local affairs, not so much on behalf of scholarly activities, but as landlords and employers. Here the campus qualifies as a large, "smokeless" industry.

To say that these cases point to a national trend of institutional proliferation and expansion is to say little. The intriguing and significant question is how does this take place within a community? Do Princeton, Palo Alto, and Cambridge share historical patterns of urban development with, say, Columbus, Ohio, or Columbia, Missouri? Our tentative finding of a recurrent and widespread pattern is that a 19th-century college town often becomes a multi-institutional university town in the 20th century.

To illustrate this pattern, consider the case of Amherst, a small Massachusetts town which has been the setting for Amherst College since 1820. As noted in Chapter 5, many state land-grant facilities were established near or as part of existing private colleges. Such was the situation in Amherst. In the 1870s, the town became the site for the state agricultural college, later renamed the University of Massachusetts and expanded in curricula. In the last twenty years, the University of Massachusetts has increased its enrollment from 7000 to approximately 25,000 students.

For the study of institutional impact in higher education, such change raises several questions central to community and regional development. How has the traditional town-gown balance changed? Has the small, selective private college maintained its influence and prestige in local affairs? Can the town integrate the state university's growth and transformation into its traditional, historic personality? Above all, what are the relations among institutions which cluster in the same locale: hostility, avoidance, reciprocation, or cooperation?

The historical development of Amherst seems to have credence for some other academic communities. Lexington, Kentucky, is an interesting example. Transylvania University, an old private institution, has played an integral part in the education, social life, and community character of local leaders and gentry since the early 19th century. As did Amherst, Lexington became the home of the state land-grant university after the Civil War. In the course of the past half-century, the newer University of Kentucky has stimulated construction, encouragement of national companies and industries, and large-scale residential and commercial development. On the one hand, such growth transforms (and economically benefits) the entire metropolitan and county area. At the same time, a neighborhood-by-neighborhood analysis of development patterns indicates growth away from Transylvania and the city's historic core, which significantly transforms the identity and spatial arrangement of the community.[21]

RESEARCH SUGGESTIONS

The fine edges of the relations between institutions and culture, colleges and communities are rubbed off when higher-education research and thinking are confined to preoccupation with national trends.[22] Review of and hypotheses about the university town and the ethnography of campuses and communities serve to draw attention to two distinct areas which, taken together, might reorient our conception of American social development. First, the aim is to nudge higher-education researchers toward increased interest in the structural and organizational behavior of academic institutions over long periods of time. Second, the focus on interaction and relations, shifting alliances between the campus and the surrounding community, is intended to rescue local and institutional history from the antiquarian and rather uncritical research and writing to which those topics often fall by default.

It is all too easy to think of higher education and social trends in terms of national institutions and national trends. Local and regional differences and distinctions have not received great attention in the research effort of the past twenty-five years. As historian C. Vann Woodward lamented in the 1950s:

> In a time when nationalism sweeps everything else before it, as it does at present, the regional historian is likely to be oppressed by a sense of his unimportance. America is the all-important subject, and national ideas, national institutions, and national policies are the themes that compel attention.[23]

One problematic consequence of inordinate attention to national institutions is a big-league syndrome in which every campus or community emulates, for instance, New York City, or (to draw from higher education) the Ivy League, or the University of California's master plan. The tendency toward disproportionate policy and news coverage for a few "national" institutions seriously distorts differntial contributions to the ranks of the learned professions. Within a metropolitan area, there may be a nationally known university or selective college whose research, publications, and advanced scholarship enhance institutional reputa-

FIGURE 10

Instant History and the American Campus: No college or university would be complete without its own monuments, including the ubiquitous "Founders' Rock." When the new Westwood campus of UCLA opened in 1926, administrators and students added a touch of historical legitimacy to the grounds by importing a 75-ton boulder.

Courtesy, Department of Special Collections, University of California at Los Angeles Library.

tion. Yet often across town, a local campus, virtually invisible or unknown outside the immediate city or neighborhood, wields considerable influence and power because its professional schools have educated most of the city's judges, lawyers, dentists, businessmen, state legislators, and school superintendents. This contribution hardly warrants national coverage in *Time* or *Newsweek*, or even a paragraph in guides to colleges, but it remains very important for determinig the conduct of local and regional affairs.

One partial explanation for this oversight and for the distortion of institutional impact has been faulty conceptualization of "national cosmopolitan elites" versus "local elites." According to one typology, the former category includes those professionals whose undergraduate or advanced education took place at prestigious "national" universities. The subsequent implication is that these people's careers tend to be in national politics, major corporations, or national associations and are pursued in a network defined by New York City, Washington, D.C., Boston, Chicago, San Francisco, and Los Angeles. This is a national network which ignores the provincial and regional cities or local communities. It is also a typology which underestimates the ascent, power, and sophistication of "favorite sons and daughters" whose arena of work, play, traditions, and alliances is *within* the community or region. Recognition of these regional cosmopolitans as a force in American life provides a path by which higher-education research and planning can lead to increased appreciation of configurations between campus and community.[24]

9

Future Tense Imperfect: "Futurology" and Higher Education's Recent Past

THE FUTURE AS HISTORY

The preceding chapters have presented resurrection of episodes and institutions which complicate the familiar conventional and contemporary"wisdom" about higher education. In so doing, we have presented the extended and underlying argument that *proper* and *careful* use of historical sources and insights has potential to be helpful, even essential, to decision-making and planning in higher education today. In other words, history need not be a discipline or research orientation that is without interest of application beyond a relatively small and closed circle of historians.

That argument has been advanced with a bittersweet sense of the limits of historical research to provide definitive and foolproof answers to institutional problems. A reconstruction of the past will seldom be wholly satisfactory to administrators, planners, and policy formulators if that information thwarts attempts at fast and direct solutions. So long as the art of administration and decision-making is accompanied by impatience, history will occupy a limited and precarious standing as an applied research area. To repeat a theme which has been both implicit and explicit in this work: historical studies and research might be of reasonable worth if and when they do stimulate those of us in the present to respect the complexities and varieties of patterns and events associated with colleges and universities.

The question persists, Why spend time studying and reconstructing the past when there is a pressing demand for analysis of present and future institutional issues? To respond to that query, we close on a curious, seemingly incongruent note for a work devoted to historical research and thinking: with some comments on "futurology," the study of higher education's future. During the 1970s, futurology emerged as a boom field; it has attracted funding and has made claims to legitimacy as an area of academic and institutional expertise. Futurology is an allegedly "relevant" research field. By contrasting the historical study of higher education with the futurological study of higher education, this chapter attempts to answer key questions: Does futurology constitute a discipline? How have its tenets, methods, and findings contributed to applied research and subsequent institutional performance? To answer the questions, we shall undertake a study of higher education's recent past by analyzing and reviewing that literature in the field of futurology which has been published in the past two decades.

Differences between the two disciplines, history and futurology, can be exaggerated. Historians must face the test of whether one can construct an accurate, significant portrait of the past. Similarly, futurologists must demonstrate that their distinctive, special research expertise enables them to construct an accurate, significant image of the future. In sum, *pre*construction and *re*construction are variations on common research tasks and assumptions. And there is the curious fact that even futurologists must gather sources and data from the past (at least from the recent past) in order to formulate projections for the future. The arrogance which tends to beset historians is that they feel they have perfect hindsight—accuracy after the fact. The comparably arrogant flaw to which futurologists are susceptible is the claim of foresight—accuracy before the fact.

It is not unreasonable for a college or university president, or for the chancellor of a university system, to decide that information about the future would be worth pursuing or purchasing. Futurological reports could serve to guide institutional development, both in pursuing certain courses and in avoiding others. The thorny problem is to identify bona fide expertse in futurology. How would one choose among candidates or proposals for such research projects? What are the prospects and promises of futurology as an institutional research tool? To illustrate the state of the field—and futurology's legitimacy as an academic or research discipline—let us examine a heralded work on the future of higher education which was published and marketed in 1978-79.

THE PROMISE OF FUTUROLOGY, 1980

During the late 1970s, one of the most highly publicized and celebrated futurology works was *The Third Century: Twenty-Six Prominent Americans*

Speculate on the Educational Future. Promotional announcements hailed the books as "a fascinating look into the educational future by some of the major actors on the stage," and noted:

> For the first time within memory, the leading figures in academic, political, and intellectual life have joined to produce a volume on the probable future of our colleges and universities and the nature and future directions of learning. . . . Whatever their particular visions of the future, these *Third Century* essays are likely to be heeded because of the positions of leadership of their authors.[1]

Herein lay clues to issues (many of which are unresolved) concerning the proper jurisdiction of futurology and its appropriate logic and validity. According to the publishers, the *Third Century* essays "are likely to be heeded because of the positions of leadership of their authors." However, one may occupy a position of leadership without being a leader and without having any skill as a researcher, writer, analyst, or forecaster. This grim observation is offered with reluctance, but must be entertained, since Laurence Peter's "Peter Principle" is plausible. According to Peter, one rises in a bureaucratic organization up to one's level of incompetence.[2] Do we have any evidence to accept or reject that pattern of organizational behavior for those in higher education? One wonders if the publishers would dare to make the claim that readers should heed *The Third Century* because the contributors are trained, certified futurologists whose research findings have passed tests of accuracy. Sorting out the claims of the promotional announcement raises the question, Will the future of higher education turn out as these authors describe because they are insightful and wise, or because they will make it do so?

Since the essayists are described as "major actors on the stage" of higher education, there is the unsettling prospect that they will work so as to fulfill or confirm projections and prophecies. This is an important observation about futurology in that it raises questions of advocacy. In other words, some futurologists claim that the task is not so much to forecast the future as to present information which will lead individuals and institutions toward certain options which might influence the future. This latter view of the field is disquieting, since there is no clear evidence that the actions and visions of the *Third Century* essayists have been especially successful, wise, or desirable in the *past*.

If we assume that the typical essayist-leader-actor noted in *The Third Century* was born around 1920, we can infer that his or her career in higher education, government, policy planning, or public service was pursued in large part during the decades from 1950 to 1980.[3] These were precisely the years in which higher education enjoyed fiscal fitness, abundance, and popular and legislative support, *and* the years in which policies and programs characterized by overbuilding, curricular fragmentation, reliance on soft money, overhiring, overtenuring of faculty were endorsed, accepted, or vigorously promoted. Looking at the future may be more comfortable for these leaders and spokesmen simply because the recent past is littered with mistakes and miscalculations. It behooves historian to look at the writings and events of the recent past along with the vision of the 21st century to posit a comprehensive appraisal of leadership and development in higher education. To do so, we will review the higher-education forecasts and projections which were published in the 1960s and early 1970s.

LOOKING BACKWARD: FORECASTS MADE IN THE 1960s AND 1970s

Recall that the publishers of *The Third Century* stated, "For the first time within memory, the leading figures in academic, political, and intellectual life have joined to produce a volume on the probable future of our colleges and universities and the nature and future direction of learning." If that is so, the publishers must have very short memories indeed. Two years before publication of *The Third Century*, in 1974-75, several *Third Century* essayists were contributors to a *Daedalus* anthology, "American Higher Education: Toward an Uncertain Future." In 1967, many of these same commentators participated in the American Academy's Commission on the Year 2000, the findings of which were published by *Daedalus* as *Toward the Year 2000: Works in Progress*. In 1968, the Academy for Educational Development sponsored a volume entitled *Campus 1980: The Shape of the Future in American Higher Education*. Edited by Alvin C. Eurich, this latter work included articles by David Riesman, John Gardner, Clark Kerr, Logan Wilson, and Nevitt Sanford.[4]

The salient point is that anthologies on the future of higher education are not a new, instantaneous product of the late 1970s. Rather, the authors are familiar faces who have been offering forecasts since at least the early 1960s. One puzzling feature which accompanies this literature is its vacillations in tone. Whereas *The Third Century* describes itself as a "volume on the probable future of our colleges and universities," the 1974-75 *Daedalus* work deals with American higher education's "uncertain future." Can the same writers posit multiple futures, with differen-

tiations between the "probable" and the "uncertain"? Do these differences demand different methods and data?

A review of the essays in *Campus 1980* and other works on the future of
higher education which were published in the late 1960s suggests a
number of recurrent themes and projections. The underlying tones were
those of dramatic change—growth, acceleration, expansion,
turnover—which was usually described in terms of optimism and excitement. Faculty the academic professionals, were depicted as a group
which was rising in income, status, social mobility, and geographical
mobility. Numerous essayists alluded to the vision of jet-setting professors who teach and consult at numerous institutions. One study
published by the American Council on Education in 1967 associated this
academic mobility with the scarcity and demand for professors. Discussion of the college teacher shortage included the following comment:
"Experts disagree on the present magnitude of the college teacher
shortage and upon when the shortage will end; but most conclude that
general shortages will prevail through the 1970s at least."[5] The corollary
of the rise and expansion of the academic professoriat was the forecast
that the demand for expansion of higher education would be stimulated
by two related yet distinct sources: the growing prestige of a college
degree, and the growing number of college-age youth (and other potential student pools). As the editor of *Campus 1980* noted in 1968:

> The size as well as the shape of higher learning will have changed
> significantly by 1980. The explosion in the student population will have
> resulted in a vastly enlarged number of undergraduate and graduate
> students, and a continuing shortage of faculty.[6]

In reinforcement of that projection, Clark Kerr of the Carnegie Commission on Higher Education stated that "swelling enrollment" was one
of three major areas of adjustment which colleges and universities would
have to make in 1980 and beyond. Quantitative growth was to be accompanied by qualitative change in the nature and character of
undergraduate education. The forecast was that students who entered
colleges and universities would be more sophisticated, and better
prepared in their academic studies than counterparts of preceding years.
One contributor to *Campus 1980* made the confident prediction that
"the college generation of the 1950s was the last 'quiet' one we will see
in a long time." This would offer partial impetus for a change in
teaching style and certification: "Moreover, the time spent on campus
will be differently organized for more effective learning. No longer will

students merely pile up credit hours through fragmented and specialized courses.''

Implicit in this genre of literature was the assertion that higher education was important and would be regarded as increasingly important by numerous constituencies in American life. As the spokesman for the Academy for Educational Development noted in 1968, ''The basic premise of this book is that across the American future is written 'Higher Education,' '' and that ''to envisage Campus 1980, then, is to consider what our society will or should soon become.''

One contributor to the 1967 *Daedalus* symposium focused on growth and change in American higher education by identifying university cities in the year 2000 as a new phenomenon, markedly different from the familiar academic ''company towns'' of mid-century Ann Arbor, New Haven, Cambridge, Berkeley, and Madison:

> What, then, is the university city of the year 2000 to be? Essentially, it will be an urban area of some size and economic importance that will shelter a significant number of strong educational institutions, broadly defined; these institutions will cooperate in ways that are now only dimly perceived. For a university city to develop, there must be a continuing relation among institutions of learning, public and private. Moreoever, the collective influence of these bodies must be greater than that of all other corporate groups in the city.[7]

If this mandate seems vague, 1967 readers received additional commentary about these projected and unprecedented cities:

> By the year 2000, however, the business of certain cities in America will be education, in the broadest sense. These cities will be as different from the commercial, industrial, and governmental cities of today as the latter are from the cathedral towns of an earlier European society. If I am correct in believing that a few cities of this sort will have established themselves in the United States by the year 2000, they must not be seen as displacing existing cities; they will co-exist with them, but will have a different sort of appeal for a growing segment of an increasingly mobile American society.

This development was anticipated by the author on the grounds that ''education, health, and leisure are all becoming 'big business,' '' and that it was reasonable to expect some concentration of these enterprises. Affluence and mobility were to mean that the new university cities would appeal to and attract great numbers of postdoctoral fellows, career-changing professionals, businessmen on sabbatical leave, and transient professors (''At a time when London will be an hour's distance from New York, scholars and teachers will divide their time between several university cities").

A few years earlier, Clark Kerr's *The Uses of the University* sketched comparable and compatible projections for the future of the "City of Intellect."[8] Kerr argued that the growth of the "knowledge industry" would in turn promote the "rise of ideopolis," that is, the clustering of university centers into ranges and networks, accompanied by related public and private services and educational enterprises. This ostensibly would make the university city into the potential "salvation of our society" and an "instrument of our national purpose." Whether for ill or good, the American university was projected as dramatic and consequential.

THE VISION OF THE YEAR 2000: A 1980s PROGRESS REPORT

Given the preceding summary of social and educational forecasts published in the 1960s, how do these authors and forecasters comment on the image of the year 2000 which they espoused about a decade ago? In other words, as we proceed on the trajectory toward 2000, can we pause to review the data and arguments which were made in the recent past? Feedback—knowledge of results—is, after all, integral to systems analysis.

In 1966, *The Wall Street Journal* published a series of articles dealing with life in the year 2000. Ten years later, the newspaper's editors noted in a prelude to a series entitled "The Future Revised" that "developments in the past decade have changed the outlook". According to *The Wall Street Journal* reporters, the educational forecasters of 1967 had returned to the drawing board:

> The future of education now seems a bit different from the one most educators predicted 10 years ago. They correctly foresaw major trends: Increasing demand for adult education. New flexibility in the content and structure of education. A great expansion in corporate education and training.
>
> The experts perceived the impact of computers and other electronics advances. But they didn't perceive the time it would take to get new technology into widespread use.
>
> They went wrong in other ways, too. They thought the outpouring of government and foundation money into education would never stop growing. They conceived of education as the new growth industry. They expected school enrollments to continue soaring at all levels. And they worried about how to manage the staggering amount of new construction all this would require.[9]

One president of an educational research and development organization (who was, incidentally, a contributor to *Campus 1980*) told reporters, "I shudder at how cloudy was that crystal ball." Along with the unexpected drop in the birthrate, he explained, "what we all failed to observe was that we were about to pass out of the era of cheap labor, cheap energy, and cheap money. No one seemed to foresee that education and economics were on a collision course."[10]

This apologia is incomplete. There is, for example, reasonable evidence that there were some research projects in the late 1960s which did forecast economic collision and social disruptions for the 1970s, but such reports were unpleasant for government and political sponsors and funding agencies and led to withdrawal of the projects' support. One such case was the project undertaken by Stanford University Research Institute, funded in 1967 by the United States Office of Education, to "examine the future for the next 20 to 30 years in order to determine its educational policy." The project director noted, "We forecast a time of trouble and social disruption in the mid-'70s, and predicted that the problems would appear to have individual causes, but in reality would be symptoms of a fundamental social wrenching. As a result, "the USOE response was to withdraw further support of general futures research."[11] general futures research."[11]

The apologia is unsatisfactory on another point. There is a tendency to minimize errors in forecasting by appealing to collective oversight. In other words, since all the expert forecasters failed to see the collision course of economics and education, it is understandable and forgivable that no one expert identified the development. If that crystal ball was so cloudy, why did not the 1967 forecasters refute any claims to professional expertise? Finally, if the 1966 vision of the year 2000 can be altered by 1976, why cannot the revision be changed again in 1986, and again in 1996? By definition, each subsequent revision will be closer in time and reality to the "correct" vision of 2000. The logical extension is that researchers in the year 2010 will be more likely to posit an accurate image of the year 2000.

The preceding case of the "cloudy crystal ball" was not an isolated or unrepresentative rush to apology and revision. By 1973, for example, research institutes and foundations publicly announced that many of their projects and predictions undertaken in the 1960s were unsuccessful and incorrect, and these announcements were accompanied by prospecti for new directions and insights to guide subsequent projects. The program officer for the Ford Foundation's public education sector wrote as follows: "Nineteen-sixty was a time when nearly everyone thought that with more money, more buildings, and more teachers, our nation's schools could, indeed, make a few adjustments and changes to produce a better society."[12] In an article on "What Went Wrong in the '60s," a Ford Foundation spokesman told reporters that the unsuccessful projects which had been funded by the foundation would be replaced by new directions. "Educational emphases in the 1970s will be on decentralization, students' rights, teacher militancy, full state funding, free schools outside the public system, and the effects of Vietnam on youth."[13]

Apart from these redirections within the field of education, many state legislators and federal programs of the 1970s treated higher education as a risky area which had lost the alleged popular enthusiasm it had enjoyed in the 1960s. Contraction and stagnation, not expansion, were the characteristics of a decade in which "steady-state growth" emerged as the dominant slogan to describe administrative style.

The striking and alarming aspect of these self-evaluations by the forecasters is not that their 1960s predictions appeared to have gone awry. Rather, it is the vacillation in outlook on the part of the forecasters toward their own writings and announcements. In less than a decade, they had become defensive and apologetic about their vision of the 21st century. Despite their apologies and revisions of the mid-1970s, we do not yet know for certain that they were incorrect. True, many of the essays written in 1967 strike us today as utopian images unrelated to surrounding institutions and cities—but we are still several years from 2000. Economists talk about the "blip" phenomenon, on intense, drastic, short-lived alteration to a plotted course. It may well be that the events and situations of 1968-78 constitute a "blip" and that we may well regain the trajectory which was forecast in 1967. What if that image of the year 2000 takes several years longer to achieve than the forecasters said it would take?

Nonetheless, the futurologists seem to be unsure of their own expertise. One indication is that the forecasts tend to offer linear projections of the present; in other words, forecasts made in a time of growth, abundance and confidence (1967) report on abundant, expanding, and confident higher education in 2000. Forecasts announced in a year of "stagflation," declining SAT scores, and taxpayer discontent with school bond issues (1979) will tend to conjure an image of the year 2000 which is bleak and unreceptive to support of colleges and universities. The danger is that futurology becomes an unstable, chameleonlike undertaking.

This reasonably close look at the higher-education futurology literature of the 1960s and 1970s is meant to suggest that these were the years in which the discipline gained entrance to academic and educational research and planning. Yet these particular application, prospects, and problems are not the sole domain of either higher education or the past two decades. To understand the identity crises which futurological research encounters as a part of higher-education administration, we must look back at various kinds of literature from which futurology has gathered inspiration and methods.

THE FUTUROLOGY INHERITANCE

Antecedents to higher-education futurology can be found in several traditions, ranging from utopian novels, and oracles and prophecy to science fiction and social-science research. Contemporary forecasters may be reluctant to be associated with soothsayers, as the latter's skills were attributed to mystical insights, not research and analytic expertise. However, the lack of data, documentation, and discernible research procedure in many essays of conjecture about higher education suggest that 20th-century writers are kindred to medieval prophets. There exists today in the academy a tendency to ridicule or dismiss science-fiction writers as hacks and charlatans. But such offhanded dismissals warrant careful reconsideration.

A revisionist view of the science-fiction genre acknowledged that the creators of Flash Gordon and Buck Rogers comic strips in the 1930s and 1940s were reasonably accurate in their anticipation of many scientific developments. Many of the projections predisposed the American public to support and accept projects associated with space programs in the 1950s and 1960s. Often overlooked is the fact that the craft of science fiction, properly understood, demands that an author adhere to strict ground rules which prevent pure indulgence in fantasy. Social and technical features must be plausible, and grounded in known fact and capability. Arthur Clarke (*2001 : A Space Odyssey*), for instance, has been a scientist who worked directly on space programs. The residual point is that the science-fiction craft or guild has established internal safeguards against writers' futuristic whims. As suggested by preceding anecdotes and examples, similar ground rules and checks have not always been built into the forecasts made by higher-education professionals who write about their own institutions.

The recent past brings us to familiar turf: what may be termed "applied social research" for the future. A landmark effort in this area took place during the years 1928-31, under the commission of President Herbert Hoover.[14] Although a number of business and economic writers of that period were outrageously optimistic in contending that the 1929 stockmarket crash was a temporary unpleasantness, the President's team of psychologists and social scientists constructed an interesting and reasonably sound multivolume forecast for American society. Published in 1933 (after Hoover was out of office), *Recent Social Trends in the United States* provided both a massive compilation of existing patterns and practices and a discussion of implications for the future. This was an adventurous project, but the use of its findings for guiding policy or for anticipating social problems remains unclear. For example, the presidential commission research team was quite correct in observing that radio, automobiles, and mass production would be increasingly important in American life. But, it is important to note that these were already available and influential in America in the late 1920s; that is, the projections were obvious and safe. In the case of the automobile, the researchers *under*estimated its impact and expanded use. As for mass communications and broadcasting, there is indication that the official discussion misread the national pulse. The recommendation for restraint in federal regulation of radio broadcasting grew from the idea that there was little need to monitor or restrict advertisements on radio because radio waves were in the public domain and were not "commercial," and the American listening audience would not tolerate interruptions in programs by frequent sponsor messages. It is an understatement to say that the future of American broadcasting has taken a markedly different turn from the one projected in this study published less than half a century ago.

As a spinoff from the Hoover Commission, popularizations of forecasts were prevalent in the 1930s. Thematic publications released as part of the Chicago World's Fair included elaborate, dramatic projections of life in the 1980s. The predictable formula was to seize a contemporary item or practice and paste on a fantasy projection. For example, the existing technology (automobiles and airplanes) was combined into a product which would be readily available to the American consumer: a 1934 Packard with wings which would carry Mr. and Mrs. America home to New Jersey after a morning visit to Moscow ("Look, dear, there's Paris!"). The temptation is to ridicule these naive projections, but in fairness to the optimistic writers and artists of the World's Fair, we ought remember that in 1967, a prominent higher-education commentator pointed out that faculty mobility in 2000 was probable, as

London and New York would be only an hour away from each other.

Futurology of the 1960s and 1970s has been a hybrid field in that it has been interdisciplinary and multidisciplinary, or, at worst, non-disciplinary. Part of its claim to legitimacy has been its ability to draw from and enlist methods and findings from systematic research disciplines such as economics, sociology, and demography (the study of population changes). Yet most futurology research units converge on the model of a discussion group or thinktank. Here the example which comes to mind is the Rand Corporation, or the Club of Rome, an exclusive association of 100 policy-makers from 25 nations which has been founded by the governments of Canada, West Germany, the Fiat Corporation, and the Volkswagon Foundation.[15] The United States' academic version was the already noted 1966-67 gathering chaired by Daniel Bell and sponsored by the American Academy of Arts and Sciences.

One warning that these select groups have issued from time to time is that futurological research is susceptible to vulgarization and faddishness. That, however, is a problem which any creative or advanced endeavor faces, and ought be accepted as a normal feature in the sociology and diffusion of knowledge. Implications for the 1970s included resumption of government funding for futurological research after withdrawal of support in the late 1960s; establishment of university programs and degrees in some variant of "future studies"; widespread sales of an electric work which popularized futurology, namely, Alvin Toffler's *Future Shock*. Were one to identify those variants which seem to be most comprehensive and thorough in data collection and analysis, the discipline of demography and the enterprise of census-bureau research are impressive. Yet for all the increments in methodology, analytic tools, and information storage, the image of the futurologist as prophet or sage has had enduring appeal. And despite differences among these tributaries, there are enduring problems of logic and working assumptions to which futurological research, in higher education and other areas of social-institutional development, remains susceptible.

ACCOUNTABILITY AND SIGNIFICANCE IN HIGHER EDUCATION'S FUTURE

Preceding examples have alluded to futurology as a professional endeavor which might attract charlatans; one can always move on to virgin territory before the due date of one's earlier forecasts is reached. This is not appealing to clients who have paid for futurological research, however. How might one build in a measure of accountability and consumer protection for futurology? Here we look to three disparate areas—baseball, architecture, and the military—for professional models which guard against research malpractice.

One deterrent to research malpractice could be to have futurologists monitored according to the equivalent of a batting average. This would involve a prorated, sliding fee structure in which research contracts would include a clause whereby the hired expert in futurological research would itemize his projections. If and when two-thirds of the recommendations or forecasts were realized, the researcher-forecaster would receive two-thirds of the grant or fee. The attractions of this mechanism are many. First, futures experts would not risk their reputations or income potential on unfounded projections and cloudy crystal balls. Second, unless a researcher expected to live an inordinately long time (this in itself would entail shrewd futurological anaylsis), reports would tend to be confined to the not-too-distant future. Third, the batting-average incentive would instill an "up-or-out" career pattern among alleged futurology experts.

A related mechanism to promote accountability owes its inspiration to Henry Churchill, an architect and urban historian who wrote in the 1930s a remarkable and enduring book on city planning, *The City is the People*. Churchill was tired of architectural design which indulged the architect's whims at the expense of thoughtful social and spatial planning. To counter the syndrome, he suggested municipal ordinances which would require an architect to live for at least six months in a building or environment which that architect had designed. Similarly, one could have requirements, through professional, academic, or legislative codes, that futurologists for educational institutions be bonded and required to remain at the college or university whose future they were contracted to forecast. Analysts and advocates of institutional options would then be more apt to use care and thought in reports—a healthy antidote to researchers' capricious hopping from one consulting situation to another, with limited concern for the consequences of their research.

Finally, there is the approach of gentle suasion within the research profession, a voluntary campaign whereby researchers are reminded to use restraint in constructing utopian futures for higher education. This is an approach inspired by World War II public information campaigns, in which billboards and graphic posters daily warned civilians and sailors that "Loose Lips Sink Ships." For potentially flamboyant futurologists whose unfounded projections are expensive to clients, a fitting motto would be "Talk is *Not* Cheap."

One can justifiably protest that these proposed measures would be so strict as to stifle imaginative discussion about the future of institutions and society. That is a worthy point which warrants concession, but it ought to be accompanied by the understanding that futurological research and reports fall outside the domain of the "hard" or exact sciences and are more akin to discussions among philosophers, historians, and members of other disciplines.

Whether one favors the preceding proposals or opts for other regulation of futurological research, there are tendencies in futurology which raise questions of dubious logic. We will now turn to these.

OVERDRAMATIZATION OF THE FUTURE

By this is meant the tendency for futurological researchers, whether optimistic or pessimistic, to see future situations as unprecedented in terms of complexity and importance. One recurrent statement is that the 21st century will be a period of "accelerating change" characterized by a "knowledge explosion." The result is that stagnation, gradual erosion, and unspectacular institutional existence are seldom worked into the forecast, if for no other reason than that such conditions are not welcomed or exciting for authors to convey.

A logical corollary of overdramatization of the future is a susceptibility to dismissing past institutions and individuals as belonging to a simpler era. This can be faulted in specific terms by looking at American higher education in the situation of a century ago. One can argue with sound documentation that the participants in higher education from 1880 to 1910 witnessed, experienced, or planned sizable changes in the structure, administration, and scope of campuses which were more unsettling than the situations encountered in the late 1970s. And one must consider the place of perennial problems in education and institutions; that is, that each generation must confront limits of finance, support, cohesion, and purpose within the context of its information sources and methods. How do we know that the demands of compliance with federal regulations and data systems in 1980 hold more or fewer frustrations and chances for failure than, for instance, the task of establishing a college in the western reserve country of 1810 did? If one reads through annals of crucial court cases and decisions, one finds that the legal arguments, institutional issues, and educational principles with which our predecessors dealt in the 18th and 19th centuries do match the importance and complexity of those encountered in our own age. The futurologists go awry when they wholly invert the medieval world view and depict the present and future as a giant who stands on the shoulders of a dwarflike past.

FASCINATION WITH TECHNOLOGY AND GADGETRY

In futuristic novels, this abuse often takes the form of predictions that familiar tasks and tools will be obsolete and related nuisances and problems will be eliminated through technological improvements.[16] The weakness is that such gadgets do not insure removal of work or chores and are not always readily available to the public. Note, for example, that the advent of "labor-saving" devices through household appliances did not necessarily reduce the amount of human time spent in cleaning, repairing, or tending; to the contrary, new appliances often created new household tasks. For education and schooling, a number of writers in the 1960s looked to "ed tech" (educational technology) as a panacea which would both transform and save mass education. Such grandiose hopes for a 21st century *deux ex machina* gloss over complexities of social situations. As one political scientist warned the American Academy Commission on the Year 2000:

> Today, for instance, almost everyone who makes predictions about the next few decades emphasizes the future exploits in outer space. This seems like a safe prediction, since our boys now are so interested in outer space. But how do we know that by the year 2000 people will not look at a new space exploit by NASA in the same way that we now look at the completion of a new dam in Oklahoma by the Corps of Engineers: The contractors and NASA will be keenly interested, but our grown-up boys may not even notice the event buried in the back sections of their newspaper.[17]

To this we add the observation that new technology seldom wholly replaces old technology, customs, and practices. A comprehensive portrait of life within colleges and universities grasps the coexistence of conflicting practices and recognizes the notion of lag—that is, archaic patterns and practices are not automatically phased out. An issue which (deservedly) receives continuing debate is whether social or technological change is most likely to be projected with accuracy. In any event, it is important to note that a technological innovation may initiate latent functions or unexpected consequences in social patterns and cultural life. This leads to a final source of irritation in 1960s and 1970s higher-education futurology, and "institutional imperative."

INSTITUTIONAL DESTINY

During the 19th century, an arrogant historian concluded his university lectures with the disclaimer, "It is not I who speaks, but history who speaks through me." A sense of restraint, humility, and increased knowledge led subsequent generations of historians to squirm with discomfort at such pretentious statements. Equally unsettling is the following futurological disclaimer presented by Clark Kerr in his influential 1963 work, *The Uses of the University*. After mapping out a course by which there would be a unique model for the future American university, Kerr noted, "This is not said in boast. It is simply that the imperatives that have molded the American university are at work around the world." In his concluding chapter on the future growth of the "City of Intellect," he wrote, "The process cannot be stopped. The results cannot be foreseen. It remains to adapt."[18] This writing style comes dangerously close to presentation of personal conjecture as prophecy or a statement of historical imperative. Critical reading carries the continual reminder that such descriptions hold no credence for institutional destiny. As has been shown in many preceding excerpts and anecdotes from forecasters, the institutional future projected for higher education has often been vague and/or quite incorrect.

It is fitting and proper that administrators and planners in colleges and universities do take themselves and their institutions to be serious matters. That ought not to be construed as an obsession with the present. Rather, the concept of the specious present—the idea that one can telescope several eras when looking at one's immediate situations—is useful for fusion of higher education's past, present, and future. If futurdogical research is to have a legitimate place in harmony with historical and contemporary analytic strategies, one would do well to consider the research and writing models provided by three works on higher education. Specifically, we shall briefly look at the insights, sources, and tones provided by Michael Young's *The Rise of the Meritocracy, 1870-2033* (1958); John R. Silber's epilogue for *The Third Century*, titled "The Rest Was History" (1976); and Sir Eric Ashby's convocation address for the centennial celebration of the Johns Hopkins University (1976).

RESEARCH MODELS AND EXAMPLES

The first work turns us away from the United States to Great Britain, where Michael Young constructs a model of historical sociology in the study of schooling, certification, and national development. The remarkable feature of Young's painstaking research is that he surveys the key historical documents and issues of the period from 1870 to 2033—in a book published in 1958. *The Rise of the Meritocracy* reviews the landmark legislation in expansion and educational opportunity which accumulated in the late 19th and early 20th centuries and follows that with a satirical yet seemingly plausible account of the years from 1960 to 2033, described as if mid-20th-century policies were carried to logical and illogical extremes.

According to Michael Young, the problems of the 21st century will be rooted in an over sight of educational reformers and national leaders of the 20th century, who pursued the notion that the talented, intelligent, and educated should be identified, groomed, rewarded, and placed in positions of responsibility. In Young's book, this dream is realized, and its policies work too well, upsetting familiar forms of hereditary wealth, family position, and job promotion on the basis of seniority. Historical sociologist Young resurrects a "dirty little secret" which enabled 18th- and 19th-century British society to function reasonably well: that talent must be distributed throughout all social classes and occupations. Concentration of talent in the officer corps of the army and navy, for example, would strip those services of the truly talented (yet less than privileged) soldiers and sailors without which no army or navy can be effective.

Yet for those generations after World War II, that particular social fact was either obscured or forgotten. According to Young, Great Britain developed and refined a truly accurate system of testing centers and schools in which citizens were sorted, tested, certified, taught, and recertified according to intelligence. An illusory half-century of national progress and peace was to be followed by a revolt of the "leftovers"—the stupid children of old wealth who (according to the redistribution of meritocracy) rudely found themselves to be "lower class." Young also alludes to late-20th-century civil war, in which the nation's resurgence as a world power would lead to heated debates and violence over the issue of teaching Chinese as a second language in public schools. Writing from the vantage point of 2033, meritocrat Young points out that popular uprisings are destined to fail, since the lower classes are truly less able and less intelligent, thanks to efficient testing and policy. Despite rumblings of unrest and revolt, Young offers the confident conclusion that such movements might have succeeded in 1933, but not in 2033. He notes, "This is the prediction I shall expect to verify when I stand next May listening to the speeches from the great rostrum at Peterloo."

But 2034 is a very different story, as the publisher and editor follow Young's prediction with a note that Young has been killed at Peterloo, a victim of the violence and revolt he confidently predicted would not occur. The unexpected turn of events, familiar to forecasters and futurologists, leads the editor to provide a fitting epitaph for the mistaken author: "The failings of sociology are as illuminating as its successes."[19]

At the start of this chapter, we discussed the congratulations and great expectations which accompanied publication of *The Third Century: Twenty-Six Prominent Americans Speculate on the Educational Future*. Readers, of course, will disagree in their evaluations of the numerous authors' essays. One selection worth special note is John R. Silber's epilogue, "The Rest Was History," a brief essay which provides an American variation on developments and problems to which Michael Young alludes in his study of Great Britain.[20] Silber, famous in the 1970s as president of Boston University, looks backward from the year 2025 and writers that this was the "watershed year in the history of higher education in the United States."[21] According to his summary, educators in the last part of the 20th century were myopic in that they did not foresee the affluence and prestige which higher education would come to enjoy in the 21st century.

According to Silber, crucial events and developments will include faculty unionization with the Teamsters and the International Workers of the World, creation of a national Department of General Welfare, and a new egalitarianism. The main feature of this latter phenomenon was the insistence that equality of opportunity in education must be accompanied by equality of results in higher-education instruction and certification. Silber elaborates:

> Behavorial objectives and competence-based programs were instrumental in this development: Once it was decided that the time it took to learn something was irrelevant to learning, it was possible for medical students who took five years to master organic chemistry not only to practice alongside their fleeter collegues, but also to buy the same no-fault malpractice insurance.

The extreme consequence of the new equality was to be that higher education came to be known as "postsecondary education," and the award of a bachelor's degree in many states will accompany passing the examination for a driver's license. The happy recovery from this nadir will come at the turn of the century, when a Robert Maynard Hutchins clone will establish an innovative university and restore the term *higher education* to schooling vocabulary.

Both Michael Young and John R. Silber employed satire and historical, social-science fiction to illuminate the issues and complexities which will face higher education in the future. In a more solemn yet graceful and witty essay, Sir Eric Ashby chose to focus on the role of universities and futurological research in his 1976 address at the centennial celebration of the Johns Hopkins University.[22] Ashby, historian at Clare College of Cambridge University in England, acknowledged that the Johns Hopkins University carried the burden and glory of an institution which pioneered modern research disciplines in the United States. It would be proper and fittng, he continued, that the pioneering tradition would include the mandate of incorporating the study of the future into the familiar activities of studying the past and the present. To do so, however, would not be obvious or easy, given the character of academic disciplines. Noting that the university curriculum is discipline-oriented, while most students pursue careers which are problem-oriented, Ashby commented:

> The discipline-oriented approach had led to staggeringly successful predictions *within* disciplines, in astronomy, for instance. But to make predictions within a discipline is to scan reality only one facet at a time. It is when you try to make predictions about problem-oriented issues, which require the appreciation of the crystal reality as a whole—the sensate as well as the rational facets—that you find no such record of success; indeed, a record of humiliating failures.

Ashby argued that university-sponsored study of the future must be "stripped of all speculation unsupported by rational argument." Here it is important to distinguish the unknown from the unknowable. If there is a discipline which provides a sound model for academic study of the future, Ashby favored biology:

> Why biology? Because it illustrates both the overriding constraint and the exciting opportunity in the study of the future. The overriding constraint is that nothing we can discover in the present will enable us to plot the future course of evolution, whether of bacteria or wheat or Man. Phenomena of evolution, unlike phenomena of, say, gravitation, really are unpredictable. Nevertheless (and this is the exciting opportunity), the evolutionary process can be "tamed" by plant and animal selection to produce domesticated varieties of enormous benefit to society. . . . Can we—and this is the practical challenge of futurology—similarly tame the

evolution of social values: from cruelty toward compassion, from superfluous consumption toward conservation, from greed toward altruism?

THE EDUCATION OF LEADERS: AN APPROACH

The prospectus which Ashby offers for the sound and proper study of the future brings to mind the very attributes (and challenges) by which the 19th-century writers distinguished civilization from barbarism. That ideal, dusted off and rediscovered, is an appealing addition to the vocabulary and terminology we now associate with the proper education of leaders in higher-education institutions. Critical analysis, an invaluable dimension which academic disciplines of the 20th-century university have polished, coupled with restraint, humility, and respect for the complexities of issues and institutions, is an element which can help revitalize morale and purpose among higher-education leaders and professionals in the last quarter of the 20th century.

Twenty years ago, college and university administrators hailed the managerial revolution in higher education as a development suited to problem-solving and campus expansion. Today, those buoyant claims and expectations have often been deflated, and college and university deans and presidents increasingly are seen (and see themselves) as specialists in the management of decline. It is an ethos which is unfortunate, unnecessary, and unhealthy for those who look at, work, and live in colleges and universities.

John R. Silber's epilogue in *The Third Century* enjoys the advantages of satire to look *back* on the higher-education problems of the 1980s and 1990s, a point which enables Silber to observe with matter-of-fact confidence, ''The rest was history.'' Even though we do not know the outcome of events for those years, Silber's humorous tone of criticism of the abuses and grandiose claims of policy and programs in our own era is useful. For those of us who will now participate in and observe the higher education of the late 20th century, this leads to a modest proposition: that we find the courage to rid ourselves of an arrogant and deceptive sense of control over the future and kindle the careful inquiry, observation, and thoughtful actions by which we may serve responsibly in educational institutions and in society.

EPILOGUE

To understand institutions or individuals calls for patience, since even colorful personalities have tedious streaks. Consider the mixed reviews which Barbara Tuchman leaves for the Duke of Devonshire, an influential figure in late 19th century British politics: "Even his own speeches bored him and once when speaking on the budget for India he paused, leaned over to the colleague nearest him on the bench, and suppressing a yawn, whispered, 'This is damned dull. . .' "

The study of colleges and universities, too, suffers its dull moments. I have set out to show readers that the topic need not be as stifling as discourses on the 19th century imperial budget for India. Provocative use of historical materials can develop curiosity and delight as a part of serious thinking about higher education.

A work which aspires to leaving readers with a desire for more sources has special obligations in its closing comments. First, I repeat my early warning that this is not a comprehensive encyclopedia; it is an invitation to the study of higher education. Second, I wish to suggest bring attention to works which I have found useful for additional reading, reading, research, and reflection.

SUGGESTED READINGS

Notes which accompany each chapter provide one guide to readings. The following annotations comprise a brief bibliography and an essay on sources which allow me to acknowledge my debt to numerous authors.

Readers intrigued by original documents may find the following edited anthologies helpful both in content and as a model for the kinds of reports, letters, notebooks, tracts, legislative materials, court decisions, institutional records, and charters from which historians reconstruct higher education's past:

Richard Hofstadter and Wilson Smith, editors, *American Higher Education: A Documentary History* (University of Chicago Press, 1961) 2 volumes.

Edward C. Elliott and M.M. Chambers, *Charters and Basic Laws of Selected American Universities and Colleges* (Carnegie Foundation for the Advancement of Teaching, 1934) 640 pages.

Lynn Thorndike, editor, *University Records and Life in the Middle Ages* (Columbia University Press, 1944) 476 pages.

Helene Wieruszowski, *The Medieval University* (D. Van Nostrand, 1966).

Indicative of the advanced and revised approaches to the social and historical study of European higher education are the coherent collections of monographs prepared under the auspices of the Shelby Cullom Davis Center at Princeton University and the anthology guided by editors of the *Journal of Contemporary History:*

Lawrence Stone, editor , *The University in Society*   (Princeton University Press, 1974), 2 volumes.

Walter Laqueur and George L. Mosse, editors, *Education and Social Structure in the Twentieth Century, Journal of Contemporary History* (Spring 1967) vol. 2, no. 3, 218 pages.

For those who seek comprehensive and enduring histories of American higher education which provide greater depth than this work, classic sources include the following:

Frederick Rudolph, *The American College and University: A History* (Random House, 1962) 516 pages.

John S. Brubacher and Willis Rudy, *Higher Education in Transition: A History of American Colleges and Universities, 1636-1976* (Harper and Row, 1976) (third edition) 536 pages.

Laurence R. Veysey, *The Emergence of the American University* (University of Chicago Press, 1965) 505 pages.

The debates over and mysteries about *which* topics and *which* methods gain support in large-scale education research receive fair hearing in the selections noted below:

Harold Howe II, "Education Research—The Promise and the Problem," *The Educational Researcher* (June 1976) vol. 5, no. 6, pp. 2-7.

Lee Cronbach and Patrick Suppes, editors, *Research for Tomorrow's Schools: Disciplined Inquiry for Education* (Report of the Committee on Educational Research of the National Academy of Education) (Macmillan, 1969) 281 pages.

Ellen Coughlin, "Where Are the Jobs? Outside Academe, More and More Historians Find," *Chronicle of Higher Education* (8 January 1979) pp. 1, 11.

One unusual work which provides both autobiographical information and revelation of historians' varied research strategies and methods is an anthology whose contributors are "working" historians:

L.P. Curtis, Jr., editor, *The Historian's Workshop* (Alfred A. Knopf, 1970) 326 pages.

Higher education students and analysts would do well to keep abreast of good writing and research design in several disciplines. Below, the small books by Cipolla and Hemenway suggest *economists'* sensitivity to "external factors" and the "irrationalities" of culture which should delight social historians while complicating institutional evaluation. Webb's pioneering collection of unobtrusive measures has import for all the social studies disciplines:

Carlo M. Cipolla, *Literacy and Development in the West* (Penguin Books, 1969)

David Hemenway, *Prices and Choices: Microeconomic Vignettes* (Ballinger, 1977) 196 pages.

Eugene Webb, *et al. Unobtrusive Measures: Nonreactive Research in the Social Sciences* (Rand McNally, 1966).

Preoccupation with surveys, scores, and test results as the bases from which education research and evaluation should generate tends to obscure other sources of data from which one might reconstruct, describe, and interpret "learning" and "intelligence." One splendid historical work whose methods and assumptions could be transposed to contemporary higher education is as follows:

Daniel H. Calhoun, *The Intelligence of a People* (Princeton University Press, 1973) 408 pages.

Historical orientation has, in fact, already made important in-roads on the sociological study of colleges and universities. Here are two memorable essays in what might be termed "historical sociology":

> Burton R. Clark, *The Distinctive College: Antioch, Reed, & Swarthmore* (Aldine, 1970) 280 pages.

> Christopher Jencks and David Riesman, *The Academic Revolution* (Doubleday and Company, 1969) 580 pages.

In chapter 1 and elsewhere readers have been urged to consider the *visual* legacy of higher education as a dimension of institutional study. That is no easy task, but there are some works which afford direct and indirect guides. How, for example, might a researcher consider certain categories of snapshots, formal photographs, and mementos as a part of a campus' liturgy? An obvious choice to approach that question is the volume prepared by Oliver Jensen and the editors of *American Heritage* magazine. Apart from the specific concerns of higher education, the collections assembled by Norfleet and Paros address the monumental importance of "everyday events" as preserved in photographs:

> Oliver Jensen, *A College Album: Or, Rah, Rah, Yesterday* (McGraw-Hill, 1974) 112 pages.

> Lawrence Paros, *The Great American Cliche: Our National Experience, So To Speak* (Workman Publishing Company, 1976).

> Barbara Norfleet, *The Champion Pig: Great Moments in Everyday Life* (Godine, 1979) 128 pages.

Chapter 8 on "Alma Mater" includes elaborate discussion of the strengths and weaknesses of collegiate fiction as sources of institutional data. And, as noted in chapter 8, A.C. Spectorsky's collection of short stories, excerpts from novels, and memoirs is an excellent single-volume reference on the topic. "Personal history" and autobiography carry both attraction to and warnings about campus nostalgia:

> A.C. Spectorsky, editor, *The College Years* (Hawthorn, 1958) 509 pages.

> Henry Seidel Canby, *Alma Mater: The Gothic Age of the American College* (Farrar and Rinehart, 1936) 259 pages.

> Irving Stone, editor, *There Was Light: Autobiography of a University, Berkeley: 1868-1968* (Doubleday, 1970) 454 pages.

Provocative and well-written journalism on American higher education is not abundant. An important exception are selected works from the periodicals of the late 19th and early 20th centuries:

> Edwin E. Slosson, *Great American Universities* (Macmillan, 1910) (originally appearing in *The Independent*) 528 pages.

> James C. Stone and Donald P. DeNevi, *Portraits of the American University, 1890-1910* (Jossey-Bass, 1971) 380 pages.

Approaches to research and reconstruction of the factors which influenced the features of college and university architecture and campus planning utilize archival documents and external reports and sources—as these samples from varying eras and publications suggest:

> A.D.F. Hamlin, "Recent American College Architecture," *The Outlook* (August 1903) 10 pages.

> Agnes Lynch Starrett, *The Cathedral of Learning, 1921-1937* (University of Pittsburgh, 1937) 30 pages.

> Bryant Franklin Tolles, Jr., "College Architecture in New England Before 1860 in Printed and Sketched Views," *Antiques* (March 1973) Vol. CIII, No. 3, pp. 502-509.

The tendency to berate and dismiss "house histories" may be convenient and often correct. Nonetheless, it is an indulgence which can cause students and readers to gloss over imaginative approaches within the genre. One pleasant surprise from the University of California, Santa Cruz is a book which started out as a history seminar for undergraduates who had been members of the campus' first entering class. John Whitehead's study, to which I refer in several chapters, demonstrates the manner in which sharp internal analysis of institutions can be used to gauge historically changing campus identities. Earl Cheit resists the temptation to dwell on the campus unit; instead, he looks at some neglected yet significant componenets—schools of agriculture, business administration, forestry, and engineering—and assembles a sorely needed introduction to the "multiple parts" of the so-called "multi-versity":

> Cowell History Workshop 144G, *Solomon's House: A Self-Conscious History of Cowell College* (Big Tree Press, 1969).

> John Whitehead, *The Separation of College and State* (Yale University Press, 1973).

Earl F. Cheit, *The Useful Arts and the Liberal Tradition* (Carnegie Foundation for the Advancement of Teaching, 1975) 166 pages.

Incorporation of sports into the systematic study of higher education faces two major, divergent avenues of inquiry. For admittedly chauvinistic celebration of football as part of campus identity and institutional pride, see numerous works published by Strode Publishers. Guttman's recent survey brings analysis of sports into the realm of American Studies and the social and philosophical disciplines. Primary source material on external investigations into institutional practice in intercollegiate athletics is readily available from the Carnegie Foundation's reports of the late 1920s and early 1930s:

Allen Guttmann, *From Ritual to Record: The Nature of Modern Sports* (Columbia University Press, 1978) 198 pages.

Howard J. Savage, *et al. American College Athletics* (Carnegie Foundation for Advancement of Teaching, 1929) 382 pages.

Relatively few non-historians read *History of Education Quarterly,* but those who do will be rewarded with some excellent innovations in the framing of higher education issues. Listed below are articles which have dealt, respectively, with *alleged* indicators of institutional decline; patterns of student life within the campus organization; the phenomena of campus clustering and institutional configurations. Regardless of the particular era or institutions with which the articles deal, these are topics in higher education which should have widespread significance for and application to institutional research. The first selection noted below features lucid, original approaches by four first-rate historians—James Axtell, Hugh Hawkins, David Potts, and David Allmendinger, Jr.—whose combined scholarship stands as a classic yet underappreciated work:

"The Liberal Arts College in the Age of the University," *History of Education Quarterly* (Winter 1971) vol. XI, no. 4, pp. 339-389.

W. Bruce Leslie, "Localism, Denominationalism, and Institutional Strategies in Urbanizing America: Three Pennsylvania Colleges, 1870-1915" *History of Education Quarterly* (Fall 1977) vol. 17, no. 3, pp. 235-256.

Kathryn McDaniel Moore, "The War with the Tutors: Student-Faculty Conflict at Harvard and Yale, 1745-1771," *History of Education Quarterly* (Summer 1978) vol. 18, no. 2, pp. 115-128.

Controversy and clarity in discussion of "Futurology" within the higher education research enterprise can be found in the following works which bring markedly different tones and approaches to the topic:

> Daniel Bell, editor, "Toward the Year 2000: Works in Progress," *Daedalus* (American Academy of Arts and Sciences) (Summer 1967).

> William Irwin Thompson, *At The Edge of History: Speculations on the Transformation of Culture* (Harper and Row, 1971) 252 pages.

> Michael Young, *The Rise of the Meritocracy, 1870-2033: An Essay on Education and Equality* (Thames and Hudson, 1958) 160 pages.

APPROACHES TO RESEARCH AND REFLECTION

There persists the misguided notion that length and volume of reports contribute validity and significance to higher education research. To the contrary, I argue that bulk often represents easily detected attempts to obscure either unwanted findings or the inconclusiveness of shoddy research design. At the 1976 American Educational Research Association conference, Howard Howe II of the Ford Foundation (and, former U.S. Commissioner of Education) commented that the proliferation of second-rate and third-rate education research was due to either dull research tools or lack of disciplinary tools.

To remedy that situation, faculty and students in graduate higher education programs might re-think the assumptions and accomplishments brought about by the ubiquitous "lengthy term papers" and herculean dessertations. That such assignments aim to expose a student to comprehensive investigation and independent work is valuable—but not clearly effective. Dissertations and end-of-semester term papers can be over-rated in both educating function and contribution to professional preparation.

Therefore, I favor two kinds of assignments both for course work and for inclusion in comprehensive examination requirements: essays in which one responds to a particular document, or a critical review of a major work; second, relatively small-scale exercises in which the student must gather and analyze historical information. Here the intent is to encourage clarity and brevity, and to avoid the "mental blocks" and trauma which all too often pervades the dissertation. Few architects will even receive commissions to plan Brazilia or design the Superdome—to spend five or more years in graduate school with such a project may well deter talented people from entrance into the public and professional realm. A comparable situation exists in many higher education master's and doctoral degree programs where a shrinking number of students are able to devote full time to courses and assignments. Taking a cue from the so-called "public historians" employed by numerous museums, consulting firms, government agencies, and civil service areas, I urge faculty planning committees in Higher Education programs to ask, "Does our program prepare students to handle a variety of problematic assignments, to work with data and sources on a day-to-day basis, to be able to cooperate with interdisciplinary research teams, and to write clearly and promptly so as to meet the kinds of deadlines one would encounter in professional projects and assignments?" That capacity to digest information, to analyze, and to write clearly combines nicely with the heritage and storehouse of knowledge afforded by enduring, classic works and issues in higher education to which this book has been addressed.

The potential for the historical study of higher education to develop and sharpen the imaginative and analytic capacities of college and university administrators and planners can be fulfilled, in part, via essays which demand gamesmanship, reflection, review of secondary sources, and some confrontation with frest data. The following are presented as samples which I have found to be received by students as both enjoyable and demanding:

1. Compile a list of landmarks and associated legends and rituals on your campus. Trace these landmarks and legends as far back as possible. Using interviews, oral history, gossip, rumors, and archival sources, identify the origins of a practice. As you survey the landmarks and rituals, comment on modifications, fluctuations, disappearances, and revivals of these celebrations, symbols, and practices within the campus constituency.

2. You have been appointed as Advisor and Assistant to a newly appointed University President who is a newcomer to the campus. Assuming confidentiality, what are the practices, lore, historical events, matters of local and institutional etiquette that the new President should know if he wishes to live and work effectively in this particular campus community?

3. How would a modern-day accreditation team appraise, respectively, such institutions as 13th century University of Paris, or 19th century Oxford? Obtain a regional accrediting agency's handbook and guidelines for campus evaiuation and compile appropriate historical information by which to represent the aforementioned universities. After having filled out the surveys and filed related reports, prepare what you think the respective responses would have been from the 13th century faculty and the 19th century faculty who were objects of review?

4. Construct and assemble a time-line of campus portraiture. In other words, for each decade, gather the drawings, aerial photographs, master plan recommendations, architectural proposals, and maps for the college's or university's design. Can you posit explanations for relations among architectural changes, curricular innovations, and administrative policy? How have residential and social patterns changed over the years?

5. You have been named Research Director for a large foundation concerned with the study of higher education. Given an ample budget and five years in which to conduct your studies, what are research topics which you think ought to be addressed—yet which are conspicuously avoided heretofore? Although you have license to pursue these topics, what problems do you foresee in terms of obtaining data, gaining cooperation, over-coming resistance?

6. You have stumbled upon a dusty, first edition copy of a novel about "college life." How useful and/or valid is this novel as an historical source in the study of colleges and universities? What kinds of information, records, documents, manuscripts, photographs and secondary sources might you use to check and counter-check the novelist's alleged "inside view" of the college during a particular era? What do you consider to be the author's biases, credentials, and insights which qualify him to comment on the campus? What difficulties do you encounter in the student jargon, argot, practices, and allusions of that earlier period which are not readily comprehensible nor clear to the modern reader?

7. The year is 2020 and you have completed more than a half-century of distinguished service in higher education. At the ceremony and reception in your honor, you are awarded *Emeritus* standing and a commission to write your memoirs. Review the preceding decades with special attention to the fads, myopias, heroes, villains, and enduring developments which shaped American higher education.

In deference to the brevity which I have advocated in Higher Education research and writing assignments, this *invitational* work comes to a close. Those whose interest in the uses of historical study for research and planning in higher education has yet to be exhausted can take heart in that they can look forward to reading *and* writing about the useful past noted here.

Notes

CHAPTER 1

1. Edwin Slosson, *Great American Universities* (New York: MacMillan, 1910), pp. 136, 345.

2. Harvey K. Jacobson, "Seven Ways to Improve Our Accountability," *Case Currents,* (January 1978), pp. 4-7. See also Kenneth S. Lynn, ed., *The Professions in America,* (Boston: Beacon Press, 1967); Christopher Jencks and David Riesman, "The Professional Schools," *The Academic Revolution,* (Garden City, New York: Doubleday, 1968), ch. V; John R. Thelin, "Higher Education's 'Useful Past': A New Use for Liberal Studies," *Liberal Education,* (December 1976), pp. 568-575.

3. Eugene Webb, *et al., Unobtrusive Measures: Nonreactive Research in the Social Sciences* (Chicago: Rand McNally, 1966). See also John R. Thelin, "Beyond the 'Factory Model': New Strategies for Institutional Evaluation," *College and University* (Winter 1976) pp. 161-164.

4. Gray Brechlin, "Classical Dreams, Concrete Realities," *California Monthly,* (March 1978), pp. 12-15.

5. Philip C. Schlechty and James L. Morison, "The Role of the Social Scientist in the School of Education," *Educational Studies,* (Fall 1977), pp. 241-252.

6. Quoted in Don Speich, "Study on Lost Jobs, UC Research Asked," Los Angeles *Times,* 17 February 1978. See also Douglas Zoloth Foster, "The Faces of the University of California at Davis," *Change,* (February 1978), pp. 15-16.

7. Carlo M. Cipolla, *Literacy and Development in the West,* Baltimore: Penguin Books, 1969). See also Cipolla's autobiographical essay, "Fortum Plus Homini quam Consilium Valet," in *The Historian's Workshop,* edited by L.P. Curtis, (New York: Knopf, 1970), pp. 67-76.

8. Daniel Boorstin, *The Image: A Guide to Pseudo-Events in America* (New York: Harper Colophon, 1961); John R. Thelin, "California and the Colleges," *California Historical Quarterly,* (Summer 1977), pp. 140-163, esp. pp. 144-150.

9. Council for Financial Aid to Education, Inc., announcement appearing in *Newsweek,* November 1976.

10. For example, see Elaine H. El-Khawas, *New Expectations for Fair Practice: Suggestions for Institutional Review,* (Washington, D.C.: American Council on Education, 1976); Joan S. Stark, ed., *Promoting Consumer Protection for Students,* (San Francisco: Jossey-Bass, 1976).

11. For period piece college photographs and discussion of campus images see Oliver Jensen, *A College Album: Or, Rah, Rah, Yesterday,* (New York, Avon, 1974).

12. For example, see Wilson Smith, "The New Historian of American Education: Some Notes for a Portrait," *Harvard Educational Review,* (Spring 1961), pp. 136-143; John Talbott, "History of Education," *Daedalus,* (Winter 1971), pp. 133-150; Lawrence Stone, ed., *The University in Society,* (Princeton: Princeton University Press, 1974).

13. Burton R. Clark, "Belief and Loyalty in College Organization," *The Journal of Higher Education,* (June 1971), pp. 499-516; Burton R. Clark, *The Distinctive College: Antioch, Reed, & Swarthmore,* (Chicago: Aldine, 1970).

14. D.H. Kamens, "The College 'Charter' and College Size: Effects on Occupational Choice and College Attrition," *Sociology of Education,* (1971), pp. 270-296.

CHAPTER 2

1. Ernest Earnest, *Academic Procession: An Informal History of the American College, 1636-1953* (New York: Bobbs-Merrill, 1953) p. 213.

2. Attributed to Daniel Webster (1819) in "The Trustees of Dartmouth College vs. Woodward," in Richard Hofstadter and Wilson Smith, editors, *American Higher Education: A Documentary History,* vol. 1 (Chicago: University of Chicago Press, 1961) pp. 202-213.

3. Incident cited in Johan Huizinga, *The Waning of the Middle Ages* (London: Edward Arnold, 1955) pp. 7-8. Huizinga's work first was published in 1925.

4. R.W. Southern, *The Making of the Middle Ages* (New Haven: Yale University Press, 1953).

5. Usamah, "An Arab Opinion of the Crusaders: Their Curious Medication," in James Bruce Ross and Mary Martin McLaughlin, editors, *The Portable Medieval Reader* (New York: Viking Press, 1949) pp. 447-451.

6. Carlo Cipolla, "Illiteracy, Semi-Illiteracy, and Related Problems," *Literacy and Development in the West* (Baltimore: Penguin, 1969) ch. I.

7. Huizinga, *Waning of the Middle Ages,* ch. 1, "The Violent Tenor of Life," and ch. 2, "Pessimism and the Ideal of the Sublime Life."

8. Charles Homer Haskins, *The Rise of the Universities* (New York: Henry Holt, 1923). See also the classic three-volume work by Hastings Rashdall, *The Universities of Europe in the Middle Ages* (Oxford: Clarendon Press, 1895) and F.M. Powicke's introductory essay to Rashdall's work in the 1936 Oxford edition.

9. "The Privileges of Philip Augustus in Favor of the Students at Paris," (1200) in Helene Wieruszowski, *Medieval Universities* (Princeton: Van Nostrand, 1966) p. 137.

10. "King Henry III of England Confirms Privileges Protecting the Clerical Status of the Scholars," in Wieruszowski, *Medieval Universities,* p. 139.

11. John of Salisbury to Thomas Becket (1164) in Wieruszowski, *Medieval Universities,* p. 135.

12. Jacques de Vitry, quoted by Haskins, *Rise of the Universities,* pp. 24-25.

13. "Pope Innocent III mentions the Earliest Written Enactment of University Regulations," (1209) in Wieruszowski, *Medieval Universities,* p. 138.

14. "Statutes of the Papal Legate Robert de Courcon for the Masters in Arts and in Theology," (1215) in Wieruszowski, *Medieval Universities,* pp. 138-139.

15. Quoted in Haskins, *Rise of the Universities,* pp. 59-61.

16. "Regulations Concerning Academic Dress: From the Book of the Chancellor at Oxford" (1358) in Wieruszowski, *(Medieval Universities,* p. 196.

17. Quoted in "The Medieval Student," Haskins, *Rise of the Universities,* ch. 3.

18. Anthony Wood, "Riot at Oxford," in A.C. Spectorsky, editor, *The College Years* (New York: Hawthorn, 1958) pp. 25-30.

19. Philippe Aries, *Centuries of Childhood: A Social History of Family Life* (New York: Knopf, 1962). See also Eileen Power, *Medieval People* (Boston: Houghton, 1930).

20. Sloane Wilson, "G.I.," in A.C. Spectorsky, editor, *The College Years,* pp. 160-167.

21. Haskins, "The Earliest Universities," in *Rise of the Universities,* ch. 1.

22. Andrew Hamilton and John B. Jackson, *UCLA On the Move: During Fifty Years, 1919-1969* (Los Angeles: Ward Ritchie Press, 1969) pp. 51-57. See also John R. Thelin, "California and the Colleges, Part I," *California Historical Quarterly* (Summer 1977) pp. 140-142.

23. Robert A. Haslun, "Commencement and Tradition at Oberlin College," *Oberlin College Commencement Exercises* (May 23, 1973) pp. 13-15.

24. See Robert E. Dallol, "Nongraduates: Phony School Claims Rising by Degrees," *Los Angeles Times* (March 14, 1978); "For $45 You Can Buy a Fake Stanford Degree," *Chronicle of Higher Education* (May 8, 1978) p. 14.

25. Appearing in *Chronicle of Higher Education* (March 6, 1978).

CHAPTER 3

1. For desciption of the distinctive traditions of Oxford as a collegiate university, see B.A.O. Williams, "College Life," in *The Handbook to the University of Oxford* (Oxford: Clarendon Press, 1968) pp. 275-288. See also Frederick Rudolph's discussion of the collegiate way in *The American College and University: A History* (New York: Vintage Books, 1962) ch. 5.

2. Gerald W. Johnson, "Should Our Colleges Educate?" in A.C. Spectorsky, editor, *The College Years* (New York: Hawthorn, 1958) p. 392.

3. Lord Murray of Newhaven, *Choosing a British University* (London: n.p., 1967).

4. Noel Annan, "Introduction," in Michael Grant, *Cambridge* (London: Weidenfeld and Nicolson, 1967) pp. 8-27.

5. Annan, *op. cit.* An early example of the American view of Oxford and the Rhodes Scholarships is found in William C. Crittenden, "The Invasion of Oxford," *Sunset Magazine* (September 1907). One important exception to the Oxbridge imbalance is presented by Jasper Rose and John Ziman, *Camford Observed* (London: Gollancz, 1964).

6. Lawrence Stone, "The Ninnyversity?" *New York Review of Books* (January 28, 1971).

7. Robert Merton, *Social Theory and Social Structure* (New York: Free Press, 1968).

8. Hugh Kearney, *Scholars and Gentlemen: Universities and Society in Pre-Industrial Britain* (Ithaca: Cornell University Press, 1970) ch. 1.

9. Quoted in Felix Markham, *Oxford* (London: Weidenfeld and Nicolson, 1967) p. 84.

10. Markham, *Oxford,* pp. 64-93.

11. Anthony Wood, quoted in Markham, *Oxford,* p. 94

12. Anthony Wood, quoted in Markham, *Oxford,* p. 94

13. Samuel Johnson, quoted in Markham, *Oxford,* p. 125.

14. Kearney, *Scholars and Gentlemen;* see especially the discussion of Scotland in ch. VIII.

15. Sheldon Rothblatt, *The Revolution of the Dons: Cambridge and Society in Victorian England* (New York: Basic Books, 1968).

16. Abraham Flexner, *Universities: American, English, German* (New York: Oxford University Press, 1930) ch. III.

17. Lawrence Stone, "The Size and Composition of the Oxford Student Body, 1580-1909," in L. Stone, editor, *The University in Society: Oxford and Cambridge from the 14th Century to the Early 19th Century* (Princeton: Princeton University Press, 1974) vol. II, pp. 3-110.

18. Master of Oriel College, quoted in Markham, *Oxford,* p. 166.

19. Rudolph, *American College and University,* p. 4.

20. Oscar Handlin and Mary F. Handlin, "Colonial Seminaries, 1636-1770," *The American College and American Culture: Socialization as a Function of Higher Education* (New York: McGraw-Hill, 1970) p. 6.

21. John S. Brubacher and Willis Rudy, *Higher Education in Transition A History of American Colleges and Universities, 1636-1976* (New York: Harper & Row, 1976) pp. 4-5.

22. Bernard Bailyn, *Education in the Forming of American Society* (Chapel Hill: University of North Carolina Press, 1960).

23. Richard Hofstadter and Wilson Smith, editors, *American Higher Education: A Documentary History,* vol. I (Chicago: University of Chicago Press, 1961) pp. 1-2.

24. Rudolph, *American College and University,* ch. I.

25. Quoted in Rudolph, *American College and University,* p. 8.

26. Edward S. Martin, "Undergraduate at Harvard," *Scribner's Magazine* (May 1897). See also Samuel Eliot Morison, *Three Centuries of Harvard* (Cambridge: Harvard University Press, 1936).

27. Christian Gauss, "How Good Were the Good Old Times?" (1929) appearing in A.C. Spectorsky, editor, *The College Years,* pp. 81-88.

28. John Witherspoon, "Address to the Inhabitants of Jamaica and Other West-India Islands in Behalf of the College of New Jersey" (1772), in Hofstadter and Smith, editors, *American Higher Education,* p. 137.

29. Quoted in Rudolph, *American College and University,* p. 7.

30. "The Testimony of the Harvard Faculty Against George Whitefield" (1744), in Hofstadter and Smith, *American Higher Education,* pp. 62-63.

31. Ralph Turner, "Sponsored and Contest Mobility and the School System," *American Sociological Review* (December 1960) pp. 855-867.

32. William W. Clary, *The Claremont Colleges: A History of the Development of the Claremont Group Plan* (Claremont: Claremont University Center, 1970). See also, John R. Thelin, "Life and Learning in Southern California: Private Colleges in the Popular Culture," *History of Education Quarterly* (Spring 1975) pp. 111-117.

33. Lyman Hotchkiss Bagg, *Four Years at Yale: By A Graduate of '69* (New Haven: Charles C. Chatfield, 1871).

34. For example, see the student commentary in George Weller, *Not to Eat, Not for Love* (New York: Smith and Haas, 1931) p. 245; Uther Capet [Arthur Head], "Education: A Poem," *The New Yale Guide* (New Haven: Profile Press, 1930); Harvard College, Class of 1931, *First Report* (Cambridge: Crimson Printing, 1932) p. 69.

CHAPTER 4

1. For example, C. Arnold Anderson and Mary Jean Bowman, "Education and Economic Modernization in Historical Perspective," in Lawrence Stone, ed., *Schooling and Society: Studies in the History of Education* (Baltimore: Johns Hopkins University Press, 1976), pp. 3-20.

2. Robert Holmes Beck, "Sturm's Gymnasium and Its Significance for the Future of

Humanism," *A Social History of Education* (Englewood Cliffs, N.J.: Prentice-Hall, 1965, pp. 59-62.

3. This discussion draws heavily from Richard L. Kagan's extensive study, "Universities in Castile, 1500-1810," in L. Stone, ed., *The University in Society* (Princeton, N.J.: Princeton University Press, 1974), pp. 355-406.

4. Nicholas Phillipson, "Culture and Society in the 18th Century Province: The Case of Edinburgh and the Scottish Enlightenment," in Stone, *University in Society*, pp. 407-448.

5. Theodore Zeldin, "Higher Education in France, 1848-1940," in Walter Laquer and George L. Mosse, ed., *Education and Social Structure in the Twentieth Century* (New York: Harper and Row, 1967), pp. 53-80.

6. See for example, Allan Mitchell, "German History in France after 1870," in Laquer and Mosse, *Education and Social Structure*, pp. 81-100.

7. Fynes Moryson, quoted in Carlo Cipolla's autobiographical essay, appearing in L. P. Curtis, Jr., ed., *The Historian's Workshop* (New York: Knopf, 1970), p. 70.

8. Carlo Cipolla, *Literacy and Development in the West* (Baltimore: Penguin Books, 1969), pp. 30-31.

9. Laurence Veysey, *The Emergence of the American University* (Chicago: University of Chicago Press, 1970), pp. 125-132.

10. Charles E. McClelland, "The Aristocracy and University Reform in Eighteenth-Century Germany," in Stone, *Schooling and Society*, pp. 146-176.

11. Theodore Ziolkowski, "Yesterday's Model for Today's University," *Chronicle of Higher Education*, April 24, 1978, p. 44.

12. Ziolkowski, p. 44.

13. Ziolkowski, p. 44.

14. J. C. G. Rohl, "Higher Civil Servants in Germany, 1890-1900," in Laquer and Mosse, *Education and Social Structure*, pp. 101-122.

15. Letter from George Ticknor to Thomas Jefferson (October 14, 1815) on freedom and advanced scholarship in Germany, appearing in Richard Hofstadter and Wilson Smith, ed., *American Higher Education: A Documentary History* (Chicago: University of Chicago Press, 1961), vol. 1, pp. 257-259; James Morgan Hart, *German Universities: A Narrative of Personal Experience* (New York, 1874); Lincoln Steffen, "Semester at Heidelburg," in A. C. Spectorsky, ed., *The College Years* (New York: Hawthorn, 1958), pp. 69-74.

16. Edwin Slosson, *Great American Universities* (New York: MacMillan, 1910), pp. 373-404.

17. Abraham Flexner, in *Universities: American, English, German* (New York: Oxford University Press, 1930), pp. 305-361.

18. Christopher Jencks and David Riesman, "Social Stratification and Mass Higher Education," in *The Academic Revolution* (Garden City, N.Y.: Doubleday, 1969), pp. 61-154.

CHAPTER 5

1. Carlo M. Cipolla, "Fortuna Plus Homini Quam Consilium Valet," autobiographical essay appearing in L. P. Curtis, Jr., ed., *The Historian's Workshop* (New York: Knopf, 1970), pp. 65-76.

2. Philip Lindsley, "1832 Baccalaureate Address," in Richard Hofstadter and Wilson Smith, ed., *American Higher Education: A Documentary History*, vol. 1 (Chicago: University of Chicago Press, 1961), p. 376.

3. Tom Robbins, *Another Roadside Attraction* (New York: Ballantine Books, 1971), p. 114.

4. John R. Thelin, "California and the Colleges: Part II," *California Historical Quarterly* vol. 56, no. 3 (Fall 1977), p. 235.

5. Leon Burr Richardson, *History of Dartmouth College* (Hanover, N.H.: Dartmouth College, 1932); see also, Ralph Nading Hill, ed., *The College on a Hill: A Dartmouth Chronicle* (Hanover, N.H.: Dartmouth, 1964); John S. Whitehead, "Dartmouth: A Small College," in *The Separation of College and State: Columbia, Dartmouth, Harvard, and Yale, 1776-1876* (New Haven, Conn.: Yale University Press, 1973), ch. 2.

6. Frederick Rudolph, *The American College and University: A History* (New York: Vintage Books, 1962), p. 264.

7. Merle Borrowman, "The False Dawn of the State University," *History of Education Quarterly* (1961), pp. 6-20.

8. James Axtell, "The Death of the Liberal Arts College," *History of Education Quarterly,* 11, no. 4 (Winter 1971), pp. 339-354; see also George Peterson, *The New England College in the Age of the University* (Amherst, Mass.: Amherst College Press, 1964).

9. David F. Allmendinger, Jr., "New England Students and the Revolution in Higher Education, 1800-1900," *History of Education Quarterly* vol. 11, no. 4 (Winter 1971), pp. 381-389.

10. John Whitehead, *Separation of College and State,* pp. 191-240.

11. For example, James Bryce, *American Commonwealth* (n.p.: London, 1888); See also Hugh Hawkins, "The University-Builders Observe the Colleges," *History of Education Quarterly,* vol. 11, no. 4 (Winter 1971), pp. 353-362.

12. *Reasons Against Founding a College, or Collegiate School in the County of Hampshire. . . by the Overseers of Harvard College, in New England,* appearing in Hofstadter and Smith, *American Higher Education: A Documentary History,* pp. 131-134.

13. See for example William R. Davie's 1795 plan of education for the University of North Carolina, in Edgar W. Knight, ed., *A Documentary History of Education in the South Before 1860* (Chapel Hill: University of North Carolina Press, 1952), pp. 23-26; Charter of the University of Georgia (1785), in Hofstadter and Smith, *American Higher Education: A Documentary History,* pp. 150-152; Whitehead, *Separation of College and State,* passim.

14. Borrowman, "False Dawn of the State University," pp. 6-20.

15. "Big Missouri," *Life,* June 7, 1937, pp. 32-34.

16. John Kenneth Galbraith, essay, in Irving Stone, ed., *There Was Light: Autobiography of a University: Berkeley 1868-1968* (Garden City, N.Y.: Doubleday, 1970), p. 25.

17. Quotations and incidents from James Thurber, "University Days" (1933), in A. C. Spectorsky, ed., *The College Years* (New York: Hawthorn, 1958), pp. 436-441.

18. Earl F. Cheit, *The Useful Arts and the Liberal Tradition* (New York: McGraw-Hill, 1975); see especially, "Agriculture: The Search for a Dual-Purpose Cow," pp. 31-56.

19. For discussion of the local and regional gentry of the late nineteenth century, see Robert Wiebe, *The Search for Order, 1877-1920* (New York: Hill and Wang, 1968). Accounts of snobbery and schisms at the University of Nebraska before World War I are recalled by Alvin Johnson, quoted in Laurence Veysey, *The Emergence of the American University* (Chicago: University of Chicago Press, 1965), p. 292; see also Earle D. Ross, *Democracy's College: The Land-Grant Movement in the Formative Stage* (Ames, Iowa: Iowa State College Press, 1942).

20. Henry Seidel Canby, *Alma Mater: The Gothic Age of the American College* (New York: Farrar and Rinehart, 1936), p. xi.

21. Allan Nevins, *The State Universities and Democracy* (Urbana: University of Illinois Press, 1962), p. 82.

22. Philip Lindsley, "On the Problems of a College in a Sectarian Age, 1829," in Hofstadter and Smith, *American Higher Education: A Documentary History*, vol. I, pp. 232-237.

23. Lyman Bagg, "Concluding Chapter: A Matter of Opinion," in *Four Years at Yale: By a Graduate of '69* (New Haven, Conn.: Charles C. Chatfield, 1871), p. 706.

24. Charles Eliot Norton, "Harvard," in *Four American Universities* (New York: Harper and Brothers, 1895), p. 7.

25. Daniel J. Boorstin, "The Booster College," in *The Americans: The National Experience* (New York, 1965), pp. 152-161; see also David B. Potts, "American Colleges in the Nineteenth Century: From Localism to Denominationalism," *History of Education Quarterly*, vol. 11, no. 4 (Winter 1971), pp. 363-380.

26. Thelin, "California and the Colleges," *California Historical Quarterly*, pp. 235-240.

27. Edwin Slosson, *Great American Universities* (New York: MacMillan, 1910); see especially pp. 374, 456.

28. Morris Bishop, "—And Perhaps Cornell," in Raymond Floyd Hughes, ed., *Our Cornell* (Ithaca, N.Y.: Cayuga Press, 1939), pp. 76-77. See also letter from Andrew D. White to George Burr and Ernest Huffcut (September 18, 1893), reviewing Cornell's pioneering achievements, in Carl Becker, ed., *Cornell University: Founders and Founding* (Ithaca, N.Y.: Cornell University Press, 1943), pp. 173-180.

29. E. L. Godkin, "Yale and Harvard," *The Nation* (January 19, 1882), pp. 50-51.

30. For example, Abraham Flexner, *Medical Education in the United States and Canada* (New York, 1910).

31. James A. Thomas, "Heavy Traffic on the Purple Brick Road: The Route to Law School," in Herbert Sacks, M.D., et al., *Hurdles: The Admissions Dilemma in American Higher Education* (New York: Atheneum, 1978), pp. 212-238, especially p. 225.

32. Veysey, *Emergence of the American University*, pp. 342-380.

33. Dick Corten, "Our Gift to Santa," *California Monthly* (June-July 1978), p. 16.

CHAPTER 6

1. Henry Suzzallo, president of the Carnegie Foundation for the Advancement of Teaching, April 1931.

2. Document in Lynn Thorndike, ed., *University Records and Life in the Middle Ages* (New York: Columbia University Press, 1944), p. 291.

3. Allison Danzig, *The History of American Football* (Englewood Cliffs, N.J.: Prentice-Hall, 1956), pp. 9-10. Sections and a revised version of this chapter have been drawn from John Thelin, "Higher Education and Athletics: Probing an American Ethos," *The Journal of Educational Thought*, in press.

4. Nancy Scannell, "NCAA Bemoans Title IX, While Women are Skeptical," *Louisville Courier-Journal*, June 10, 1975.

5. Frederick Rudolph, "The Rise of Football," *The American College and University: A History* (New York: Random House, 1962), ch. 18. See also David Riesman and Reuel Denny, "Football in America: A Study in Culture Diffusion," *American Quarterly* (1951), pp. 309-325.

6. John Davies, *The Legend of Hobey Baker* (Boston: Little, Brown, 1966).

7. James Cain, "The Man Merriwell," *Saturday Evening Post*, June 11, 1927, p. 129; see

also Richard O'Donnell, "America's Most Popular Character," *National Retired Teachers Association Journal* (November-December 1969), p. 61.

8. George Santayana, "A Glimpse of Yale," *Harvard Monthly* (December 1892), pp. 89-97.

9. Walter Camp, *Walter Camp's Book of College Sports* (New York: Century, 1893), pp. 2-4.

10. "Sports Records Move West," *Life,* June 7, 1937, p. 72.

11. Edwin Slosson, *Great American Universities* (New York: MacMillan, 1910), pp. 137-139, 160.

12. Howard J. Savage, *et al., American College Athletics,* Bulletin no. 23 (New York: Carnegie Foundation for the Advancement of Teaching, 1929); see also Savage, *Current Developments in American College Sport,* Bulletin no. 26 (1931).

13. Robert Hutchins, *The New College Plan* (Chicago: University of Chicago Press, 1931), p. 16. For criticisms of Chicago's football program before Hutchins's reforms, see Abraham Flexner, *Universities: American, English, German* (New York: Oxford University Press, 1930), pp. 65-66.

14. Slosson, *Great American Universities,* pp. 508-509.

15. Examples of titles in the genre of sports exposé include Gary Shaw, *Meat on the Hoof* (1971); Kenneth Denlinger and Leonard Shapiro, *Athletes for Sale: An Investigation into America's Greatest Sports Scandal—Athletic Recruiting* (1975); Joseph Durzo, *et al. The Sports Machine* (1975).

16. Mark Asher, "Play and Not Pay?" Maryland's Kehoe Blasts Title IX, Says Women Can't Produce Income," *Louisville Courier-Journal,* June 10, 1975.

17. Figures and quotations from "A Majors Success," *Time,* December 2, 1974, p. 84.

18. News release, *Los Angeles Times,* August 5, 1978.

19. Ike Balbus, "Politics as Sports: The Political Ascendency of the Sports Metaphor in America," *Monthly Review* (March 1975), pp. 27-39.

20. John Majors, quoted in Dan Hruby, "Football Degree May Be Next," *San Jose Mercury-News,* June 25, 1978.

21. Liva Baker, *I'm Radcliffe! Fly Me!: The Seven Sisters and the Failure of Women's Education* (New York: Macmillan, 1976), especially pp. 101-106.

22. Liva Baker, *ibid.*

23. Gene Lyons, "A Few Words in Praise of the Red-Swine Cult," *Los Angeles Times,* January 1, 1978. For additional approaches to the importance of logos and symbols for organizations, see Henry Dreyfuss, *Symbol Source Book* (New York: McGraw-Hill, 1972); Margaret Mead, "Symbols Speak Their Own Language," *Smithsonian,* vol. 3, no. 1, (April 1972), pp. 51-59.

24. Jo Lux, "Lexington Red, Not Tennessee Orange, Designates Color for New Civic Center," *Kentucky Kernel* (University of Kentucky), August 30, 1976.

25. Beverly T. Watkins, "Fighting Artichokes at Heart of Arizona Controversy," *Chronicle of Higher Education,* December 13, 1976, p. 5.

26. Anita Brewer, "Education in Texas," *Atlantic Monthly* (March 1975), pp. 79-81; see also John R. Thelin, "Looking for the Lone Star Legacy: Higher Education in Texas," *History of Education Quarterly* (Summer 1977), pp. 221-228.

27. Michigan State University officials quoted in "Marginalia," *Chronicle of Higher Education,* May 10, 1976, p. 2.

28. I am indebted to Randall Dahl, formerly an assistant dean at the University of Massachusetts, for having alerted me to this case of institutional mascot etymology.

29. See for example "A Griffin Speaks Up," *The Stanford Observer* (June 1978); see also John R. Thelin, "California and the Colleges," *California Historical Quarterly,* vol. 56, no. 2 pt. 1 (Summer 1977), pp. 147-149.

30. "The Griffin," *Reed Magazine,* vol. 55, no. 5 (December 1976).

31. Robert Strauss, "Jock Shorts," *The Daily Californian* (Berkeley, California), January 17, 1974, p. 7.

32. Robert Strauss, *ibid.*

CHAPTER 7

1. Robert Benchley, "What College Did For Me," in A. C. Spectorsky, ed., *The College Years* (New York: Hawthorn, 1959), pp. 188-192.

2. Bruce C. Vladeck, "Buildings and Budgets: The Overinvestment Crisis," *Change* (December-January 1978/79), p. 39.

3. For example, see Stephan Steinberg, "How Jewish Quotas Began," *Commentary* (September 1971), pp. 67-76.

4. Lawrence Stone, "The Ninnyversity?" *The New York Review of Books,* January 28, 1971, p. 27.

5. Hugh Kearney, "A Comparative Postscript: The Nineteenth Century," *Scholars and Gentlemen: Universities and Society in Pre-Industrial Britain* (Ithaca, N.Y.: Cornell University Press, 1970), pp. 188-189.

6. Ronald Story, "Harvard Students, the Boston Elite, and the New England Preparatory System, 1800-1870," *History of Education Quarterly* (Fall 1975) (vol 15, no. 3)

7. C. H. Patton and W. T. Field, *Eight O'Clock Chapel: A Study of New England College Life in the Eighties* (Boston: Houghton Mifflin, 1927), ch. 9.

8. The case here refers to policies discussed by Dean Bruce Bigelow of Brown University in the 1930s.

9. "Laws Relating to the University of Kentucky: Statutory Provisions, Sections 463c-30 and 463-30a," in E. C. Elliott and M. M. Chambers, ed., *Charters and Basic Laws of Selected American Universities and Colleges* (New York: Carnegie Foundation for Advancement of Teaching, 1934), p. 278.

10. For example, Paul Buck, "Who Comes to Harvard? *Harvard Alumni Bulletin,* January 10, 1948; see also *Admission to Harvard College: A Report by the Special Committee on College Admission Policy* (Cambridge: Harvard University, February 1960).

11. Liva Baker, *I'm Radcliffe! Fly Me!: The Seven Sisters and the Failure of Women's Education (New York: Macmillan, 1976); see also review by John R. Thelin in Educational Studies* (Fall 1977), pp. 274-277. For analysis of disproportionate record of achievement by graduates of women's colleges, see "The Search for Talented Women," *Change* (May 1974), pp. 51-52.

12. P. J. Bickel, E. A. Hammel, J. W. O'Connell, "Sex Bias in Graduate Admissions: Data from Berkeley," *Science* (February 7, 1975) (vol. 187) (no. 4175) pp. 398-404.

13. For example, Katherine Kinkhead, *How an Ivy League College Decides on Admissions* (New York: Norton, 1961). See the following articles in *Time* concerning 1960 public controversy on selective admissions: "Ivy Harvest" May 23, 1960, p. 44; "Luck and Pluck," November 21, 1960, p. 53; "Poisoned Ivy, May 30, 1960, p. 64; "Something Has to Give, June 6, 1960, p. 42.

14. Herbert S. Sacks et al., *Hurdles: The Admissions Dilemma in American Higher Education* (New York: Atheneum, 1978).

15. For example, "This University Wants You: It is a Buyer's Market as Colleges Scramble to Fill Space," *Time,* May 29, 1978, p. 69; "U.S. Colleges: Life and Death Struggle," *U.S. News and World Report,* May 29, 1978, pp. 64-66.

16. Arthur Knaus, "Surviving the Crunch: Liberal Arts Colleges Need a Marketing Approach," *CaseCurrents* (1978), pp. 11-13.

17. John R. Thelin, "Colleges and Consumerism: False Alarms and Over-reactions," *College and University* (Fall 1978), (vol. 54, no. 1), pp. 74-77.

18. Discussion of admissions research problems has been drawn in large part from John R. Thelin, "Auditing the Admissions Office: Applied Research and Evaluation at the Small, Selective College," *College and University* (Winter 1979). (vol 54, no. 2) pp. 96-108.

19. Governor Jerry Brown of California, quoted in *Time,* July 10, 1978, p. 15.

20. Fred A. Hargadon, "A Memo to Secondary Schools, Students, and Parents," Stanford University Office of Admissions (October 1978).

21. Hargadon, *ibid.*

CHAPTER 8

1. Lyman Hotchkiss Bagg, *Four Years at Yale: By a Graduate of '69* (New Haven, Conn.: Charles C. Chatfield, 1871), iii.

2. Paul Rudnick, "Students' Needs More Important Than Classification of Campuses," *The Kentucky Kernel,* November 12, 1976.

3. Works which illustrate and summarize reseach findings and style in this area include Harold L. Hodgkinson, "The Impact of the American College on Student Values," *Education, Interaction, and Social Change* (Englewood Cliffs, N.J.: Prentice-Hall, 1967), ch. 8; Nevitt Sanford, ed., *The American College: A Social-Psychological Interpretation of Higher Learning* (New York: Wiley, 1964); Alexander Astin, *Four Critical Years* (San Francisco: Jossey-Bass, 1978).

4. Nevitt Sanford, quoted in M. Freedman, *Impact of College* (Washington, D.C.: U.S. Office of Education, 1960), pp. 16-17.

5. C. Robert Pace, *CUES: College & University Environment Scales* (Princeton, N.J.: Educational Testing Service, 1963).

6. Dwight D. Eisenhower, 1953, quoted in Ralph Nading Hill, ed., *The College on the Hill: A Dartmouth Chronicle* (Hanover, N.H.: Dartmouth College, 1964).

7. Two short stories which convey the varieties of perceptions and problems related to the impact of the G.I. Bill on American higher education are Sylvan Karchmer, "Hail Brother and Farewell," and Sloane Wilson, "G.I.," both reprinted in A. C. Spectorsky, ed., *The College Years* (Amherst, Mass.: Amherst College Press, 1964).

9. See for example Howard Miller, *The Revolutionary College: American Presbyterian Higher Education, 1707-1837* (New York: New York University Press, 1976); Frederick Rudolph, "The Extracurriculum," *The American College and University: A History* (New York: Random House, 1962) ch. 7; James McLachlan, "The Choice of Hercules: American Student Societies in the Early 19th Century," in Lawrence Stone, ed., *The University in Society,* vol. 2 (Princeton, N.J.: Princeton University Press, 1974), pp. 449-494.

10. Henry Seidel Canby, *Alma Mater: The Gothic Age of the American College* (New York: Farrar and Rinehart, 1936); Laurence Veysey, "The Mind of the Undergraduate" and "The Gulf Between Students and Faculty," *The Emergence of the American University* (Chicago: University of Chicago Press, 1965), pp. 268-316.

11. Discussion of collegiate fiction as historical documentation has been drawn in large

part from John R. Thelin, "Tales Out of School: Exposs of Elite Education," *Educational Studies,* vol. 9, no. 3, (Fall 1978), pp. 295-298.

12. Although Bagg's complaints are well taken, there was, in fact, very sound and well-written coverage of American colleges and universities. We have already cited Edwin Slosson's *Great American Universities* (1910), whose selections originally appeared in *The Independent.* For examples of first-rate campus profile journalism in *Century, Harper's and Atlantic Monthly,* see the anthology by James C. Stone and Donald P. DeNevi, ed., *Portraits of the American University, 1890-1910* (San Francisco: Jossey-Bass, 1971).

13. John O. Lyons, *The College Novel in America* (Carbondale: Southern Illinois University Press, 1974.

14. See for example Hamilton Vaughn Bail, "Harvard Fiction: Some Critical and Bibliographical Notes," *Proceedings of the American Antiquarian Society,* 68 (1958), pp. 211-347; William Bentinck-Smith, ed., *The Harvard Book* (Cambridge: Harvard University Press, 1953).

15. William Randel, "Nostalgia for the Ivy," *Saturday Review of Literature* vol. 30, no. 48, (November 27, 1949), pp. 9-11, 39. See also I. E. Cadenhead, Jr., ed., *Literature and History,* University of Tulsa, Oklahoma, Monograph Series no. 9, n.d.

16. The temptation is to argue that the movie *Marathon Man* (circa 1978) added excitement and glamour to the image of the graduate student. However, the protagonist, a graduate student in history at Columbia University, found adventure and heroism outside the campus and the familiar turf of seminar rooms and libraries.

17. A partial listing of critical essays and articles which praise Weller's novel includes Richard C. Boys, "The American College in Fiction," *College English,* 7 (1946), p. 381; Frederick L. Gwynn, "The Education of Epes Todd," *Harvard Alumni Bulletin,* 51 (1949), p. 388; Randel, "Nostalgia for the Ivy."

18. George Anthony Weller, *Not to Eat, Not for Love* (New York: Harrison Smith and Robert Haas, 1933), pp. 93-94.

19. Canby, *Alma Mater,* ch. I: "The College Town."

20. For an introductory discussion of local implications of the University of Massachusetts' changing size and character, see the section on campus ethnography by David Riesman and Christopher Jencks, "The Viability of the American College," in Sanford, *The American College,* pp. 74-192.

21. Historical reconstruction of Lexington, Kentucky's, institutional, spatial, and commercial arrangements were based in part from "Cities and Towns: Lexington," in *Kentucky: A Guide to the Blue Grass State* (Federal Writers' Project for the Works Progress Administration for the State of Kentucky, 1939), pp. 197-220.

22. For example, Christopher Jencks and David Riesman, "Nationalism versus Localism," by *The Academic Revolution* (Garden City, N.Y.: Doubleday Anchor, 1969), pp. 155-198; Robert K. Merton, "Patterns of Influence: Local and Cosmopolitan Influentials," in *Social Theory and Social Structure* (New York: Free Press, 1967), pp. 387-420.

23. C. Vann Woodward, "The Irony of Southern History," *Journal of Southern History,* 19 (1953).

24. The study of national institutions and national leadership is covered in George W. Pierson, *The Education of American Leaders: Comparative Contributions of United States Colleges and Universities* (New York: Praeger, 1969). Reconsideration of the local character of American higher education is discussed in Robert Nisbet, "The Decline of Academic Nationalism," *Change* (Summer 1974), pp. 26-31; see also David Kamens, "Colleges and

Elite Formation: The Case of Prestigious American Colleges," *Sociology of Education* (Summer 1974), pp. 354-378.

CHAPTER 9

1. *The Third Century: Twenty-Six Prominent Americans Speculate on the Educational Future* (New Rochelle, N.Y.: *Change* Magazine Press, 1976). See also promotional announcements appearing in *Change*, 1978-79.

2. C. Northcote Parkinson, famous for Parkinson's Law, has countered the Peter Principle with the argument that modern organizations do, in fact, elicit competence from employees—for instance very few pilots crash planes. Although the Peter Principle may be limited as a *general* description of organizational behavior, there is reasonable cause to assume its applicability to higher-education leaders, since Peter gathered his data from the study of educational organizations and school systems.

3. We arrive at this average age with the following logic: A 1978 compilation and survey on young leaders in higher education used age forty as the ceiling which distinguished "young leaders" from "leaders." If we assume that essayists for *The Third Century* are leaders, then it follows that each is older than forty years of age. Elder statesmen, of course, may well be septuagenarians and octogenarians. Hence, we posit the reasonable approximation that a leader in 1980 would be between forty and eighty years of age. Since customary retirement age is between sixty-five and seventy, we infer than an active yet established leader would be younger than sixty-five. Finally, we noted that if a leader is sixty years old in 1980, his year of birth would be 1920.

4. Works in this category are Stephen R. Graubard, ed., "American Higher Education: Toward an Uncertain Future," *Daedalus* (Fall 1974 and Winter 1975); Daniel Bell, ed., *Toward the Year 2000: Work in Progress* (Boston: Houghton Mifflin, 1968); Alvin C. Eurich, ed., *Campus 1980: The Shape of the Future in American Higher Education* (New York: Dell, 1968).

5. David G. Brown, "College Teacher Shortage," *The Mobile Professors* (Washington, D.C.: American Council on Education, 1967), p. 16.

6. Eurich, *Campus 1980*, pp. vii-xvii.

7. Stephen R. Graubard, "University Cities in the Year 2000," in Daniel Bell, *Toward the Year 2000*. For critique of this work, especially Graubard's essay, see also William Irwin Thompson, "A.D. 2000: The Millenium Under New Management," in *At The Edge of History: Speculations on the Transformation of Culture* (New York: Harper and Row, 1971) ch. 5.

8. Clark Kerr, "The Future of the City of Intellect," *The Uses of the University* (Cambridge: Harvard University Press, 1963), ch. 3. For update and revision of this 1963 view, see Kerr's "Higher Education in the 1980s and the Role of the Private Institution," *Pomona Today* (Pomona College, Claremont, Calif.) (Spring 1972), pp. 8-11.

9. R. Martin and R. J. McCartney, "The Future Revised: Education's Big Boom Is Ending, But Studies to Get More Diverse," *The Wall Street Journal*, April 8, 1976, p. 1.

10. Harold B. Gores, president of Educational Facilities Laboratories, Inc., quoted in Martin and McCartney, "The Future Revised." *Wall Street Journal* (8 April 1976) p. 1.

11. Willis W. Harman, director of 1967 Stanford University Research Institute project, quoted in Peter Kiernan, "Society Seen in 'Midlife Passage': Researchers Predict Identity Crisis," *Los Angeles Times*, September 3, 1978.

12. Edward J. Meade, Jr., *A Foundation Goes to School* (Ford Foundation 1973).

13. "What Went Wrong in '60s: Ford Foundation Turns Retrospective Eyes on Educational Funding, Improvement Programs," *Guidepost* (26 January 1973), p. 1.

14. *Recent Social Trends in the United States: Report of the President's Research Committee on Social Trends* (New York, 1933). One key member of that research committee, Lawrence K. Frank, was active in the 1960s and served as a contributor to the Commission on the Year 2000. See his essay, "The Need for a New Political Theory," in Bell, *Toward the Year 2000*, pp. 177-184.

15. Louis B. Fleming, "True to Form, the Club of Rome Celebrates Its Founding With the Lights Out," *Los Angeles Times*, September 3, 1978.

16. See critique of gadgetry preoccupation in Daniel Bell, "The Year 2000—The Trajectory of an Idea," in *Toward the Year 2000*, pp. 3-5.

17. Fred Charles Ikle, "Can Social Predictions Be Evaluated?" in Bell, *Toward the Year 2000*, pp. 101-126; see especially p. 117.

18. Clark Kerr, *Uses of the University*, pp. 87, 124.

19. Michael Young, *The Rise of the Meritocracy, 1870-2033: An Essay on Education and Equality* (London: Thames and Hudson, 1958).

20. John R. Silber, "The Rest Was History," in *The Third Century*, See also, publication of the essay in *Change* (September 1976), pp. 40-41.

21. As noted earlier in discussion of clichés and fallacies associated with higher-education futurology, there is a tendency for every university in every era to see itself as at a watershed, a turning point. The humor of that tendency and institutional self-deception does not escape Silber.

22. Given in Baltimore, Maryland on February 22, 1976. I am indebted to Robert Hewes, assistant vice-president for university affairs at the Johns Hopkins University, for prividing me with a copy of Ashby's address.